East Asia and Pacific Cities

Urban Development Series

The Urban Development Series discusses the challenge of urbanization and what it will mean for developing countries in the decades ahead. The series aims to delve substantively into a range of core issues related to urban development that policy makers and practitioners must address.

Cities and Climate Change: Responding to an Urgent Agenda

Climate Change, Disaster Risk, and the Urban Poor: Cities Building Resilience for a Changing World

East Asia and Pacific Cities: Expanding Opportunities for the Urban Poor

East Asia's Changing Urban Landscape: Measuring a Decade of Spatial Growth

The Economics of Uniqueness: Investing in Historic City Cores and Cultural Heritage Assets for Sustainable Development

Financing Transit-Oriented Development with Land Values: Adapting Land Value Capture in Developing Countries

Transforming Cities with Transit: Transit and Land-Use Integration for Sustainable Urban Development

Urban Risk Assessments: An Approach for Understanding Disaster and Climate Risk in Cities

All books in the Urban Development Series are available for free at
https://openknowledge.worldbank.org/handle/10986/2174

East Asia and Pacific Cities
Expanding Opportunities for the Urban Poor

Judy L. Baker and Gauri U. Gadgil, Editors

ISBN (paper): 978-1-4648-1093-0
ISBN (electronic): 978-1-4648-1103-6
DOI: 10.1596/978-1-4648-1093-0

Cover photo: © Aileen Dimatatac / World Bank

Cover design: Debra Malovany (World Bank)

Library of Congress Cataloging-in-Publication Data has been requested

Contents

Figures

Tables

Acknowledgments

This study was prepared by a World Bank team led by Judy L. Baker, Global Practice for Social, Urban, Rural, and Resilience (GSURR), and included the core team of Gauri Gadgil, Gayatri Singh, and Kimberly Burrowes. Linh Le, Natsuko Kikutate, Kamakshi Mubarack, Huong Mai Nguyen, Gayatri Sahgal, and Yasmin Zaerpoor provided inputs on specific aspects of the report. Nick Paul and Dina Towbin provided editorial support.

The case studies and household surveys in Metro Manila, the Philippines, and Ulaanbaatar, Mongolia, were led by Gayatri Singh. For the Manila case study, research inputs were provided by Gauri Gadgil and Bernice Varona-Soriano, along with data management and analysis support by Huong Dang. Fieldwork in Metro Manila was considerably strengthened by the field supervision of Bernice Varona-Soriano and Bebot Aguirre. Metro Manila slum mapping was conducted by consultants from GIM, led by Vincent Tigny. For the Ulaanbaatar study, Professor Gilvan Guedes provided analytical inputs and Joseph Mulhausen executed GIS analyses, with research and writing support from Battuya Dash and Gauri Gadgil. Obert Pimhidzai provided statistics based on the Mongolia National Household Survey 2014 data. Sabine Willach provided background qualitative information on social networks in *ger* areas in Mongolia and Bulgan Enkhbate provided ethnographic insights on vulnerable communities in Ulaanbaatar. For both the Metro Manila and Ulaanbaatar surveys, Juan Munoz provided sampling guidance.

Helene Carlson Rex and Kamakshi Mubarack led the review of the China Inclusive Cities background paper. Yang Zhang provided background research.

The work benefited greatly from the comments provided by Sudhir Shetty, Chief Economist of the East Asia and Pacific Region, who chaired the decision meeting, and by peer reviewers Johannes Linn, Maitreyi Das, Christine Kessides, and Caterina Laderchi, as well as by Bert Hofman, Elena Glinskaya, Bekele Debele, David Mason, and Clifton Cortez. At the concept stage, helpful comments were received from Valerie Kozel, Catherine Farvacque, Almud Weitz, Iain Menzies, Maraita Listyasari, Zuzana Stanton-Geddes, Abigail Baca, Patricia Fernandes, Ellen Hamilton, Megha Mukim, and Heejoo Lee.

This work program was conducted under the overall guidance of Abhas Jha, Practice Manager, GSURR, East Asia and the Pacific; Sameh Wahba, Director, GSURR; and Ede Jorge Ijjasz-Vasquez, Senior Director, GSURR.

The activity was made possible through the generous support of Australian Aid.

Abbreviations

1SF	One Safe Future
ACCA	Asia Coalition for Community Action
BKM	Badan Keswadayan Masyarakat (Community Boards of Trustees)
BRT	bus rapid transit
BSP	Bangko Sentral ng Pilipinas
CAT-DDO	Catastrophe Deferred Drawdown Option
CCT	conditional cash transfers
CODI	Community Development Organizations Institute
CRH	Cheap Rental Housing Guarantee Plan
DEWATS	Decentralized Wastewater Treatment Systems
DOTC	Department of Transportation and Communications
FDI	foreign direct investment
FESR	Framework for Economic and Social Reform
FLPP	fixed mortgage interest rates (Indonesia)
GSURR	Global Practice for Social, Urban, Rural and Resilience
GTFS	General Transit Feed Specification
HDB	housing authority
HCMC	Ho Chi Minh City
ISF	informal settler families
LGBTI	lesbian, gay, bisexual, transgender, and/or intersex
LIFT	Livelihoods and Food Security Trustfund
MDGs	Millennium Development Goals
MTDP	Mid Term Development Plan
NCD	National Capital District
NGO	nongovernmental organization
NMT	Nonmotorized Transportation
OBIA	Object-Based Image Analysis
PIR	price-to-income ratio

PKH	Keluarga Harapan Program
PNOs	piped network operators
PNPM	Program Nasional Pemberdayaan Masyarakat
PPP	purchasing power parity
PPPs	public-private partnerships
RMB	*Renminbi*
SDG	Sustainable Development Goal
SHFC	Social Housing Finance Corporation
SPSP	Social Protection Strategic Plan
SPSPs	small-scale service providers
STD	sexually-transmitted disease

Executive Summary

The Growing Case for Addressing Urban Poverty, Inequality, and Slums in East Asia and the Pacific

Urbanization in the East Asia and Pacific (EAP) region has created enormous opportunities for many. Cities create jobs and boost productivity, while urban density has the potential to lower the unit costs of public service provision, enabling governments to extend access to basic services to more people. The EAP region stands out for its impressive rate of poverty reduction over the past two decades, with much of it occurring in cities (World Development Indicators 2016).

Rapid growth in cities, however, can create challenges. It is often difficult for cities to keep up with the growing needs of their citizens, and a lack of planning and investments in physical infrastructure, housing, and transportation invariably results in congestion, pollution, and widening inequalities for urban dwellers. Urban inequality can undermine urbanization's benefits by threatening the sustainability of the growth process and slowing poverty reduction, and it can lead to social divisions, conflict, and rising crime and violence in cities.

This study focuses on urban poverty and inequality in EAP cities, recognizing that many countries of the region, particularly those with middle-income status, are at a critical juncture in the urbanization and growth process where potential social divisions in cities could harm prospects for future poverty reduction (box 1).

With an estimated 250 million people in EAP living in slums, the region has the largest slum population in the world (much of this due to the sheer numbers of people in EAP countries). Approximately 75 million people live below the US$3.10/day poverty line, with urban poverty existing in both lower-middle-income and upper-middle-income countries. The cities

---

Box 1 *East Asia and Pacific Cities: Expanding Opportunities for the Urban Poor:*
Objectives and Contents

This study aims to provide a better understanding of issues of urban poverty, inequality, and urban inclusion in East Asia and the Pacific (EAP), particularly for those living in slums, as well as presenting a set of guiding principles for creating inclusive cities through multiple, interlinked dimensions — economic (jobs), spatial (housing and services), and social (equity in rights and participation, particularly for marginalized groups). The study is aimed at policy makers, researchers, donors, and practitioners working at both the city and national levels.

A focus on urban poverty and inequality is consistent with the World Bank twin goals of ending extreme poverty and promoting shared prosperity, as well as addressing the Sustainable Development Goals (SDGs), particularly Goal 11, which focuses on "inclusive, safe, resilient and sustainable cities." It also closely aligns with the New Urban Agenda which calls for providing basic services for all citizens, ensuring that they have equal opportunities and face no discrimination, and fully respecting the rights of refugees, migrants, and internally displaced persons, regardless of their migration status, among other important priorities.

The work draws on an analysis of existing data, literature, case studies, and two specially-designed surveys of low-income urban areas of Metro Manila, Philippines, and Ulaanbaatar, Mongolia.[a] As data across countries are not always consistent, the study uses specific examples to illustrate key points. Finally, this study uses numerous good practice examples from EAP to demonstrate how cities and countries have approached specific aspects of inclusion and urban poverty reduction for consideration of possible replicability.

Chapter 1 of the main study covers broad trends related to urbanization, poverty, inequality, and slums in EAP; chapter 2 reviews economic inclusion as it relates to employment opportunities and the economic costs of natural hazards; chapter 3 discusses the factors of spatial inclusion, including housing, infrastructure and service delivery, and mobility; chapter 4 presents social inclusion, including rights for the elderly, women, and migrants; and chapter 5 outlines the guiding principles for policy in addressing urban poverty and inclusion. Appendix 1 includes country-level urban poverty profiles. The city-level poverty studies for Metro Manila and Ulaanbaatar are available as companion reports.

a. These cities were selected to coincide with parallel work that benefited greatly from new data on low-income residents.

with the highest numbers of urban poor are in China, Indonesia, and the Philippines, while the highest urban poverty rates are in the Pacific Island countries of Papua New Guinea and Vanuatu, and in Indonesia and the Lao People's Democratic Republic (PDR). Despite the concentration of urban poor in some large cities in the region, overall urban poverty is higher in small and medium-sized cities.

There are also multidimensional aspects of urban poverty that are not captured through standardized income or consumption-based poverty studies. The living conditions in slums, where many of the urban poor reside, are often overcrowded, lack adequate infrastructure and services, and present a number of resulting health and environmental risks. Mobility and access to jobs, services, and markets are constrained by limited options for affordable transportation. The high expenses in cities for food, shelter, basic services, and commuting put considerable pressure on poor households, and the gap between rich and poor can be quite stark in dense urban environments, which can lead to social tensions.

In EAP countries, there are also particularly high risks associated with natural disasters and climate change, as the region is the most disaster-stricken in the world, affected by small recurrent as well as rare high-impact events (Jha and Stanton-Geddes 2013). Exposure to these events is very high in cities, with their concentration of people and assets, and it is the urban poor who are most acutely affected (Baker 2012).

Urban Inclusion: Understanding the Dimensions of Urban Poverty and Inequality

Because traditional measures of poverty and inequality do not always capture the multidimensional deprivations and issues facing the urban poor, a more comprehensive framework is used in this study, with a focus on urban inclusion. The framework is based on three dimensions of inclusion—economic, spatial, and social—which capture important factors related to jobs and livelihoods, living conditions, and equitable rights and protection of subgroups among the urban poor; these subgroups, for various reasons, are at a disadvantage in benefiting from the opportunities that cities bring.

Economic Inclusion The economic dimension of inclusion refers to equitable access to jobs and income-generating activities in cities, which are critical to poverty reduction and economic inclusion. In cities, the poor are reliant on cash incomes, highly vulnerable to job losses and wage reductions in urban-based industries, and do not have agricultural production to fall back on as they would in rural areas. External shocks can also impact their economic inclusion, particularly if mechanisms for resilience do not exist, as is typically the case for the urban poor. Key issues related to economic inclusion for the urban poor are related to barriers to formal employment and to limited resilience, as noted below:

- **Barriers to formal employment.** Cities across EAP are a driving force in the region's economic development and are home to industries that have been critical for job creation. However, the region's high level of informality leaves many of the urban poor engaged in informal low-skill and low-wage work, without employment contracts and social insurance, and without protection against unfair dismissal. This situation results from a number of constraints related to labor markets that, in turn, stem from constraints in educational opportunities, gaps in social networks that facilitate labor market entry for specific subgroups—notably those with lower skills, such as rural migrants, youth, and women—and mobility challenges, particularly for those living in slums on the urban periphery.

- **Resilience.** Economic inclusion is also reliant on resilience to economic shocks from natural disasters or global crises. The EAP region has faced many shocks in recent years, with significant impacts on the urban poor. Examples include urban flooding, the 2008–09 financial crisis, and the devastating cyclones in a number of countries that demonstrate how one event can wipe out years of economic gain, especially for those with little protection. The current slowdown in trade and the growing protectionism in developed markets are affecting labor demand, which can have substantial impacts on the poor. For example, the 2008–09 financial crisis is estimated to have resulted in an additional 1.4 million people living below the poverty line in the Philippines, primarily because of labor income losses. Most of these individuals were the near-poor living in urban areas, with lower levels of skills than the general population (Habib et al. 2010).

Spatial Inclusion. The spatial dimension of urban inclusion links equitable access to land, housing, infrastructure, and basic public services. Mobility is particularly important, given its role in connecting low-income residents to jobs, services, and amenities. The relationship between the urban spatial structure and inclusion is important for understanding and addressing the inter- and intra-urban disparities that can hamper urban growth.

Spatial inequality in many EAP cities is high, with major divisions in access to housing, infrastructure and services, and affordable transportation. This division is exacerbated by the rapid growth of EAP cities, which have not been able to keep up with the needs of their burgeoning urban populations. Such deficiencies are particularly evident in slums where many of the urban poor live.[1] When analyzing spatial inequality, three key areas stand out as lacking for the urban poor: accessibility, affordability, and quality and safety, as explained below:

- **Accessibility.** Across the region, the urban poor's level of access to housing and basic services varies considerably. For example, in Indonesia, the Philippines, and Vietnam, 27 percent, 21 percent, and 7 percent of the urban populations, respectively, still do not have access to improved sanitation. In the two largest cities of Vietnam—while overall water access is high—only 43 percent of the lowest quintile (poorest 20 percent) have access to private tap drinking water, compared with 75 percent of the wealthiest quintile. Basic road infrastructure, at the heart of accessibility, is also often constrained in slums where roads are narrow and without sidewalks, pushing pedestrians into the street. Roads extending to the urban periphery may be too narrow or of insufficient quality to accommodate larger public transportation vehicles, further limiting access. In accessing affordable housing, a number of complex issues create limitations in the market, including high demand and restrictive land policies in cities, and a lack of finance for low-income populations. Access to basic services is further constrained by legal documentation in informal areas, preventing utilities from installing services, and by resource and capacity constraints—particularly in rapidly growing cites.

- **Affordability.** High housing costs in cities limit affordability by the urban poor. Given the informal nature of their work or residency status, the urban poor tend to be underserved by banks that might otherwise provide financing and loans for home ownership. In terms of the provision of basic services, municipalities typically have limited resources and are not able or willing to extend services to informal settlements, which are often in high-risk areas, further exacerbating costs and concerns. As a result, low-income urban neighborhoods may only be served by small-scale service providers who lack economies of scale and therefore charge higher costs for basic services than public providers do. Transportation costs can similarly be high for low-income areas, particularly in periphery neighborhoods, leaving the urban poor with costly and lengthy commutes to reach jobs in the city center. In Ulaanbaatar, Mongolia, for example, the city's sprawling spatial form means that the cost of providing network services to periphery *ger* areas where the city's poorest live is prohibitively expensive. Residents then must rely on costly private services, adding further burden to their limited resources.

- **Quality and safety.** Informality and land tenure insecurity may dissuade the urban poor from making investments to improve their houses and neighborhoods. Substandard housing gives rise to serious concerns about shoddy construction and overcrowding, and the associated health and safety risks. In areas unserved by public utilities, reliance on unregulated private vendors for water provision may leave consumers vulnerable to health problems. Finally, in regards to mobility, the EAP region leads the world in the number of annual traffic fatalities, which tend to involve pedestrians and nonmotorized vehicles. Given that these modes of transportation are favored by the urban poor, they face a higher risk of injury or death.

Social Inclusion. The social dimension of urban inclusion relates to individual and group rights, dignity, equity, and security. For this study, social inclusion in cities refers specifically to the urban poor, particularly those living in slums. Aspects of social inclusion/exclusion are most visible through their uneven recognition of their rights and their weak participation in decision making. There are also subgroups among the poor who are at higher risk and for whom the effects of urban poverty can be intensified because of their identity or place in society. These subgroups may include children, youth, the elderly, women, the disabled, the homeless, and migrant workers—although conditions differ across countries.

Social inclusion is especially important in cities where, given the high density of people, there are stark differences between income groups such as the rich and the poor. These divisions can exacerbate discontent and lead to conflict. Across EAP, the most visible forms of exclusion that affect the urban poor, both directly and indirectly, are as follows: limitations on rights to land and property; limitations on citizen participation; and exclusionary policies that prevent some from accessing urban services and social protection. These issues can be particularly acute for marginalized groups, as explained below:

- **Limited land and property rights for some.** The high informality levels in the region mean that land tenure security and land ownership are elusive for many urban poor. In countries such as Vietnam, property ownership is restricted to those with urban residency status, despite high rural-urban migration rates among low-income groups. Urban residency status is needed for more than just land ownership; it can bestow a "right to the city," which gives residency holders access to health and education services. In countries across the region, including Indonesia, Malaysia, the Philippines, and Singapore, traditional views of gender roles have been codified in inheritance and property laws to make it difficult for women to own land. This situation is particularly restrictive for low-income women who may have no other assets.

- **Citizen participation.** Across EAP, highly centralized governance structures limit participation in governance and urban planning. However, in an effort to respond to growing urban poverty, many countries have pursued citizen engagement tools to promote development. Although legal frameworks encouraging participatory planning exist in some countries, including Cambodia, the Philippines, and Vietnam, their adoption varies widely and is dependent on existing enforcement mechanisms.

- **Social protection.** Adequate social protection mechanisms are an essential tool for poverty reduction and social risk management in cities. Although spending on social assistance appears to have increased in most countries in the region, spending levels remain low, and many poor households still do not receive much-needed social assistance. In Mongolia and Thailand, for instance, coverage of the poorest stands above 90 percent because of the universal nature of the benefits; yet in Cambodia, Fiji, Indonesia, Malaysia, and Timor-Leste, are below 25 percent (World Bank 2013). Specific challenges faced in reaching the urban poor include: (1) perception that social safety nets are not required, given the vibrant labor markets in cities; (2) urban poverty numbers are underestimated, especially for migrants and informal workers; and (3) slum-upgrading and community development programs focus more on infrastructure development and less on beneficiaries.

- **Marginalized subgroups.** Among the urban poor, it is children, women, the elderly, and rural migrants that stand out as the largest groups who, for various reasons, are at a disadvantage in benefiting from the opportunities that cities bring. In some countries, youths also find it difficult to enter the labor force, particularly if they have low levels of education and skills. Low-income women disproportionately face challenges such as the following: health and safety issues; higher vulnerability to layoffs during times of economic shocks or changes in market demand; and in some countries, legal constraints to asset ownership further undermine housing security, favoring men over women. Furthermore, the proportion of elderly is rising in many parts of EAP, although there has been relatively little analysis of low-income elderly in cities; they tend to have limited access to social protection, particularly if they did not work in the formal sector. The elderly have minimal savings, growing health needs, and in some cases, disabilities. As a growing population, the elderly is a group of increasing concern in many countries. Lastly, there are a number of exclusionary policies or attitudes that discriminate against rural migrants in EAP, making it difficult for them to find housing, jobs, education, and health care. While migrants do not necessarily start out as poor, they can fall into poverty traps as they struggle to navigate the exclusionary barriers that increase the opportunity costs of integrating into city life.

The three dimensions of inclusion—economic, spatial, and social—are highly interlinked, and any approach to analyze deprivations or develop solutions to address the complexity of issues must consider all three areas. Efforts to address only one aspect of inclusion are more limited in their reach. For example, narrowly focused slum-upgrading programs may improve living conditions for specific communities, but may not open up opportunities for mobility to jobs or help to integrate these communities into the broader urban economy and amenities. Such interlinkages are also an issue at the household level and require complimentary approaches.

Guiding Principles for Public Action to Promote Greater Inclusion in the Cities of East Asia and the Pacific

This study raises a number of challenges facing cities in EAP that, if unaddressed, will put pressure on the region's future growth, stability, and social cohesion. Yet if addressed, there is enormous untapped potential for creating more inclusive, livable cities. This situation presents tremendous opportunities at the country and city levels across the region.

The study draws on global experience and presents a set of key guiding principles for policy makers' consideration and adaptation to specific country or city circumstances. Programs and policies to tackle urban poverty and social inclusion are not intended to come at the expense of addressing rural poverty, but rather are aimed at ensuring that urbanization's benefits are widely shared and can create future opportunities for those in rural areas. The guiding principles are mutually reinforcing and intended to address the multiple dimensions of inclusion.

Implementation will need to be tailored to the very diverse country and city contexts in the EAP region. Accordingly, a typology based on a country's or city's urbanization level is used to frame priorities (World Bank 2009). Priorities are defined by urbanization level in chapter 5 (see table 5.1), below, and discussed below:

Incipient urbanization refers to places that are in the early urbanization stages and typically of lower-middle-income status. Although poverty levels may be higher, at this point there is an opportunity to put in place key policies and programs that will affect future urbanization with the aim of creating inclusive, livable cities. In EAP, at the country level, these places may include Cambodia, Lao PDR, and Myanmar; and at the city level, smaller cities are included, such as Siem Reap (Cambodia), Vientiane (Lao PDR), and Hai Duong (Vietnam). These places tend to have lower density, lower levels of wealth, and lower capacity, which means they may require particular financial and technical support.

Intermediate urbanization is characterized by countries that are around 50 percent urbanized or cities that are medium to large and are growing rapidly. Examples at the country level include China, Indonesia, the Philippines, and Thailand; and at the city level, Phnom Penh (Cambodia), Yogyakarta (Indonesia), Yangon (Myanmar), Cebu City (the Philippines), and Hai Phong (Vietnam) are included. For such places, urbanization has largely taken place and middle-income status has been attained, but there is a substantial need to address substandard housing, deficiencies in service delivery, and inequality for some groups. There may be limited financial resources and capacity for such investments that require innovative financing mechanisms, as well as capacity support to design and implement programs and policies effectively.

Advanced urbanization refers to countries that are more than 75 percent urbanized. In EAP such countries include Japan, the Republic of Korea, and Malaysia. At the city level, advanced urbanization would include large highly urbanized metropolitan areas such as Beijing (China), Jakarta (Indonesia), Manila (the Philippines), Bangkok (Thailand), and Ho Chi Minh City (Vietnam). Although these places may have higher-middle-income status, much wealth, and substantial institutional capacity, there may still be high urban poverty levels in some places, and the backlog of those living in slums can be substantial, requiring urgent attention.

Key guiding principles are outlined below.

Promoting Economic Inclusion for the Urban Poor

- **Connect the Urban Poor with Job Markets.** Employment and income generation are critical to achieving poverty reduction and economic inclusion. A concerted effort by policy makers to better connect the urban poor with job markets is necessary if the urban poor are to secure "good jobs" or jobs with high enough wages to allow them and their households to meet basic needs. Labor markets across the region are shifting towards higher-skilled workers, making investments in universal primary education a key bridge between the urban poor and good jobs. At the intermediate and advanced urbanization levels, the government can bring together industry and education, and promote training programs that impart sought-after skills to meet labor market demands. Examples from Hanoi and Ho Chi Minh City in Vietnam, and Shanghai, China, show how the government can partner with the private sector in such efforts. Connecting the urban poor to jobs can require providing better transportation infrastructure and services that enable mobility in poor communities, as has been done in China and Vietnam.

- **Encourage Pro-Poor Economic Development.** Many of the urban poor are self-employed and, without access to credit, cannot easily get capital to grow their businesses. At all urbanization levels, microenterprise initiatives fill this gap, but their reach is limited. Initiatives to expand credit to vulnerable groups can be found in Indonesia and the Philippines; however, these programs often target specific communities or neighborhoods rather than the urban poor more broadly. Policies that protect and promote the rights of informal workers are also important for protecting the urban poor, particularly given the prevalence of informality in the region. Examples of such policies include legalizing space for informal work as seen in Indonesia, and creating laws that protect home-based works as in Thailand.

- **Build Resilience to External Shocks.** Risks from natural disasters are higher in this region than in other parts of the world, with the urban poor being particularly vulnerable. At all urbanization stages, community-level investments are important for building resilience. In Jakarta, Indonesia, for example, a Flood Early Warning System has been used to build local capacities to manage disaster risk using participatory planning, including in low-income communities. At the more intermediate and advanced urbanization levels, investments in social safety net and disaster planning programs can help the urban poor preserve economic gains. In China, Fiji, Indonesia, and the Philippines, for instance, social safety net programs offer disaster preparation activities for vulnerable groups and provide assistance for low-income residents affected by disasters. Also needed are programs and policies that provide formal funding both for preparedness measures (for example, insurance pools), and rehabilitation initiatives, such as building back the labor force and reconstructing damaged infrastructure.

Promoting Spatial Inclusion for the Urban Poor

- **Invest in Integrated Urban Planning.** Spatial planning that is well-integrated with transportation planning can help reduce the inequality in access to urban opportunities and amenities. This reduction has been achieved over time in places such as Korea, Japan, and Singapore. The spatial pattern within cities is one of many factors that affect the inclusion of the urban poor, and it can be influenced by ensuring geographic alignment between jobs, markets, public transportation, health and education services, recreational areas, and affordable housing. Increased attention to urban planning, especially in incipient and intermediate cities, is required to proactively influence growth patterns so that the problems of sprawl, slums, and congestion can be avoided. At the intermediate and advanced urbanization levels, elements of pro-poor urban design include the following: prioritizing public transportation corridors and connectivity to facilitate easy connections between jobs and housing; allowing for cycle lanes and sidewalks because a significant portion of the urban poor rely on cycling or walking; and involving local governments and civil society in the planning process to ensure that local needs are met and equity considerations are included. Certain sites and services projects offer a prospective approach for growing cities in EAP, where the anticipated population increases can lead to proactive investments in the rights of way and basic infrastructure services in designated locations. This approach enables low-income households to purchase lots at a relatively low price and to build housing incrementally. There are also many approaches to building resilience through urban planning and management, particularly for high-risk areas where many of the urban poor live. These approaches need to become standard practice for cities.

- **Ensure Affordable Land and Housing.** The dysfunction of urban land markets and the shortage of affordable housing options have resulted in growing slum populations across EAP cities. Low-income residents have few options for financing home purchases or for affordable rentals. To address these constraints, beginning at the incipient urbanization level, policies must be put in place that ensure property rights are protected and that enable rapid construction permitting to have positive impacts on the overall market for affordable housing. At the intermediate urbanization levels, policies that can open access to land and improve tenure security are also very important to the urban poor, as is seen in Iloilo City in the Philippines and with CODI in Thailand. A starting point is addressing the causes of high land prices in a given city—such as minimum plot sizes, maximum floor area ratio, and outdated zoning. Tools include the transfer of development rights; special assessment districts; density bonuses; mixed use development; and cross-subsidy schemes. Land pooling has been used successfully across the region to open up access to land. At the advanced urbanization levels, targeted subsidies, as well as land titling, land regularization, and land taxation policies and programs, can help to reach the poorest.

- **Provide Equitable Access to Infrastructure and Basic Services.** Aligned with pro-poor spatial planning in cities is equitable access to infrastructure and basic services. Investments in clean water, sanitation, and solid waste collection have tremendous impacts on health, productivity, and welfare, particularly at the incipient urbanization levels. As cities grow, ensuring affordable transportation provides access to income-earning opportunities as well as to services, such as schools, clinics, and hospitals, and it can reduce spatial disparities. To address priority infrastructure needs, slum-upgrading programs can use participatory approaches to identify and implement neighborhood-based interventions. Internationally recognized flagship programs in Indonesia, Thailand, and Vietnam are being scaled up. Other countries, such as Cambodia, Mongolia, and the Philippines, have a substantial need for slum upgrading, which requires urgent attention. The private sector has a significant implementation role.

Promoting Social Inclusion for the Urban Poor

- **Recognize the Rights of all Citizens to the City.** An essential part of encouraging inclusive cities is to build on the understanding that all citizens, regardless of identity, income status, or whether they were born in rural or urban areas, can have equal access to urban services or purchase property. Coupled with this is a culture of empowerment, which engenders a sense of belonging in the urban environment. Local governments can play an important role in championing the right to the city for urban residents and investing in resources to accommodate growing populations, regardless of income level. However, local governments can also create barriers when planning strategies exclude low-income communities, informal workers, and migrants. Policies such as the *hukou* in China, or other exclusionary policies for urban migrants in Cambodia, Indonesia, and Vietnam, have historically left many behind. This situation has created divisions in society and prevented many from benefiting from urbanization. In the case of China, the situation is changing, with the recent relaxation of the hukou, particularly in smaller cities. Other countries at various stages of urbanization similarly need to implement reforms to exclusionary policies to ensure equity and opportunity for urban migrants.

- **Target Marginalized Subgroups among the Urban Poor.** Funneling benefits to those who, for various reasons, cannot fully benefit from the labor market is important in promoting social inclusion. This process becomes especially important at intermediate and advanced urbanization levels as inequality rises. Social safety net programs, specifically conditional cash transfers and cash-for-work opportunities, can boost poverty reduction and inclusion in cities by providing a mechanism for vulnerable groups to achieve increased accessibility. Indonesia and the Philippines are prime examples of where these programs provide income support and training opportunities for those who fall outside the formal economy or for newcomers experiencing discrimination because of their identity. These programs have been adapted to address urban needs. Few such programs are available in other countries, particularly for those in informal settlements, leaving many excluded. Examples of programs representing groups such as low-income women, the elderly, and urban migrants in China, Indonesia, Japan, Korea, and Thailand, for instance, demonstrate how such programs can address vulnerabilities for those most disadvantaged.

- **Strengthen Local Governance and Embrace Citizen Engagement.** Building inclusive cities relies on good local governance through transparent and fair decision making at all urbanization levels. This process requires sufficient resources to successfully implement programs and policies on the ground. Research shows that the urban poor have less access and representation in the political system than the urban nonpoor; they have fewer opportunities than the nonpoor to shape and influence their governing institutions; and the urban poor endure a far more hostile and fearful relationship with institutions of urban law and order (Desai 2010). Engaging the urban poor in decision-making processes is important for strengthening policies, enhancing service delivery, and ensuring social stability in cities. Empowering urban dwellers to actively engage in and contribute to their cities is a powerful way of promoting social inclusion. One such program is the Asia Coalition for Community Action (ACCA), which targets inclusive slum upgrading for the urban poor in Thailand. And the Urban Community Driven Development Program in Indonesia (PNPM) encourages urban residents to take a proactive role to identify community priorities, improve relations with local governments, and design and implement community improvements. Ultimately such engagements can also help to empower local groups to organize for other community initiatives and benefits, which strengthens social cohesion within cities.

A Cross-Cutting Priority: Investing in Knowledge for Evidence-Based Decision Making

Committing to better data and research. A number of knowledge gaps emerged while conducting this study. Investing in reliable data and better research, as well as ensuring that results are fed back into decision making, will help to better design programs and policies aimed at reaching the urban poor and creating more inclusive, livable cities. Among the knowledge gaps identified was a clear set of priorities for evidence-based decision making, including the following:

- Evidence-based urban analysis and planning are needed to assess and understand trends and characteristics related to living conditions within cities, to identify future challenges, and to develop plans accordingly.

- A comprehensive understanding of the impacts of programs and policies on the ground is lacking. Such knowledge is reliant on good information systems and sufficient capacity to conduct an in-depth analysis that allows cities to move from making reactive decisions to creating proactive solutions for the many urban issues. It can be challenging and expensive for resource-constrained cities to collect basic information on the location of low-income settlements, high-risk areas, access to basic services, and high-growth areas. Yet the benefits of investing in this data collection is critical to good planning, and it is particularly important at the intermediate and advanced urbanization stages, including at both the country and city levels.

- The value of data in understanding issues related to urban poverty and informal settlements is evident from the case studies in Metro Manila, the Philippines, and Ulaanbaatar, Mongolia that we discussed previously. This level of detail can allow policy makers to develop more targeted interventions to address issues of urban poverty. In addition to household surveys, other important resources include remote sensing data, community mapping, census data, and new sources such as data from cell phones or citizen feedback; with these tools, policy makers can better understand their urban environment and their citizens so that they can respond to existing needs more effectively.

Investing in reliable data and better research, as well as ensuring that results are fed back into decision making, will ultimately help to design better programs and policies aimed at reaching the urban poor, and to create more inclusive, livable cities.

Note

1. Slums are broadly defined using the UN Habitat definition that refers to a slum household as individuals living under the same roof in an urban area who lack one or more of the following: durable housing of

a permanent nature that protects against extreme climate conditions; sufficient living space which means not more than three people sharing the same room; easy access to safe water in sufficient amounts at an affordable price; access to adequate sanitation in the form of a private or public toilet shared by a reasonable number of people; and security of tenure that prevents forced evictions.

References

Baker, J. 2012. *Climate Change, Disaster Risk, and the Urban Poor: Cities Building Resilience for a Changing World.* Urban Development. Washington, DC: World Bank.

Habib, B., et al. 2010. "The Impact of the Financial Crisis on Poverty and Income Distribution: Insights from Simulations in Selected Countries." *Economic Premise* No. 7. World Bank, Washington, DC.

Jha, A., and Z. Stanton-Geddes. 2013. *Strong, Safe, and Resilient: A Strategic Policy Guide for Disaster Risk Management in East Asia and the Pacific.* Washington, DC: World Bank.

Desai, R. M. 2010. "The Political Economy of Urban Poverty in Developing Countries: Theories, Issues, and an Agenda for Research (June 30, 2010)." Wolfensohn Center for Development Working Paper No. 20. https://ssrn.com/abstract=1658580.

World Bank. 2009. *World Development Report 2009: Reshaping Economic Geography.* Washington, DC: World Bank.

———. 2013. "A Diverse and Dynamic Region: Taking Stock of Social Assistance Performance in East Asia and the Pacific." World Bank, Washington.

World Bank and IMF (International Monetary Fund). 2013. *Global Monitoring Report 2013: Rural-Urban Dynamics and the Millennium Development Goals.* Washington, DC: World Bank.

CHAPTER 1

East Asia and the Pacific's Urbanizing Context

Introduction

Over the past two decades, East Asia and the Pacific (EAP) has experienced unprecedented rates of urbanization, creating an enormous opportunity for the promotion of economic growth and prosperity. The concentration of economic activity in cities attracts more firms and creates jobs that provide higher incomes for workers than they would earn on a farm. It also generates further opportunities to move up the income ladder and access schools, health services, and other urban amenities (World Bank 2009).

However, urbanization's benefits are hindered when cities are not well planned or managed, and when the needs of a growing urban population are not met. The lack of planning for physical infrastructure and housing, lagging service delivery, and inadequate transportation and connectivity within cities invariably result in widening inequalities between urban dwellers. Inequality not only threatens the sustainability of the growth process, but can also lead to social divisions and conflict, particularly in dense urban areas where there can be extreme differences in living conditions between the rich and the poor. Policies to assist low-income populations fully participate in labor markets, find affordable housing, access basic services, and have a voice in decision making help ensure that the benefits of urbanization are enjoyed widely.

This study aims to understand urban poverty issues in EAP and the extent to which the urban poor can participate in the opportunities that cities bring. While there are many definitions used to classify the urban poor, a broad definition is used here, which refers to people at the bottom end of the income distribution, particularly those living in slums, who have limited access to affordable housing and basic services.

To define a more equitable and inclusive urbanization process for the poor, this study uses a broad framework based on three dimensions of an inclusive city—economic, spatial, and social—and discusses how aspects of each dimension affect the urban poor (figure 1.1) (World Bank 2015b).

The *economic dimension* refers to equitable access to jobs and income-generating activities for the urban poor that are critical to poverty reduction and economic inclusion in cities, particularly given the heavy reliance of the urban poor on cash incomes, their vulnerability to job losses and wage reductions in urban-based industries, and the absence of agricultural production to fall back on. Economic shocks can also impact economic inclusion of low-income populations by threatening livelihoods that have few, if any, safety nets to fall back on. Approaches that are most relevant to addressing employment for the urban poor include the following: improving the state of the local economy; recognizing and integrating the informal economy; investing in education and training; broadening access to credit; and increasing resilience to economic shocks.

Figure 1.1   Multidimensional Framework for Inclusive Cities and the Urban Poor

Spatial inclusion:
Improving access to affordable land, housing and services for the urban poor

Social inclusion:
Improving the terms for the urban poor to take part in society

Economic inclusion:
Ensuring opportunities for the urban poor to contribute to and share in rising prosperity

Source: Adapted from World Bank (2015b).

The *spatial dimension* of inclusion for the urban poor links equitable access to land, housing, infrastructure, and basic public services, and is particularly relevant given that many of the urban poor live in slums. Understanding the relationship between urban spatial structure and inclusion is important in understanding inter- and intra-urban disparities. Policy tools that can improve equity and spatial inclusion for the urban poor include the following: opening access to land tenure; land use planning; providing housing and basic infrastructure; and urban upgrading.

The *social dimension* of urban inclusion encompasses individual and group rights, dignity, equity and security, in this case for the urban poor. This dimension includes policies that foster the recognition of rights to the city for everyone across the income distribution (including migrants); equitable rights to housing; a voice in decision making; and safety. There are subgroups among the urban poor that are at higher risk due to their identity or place in society, which puts them at a further disadvantage. These subgroups may include children, youth, women, the elderly, the disabled, or migrant workers, although conditions differ across countries.

The dimensions of inclusion are highly interlinked with much overlap, and any approach to analyzing deprivations or developing solutions to address urban poverty needs to take all three dimensions into account. Efforts to address only one aspect of inclusion—for example, narrowly focused slum upgrading programs that aim to address only the spatial dimensions of inclusion—can help to improve physical living conditions for specific communities, but may not open up opportunities to access jobs or may not address the needs of specific subgroups among the poor who may need other types of assistance, for example, female-headed households or unemployed youth. A more comprehensive approach would consider the economic, spatial, and social dimensions of inclusion through complementary programs such as physical upgrading coupled with job training, childcare services, and improvements in public transportation services.

The study considers the diversity of countries and cities in the EAP region in terms of economic development, and level of urbanization (table 1.1).[1] Comparing Cambodia to China, Mongolia to Malaysia, or Manila to Makassar finds much variation, which makes it difficult to generalize across countries and cities. In developing solutions, this report uses a typology drawn from the *World Development Report 2009: Reshaping Economic Geography* (World Bank 2009) to categories countries based on urbanization level—incipient, intermediate, or advanced. These categories are helpful in identifying priorities for addressing urban poverty and inequality for countries and cities at different levels, although there are also common approaches that are relevant regardless of urbanization level (see chapter 5).

Table 1.1   Diversity in EAP Countries

	Population (million)	GDP per capita current US$	Gini	Urban population (% of total)	Urban population growth rate	Year
Cambodia	14.8	946	28.6	20.1	2.5	2012
China	1357.0	7,078	36.7	53.2	2.9	2013
Fiji	0.8	4,178	43.1	51.1	1.8	2008
Micronesia, Fed. Sts.	0.1	3044	40.3	22.3	0.3	2013
Indonesia	257.6	3,346	41.0	53.7	2.6	2015
Kiribati	0.1	1152	33.2	43.6	2.1	2006
Lao PDR	6.5	1,445	37.9	35.7	4.9	2012
Malaysia	29.0	10,835	41.8	72.5	2.6	2012
Mongolia	2.9	4,202	32.9	71.2	3.0	2014
Myanmar	53.9	1,161	—	34.1	2.5	2015
Papua New Guinea	6.7	1,210	41.9	13.0	2.2	2009
Philippines	96.0	2,605	44.5	44.8	1.1	2012
Samoa	0.2	3376	43.5	20.5	-0.4	2008
Solomon Islands	0.5	882	39.8	17.8	4.8	2005
Thailand	67.5	6,225	36.4	47.9	3.1	2013
Timor-Leste	1.0	552	34.4	27.6	4.0	2007
Tonga	0.1	3076	39.2	23.3	0.8	2009
Vanuatu	0.2	2966	35.2	24.6	3.6	2010
Vietnam	90.7	2,052	33.1	32.9	3.0	2014

Source: World Bank, World Development Indicators, most recent value (2015), as reported in the *East Asia and Pacific Economic Update* (October 2016).
Note: — = not available.

The study aims to provide knowledge to better address these goals by understanding issues of urban poverty, inequality, and urban inclusion in EAP, particularly for those living in slums. The report audience broadly includes policy makers, researchers, donors, and practitioners who work at both the city and national levels. It draws on the analysis of existing data, literature, case studies, and two specially-designed surveys of the low-income urban areas in Metro Manila, Philippines, and in Ulaanbaatar, Mongolia.[2] As data across countries are not always consistent, the study uses specific examples to illustrate key points.

This introductory chapter covers broad trends related to urbanization, poverty, and inequality in the EAP region, setting the context against which to interpret the key findings and recommendations in the report's subsequent chapters.

Urbanization in the EAP region

Urbanization's Growing Importance in the EAP Region

The EAP region is the most rapidly urbanizing region globally, with the largest urban population (figure 1.2). At 3 percent for the region,[3] average annual urban population growth is significantly higher than the global rate of 2.06 percent and is second only to Sub-Saharan Africa (3.90).[4] The EAP urban population is estimated at 1.2 billion or roughly one-third of the world's urban residents/dwellers.[5] Much of this rapid urbanization is happening in China, where the government has been instrumental in strategically directing urbanization to promote growth and prosperity. China accounts for two-thirds of the region's total urban land and experienced an increase of 130 million in its urban population between 2000 and 2010 (World Bank 2015a). However, even without including China's contribution to urbanization, the EAP region exhibits high rates of urban population growth, averaging 2.5 percent per annum.

Of the world's megacities, 6 out of 10 are in EAP. Beyond the megacities, the majority of the urban population lives in small and medium cities. These areas will continue to grow, with estimates that more than of half the region's population will be living in urban areas by 2018 (UN Habitat 2015).

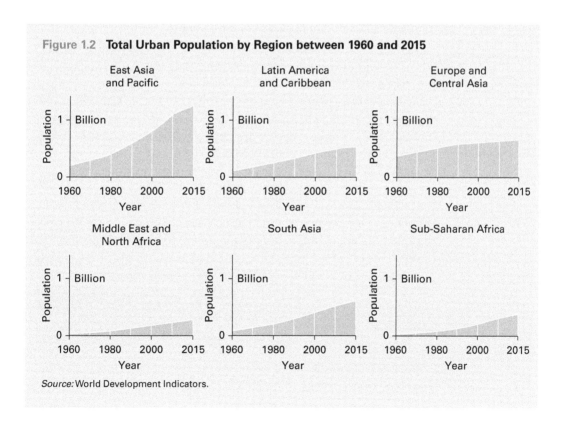

Figure 1.2   Total Urban Population by Region between 1960 and 2015

Source: World Development Indicators.

Urban population growth can be explained by a number of contributors, including: natural growth (for example, a natural increase in urban population due to births); rural-to-urban migration; net international migration; and spatial reclassification.

In most EAP countries, natural growth and spatial reclassification account for much of urban population increase (UN DESA 2012). However, in more recent times, research has indicated migration's significant contribution to the urbanization process (World Bank and IMF, 2013). China alone has experienced the greatest internal (rural-to-urban) migration in history over the past three decades. In 2013, rural migrant workers accounted for nearly half (44 percent) of total urban employment (World Bank and Development Research Center of the State Council, China, 2014). However, household registration policies put migrants at a disadvantage when they move to urban areas. In EAP, countries such as Vietnam, Indonesia, the Philippines, and Thailand have all had exclusionary policies disadvantaging migrants. Though these are changing, the prevailing attitude towards migrants often remains negative. While migrants are not always poor when they arrive in a city, they may fall into poverty traps resulting from barriers to new residents, and their contribution to the city's prosperity is not fully realized (IOM 2015).

Diversity of EAP Urbanization across the Region

Urbanization levels vary considerably throughout the region. For example, over half of the populations of China, Fiji, Indonesia, Malaysia, and Mongolia, and nearly half of the population in the Philippines, now live in urban areas.[6] Korea and Malaysia were able to achieve high urbanization levels by the 1990s, whereas China, Indonesia, and Thailand saw spurts in urban growth almost two decades later. The Philippines stands out as a unique country that was considered an early urbanizer—along with Korea and Malaysia in the 1990s—however, its rate of urban growth has dropped in recent years.[7]

Unlike other regions in the world, such as Latin America and the Caribbean, and South Asia, EAP has been slower in meeting the 50 percent threshold of urbanization, but that is now changing. EAP exhibits great diversity as urban areas develop, from the growth of megacities in China and Japan, to primate cities such as Jakarta and Manila, and medium and smaller urban areas that are now being pushed to accommodate growing populations and land expansion (figure 1.3) (see box 1.1 for a description of the measurement approach).

Substantial exposure to risk in EAP cities

The EAP region is the most disaster-stricken in the world, affected by small recurrent as well as rare, high-impact events (Jha and Stanton-Geddes 2013). Exposure to these events is particularly high in cities,

Figure 1.3   **Urban Population by Country, 2000 and 2010**

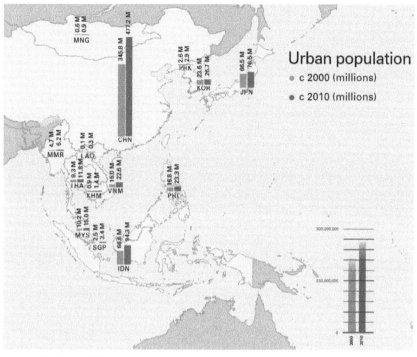

Source: World Bank 2015a.
Note: CHN = China; IDN = Indonesia; JPN = Japan; KHM = Cambodia; KOR = Korea, Rep.;
LAO = Lao People's Democratic Republic; MMR = Myanmar; MNG = Mongolia; MYS = Malaysia;
PHL = Philippines; PRK = Korea, Dem. People's Rep.; SGP = Singapore; THA = Thailand;
VNM = Vietnam.

Box 1.1   Measuring Urban Extent through New Data Sources

In an effort to create a common measure of urban expansion across different countries, the World Bank used satellite imagery and demographic data to measure expansion and population change in EAP between 2000 and 2010. To create maps of built-up areas throughout the region, change-detection methods were applied to analyze Moderate Resolution Imaging Spectro radiometer (MODIS) satellite data.[a] These maps rely on a geophysical definition of built-up areas.

The characteristics extracted from satellite imagery were then combined with the AsiaPop map, which models population distribution using census and other data as inputs. In brief, the 2000 and 2010 MODIS-derived built-up areas were integrated with detailed land cover data derived from the Landsat remote sensing project run by the U.S. Geological Survey and NASA. These refined land cover data sets were then combined with land cover–based population density weightings that were derived from fine resolution census data, and used to disaggregate the administrative-unit-level population counts to a 100-meter × 100-meter grid.

Although most of the built-up land observed by satellites is in urban areas, that built-up land also includes many small settlements that are commonly thought of as rural.

For the analysis in this section, the following definitions are used:

• Mega city: more than 10 million people
• Extra-large city: 5 to 10 million people

(Box continues on next page)

Box 1.1   **Measuring Urban Extent through New Data Sources** *(continued)*

- Large city: 1 to 5 million
- Medium city: 500k to 1 million
- Small city: 100k to 500k
- Smaller towns and rural areas

With these classifications, the location of cities and the information available from poverty maps are then spatially matched for a subset of countries. This process allows characterization of the distribution of poverty across places.

While this approach allows for a consistent definition of urban areas, it should be noted that this categorization does not coincide with national official breakdowns of urban and rural areas, and therefore, must be interpreted with some caution. However, given the lack of any other comparable resource and with the acknowledgement of a homogeneous, built area-based definition of urban, this analysis provides valuable insight into the distribution of poor within the urban category by breaking down the location of poor by city size. One limitation of the method is that it does not allow a breakdown of city categories for cities with less than 100,000 individuals.[b]

Source: World Bank 2015a.
a. Mertes et al. forthcoming.
b. This number was the threshold for the cities analyzed for the EAP Urban Expansion Report (2015).

with their concentration of people and assets. This situation is aggravated by weak regulatory and urban planning policies and practices.

There are high risks of flooding, cyclones, and earthquakes, particularly in coastal cities, where impacts include household property damages and the disruption of basic services due to the destruction of road networks and energy sources. This situation may, in turn, lead to the disruption in the availability of water, food, and other supplies, and the need to evacuate residents temporarily to other areas until the water recedes.

Six out of the 10 cities most vulnerable to coastal flooding due to sea level rise and storm surge are in the East Asia region, including Guangzhou (4), Ho Chi Minh City (5), Shanghai (6), Bangkok (7), Yangon (8), and Hai Phong (10) (Hanson et al. 2011). These cities are all key economic hubs in their respective countries and in the region as a whole. Recent flood events in Bangkok and Manila, and devastating earthquakes in China and Indonesia have resulted in a substantial loss of lives and demonstrate the debilitating impacts on the country's economy and its people (figure 1.4).

East Asia is also vulnerable to socioeconomic shocks because of its full integration in the global economy. These shocks include the 1998 Asian Financial Crisis, the severe acute respiratory syndrome (SARS) crisis in 2003, the oil price increase from 2003–08, the global food price crisis in 2007–08 and 2011, and the global financial crisis in 2008–09.

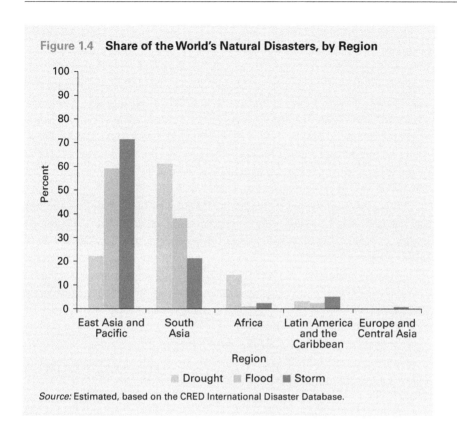

Figure 1.4   **Share of the World's Natural Disasters, by Region**

Source: Estimated, based on the CRED International Disaster Database.

All these events had major impacts on economic growth and affected many through changes in labor markets, reverse migration, and weakening social protection and capital (Bauer and Thant 2015). (See chapter 2.)

Poverty Reduction and Urbanization in the EAP Region

The EAP region stands out for its impressive rate of poverty reduction in recent years. In the past two decades, it has had the most rapid decline in poverty of any region, at any other point in time (Packard and Nguyen 2014). In 1990, EAP had the highest level of extreme poverty globally at 56.2 percent.[8] Since then, EAP has seen a reduction in its population living in extreme poverty, declining to just 12.5 percent in 2010.[9] In other words, 655 million people were lifted out of extreme poverty in this region alone within the past two decades. There has also been a dramatic reduction in the poverty gap, from 19.1 to 2.82 over the past two decades.[10] Much of this reduction occurred in China, where approximately 536 million people were lifted from extreme poverty during this period.[11]

The tremendous achievements in poverty reduction in the EAP region have largely been linked to the region's rise in labor productivity, particularly in China, where productivity has tripled since 2000 (Packard and Nguyen 2014), and in Vietnam, where it has doubled. Rising labor income in the late 2000s was also significant in Cambodia, Philippines, Mongolia, Thailand, and Vietnam, accounting for 40 percent of poverty reduction. Higher labor productivity is linked to the shift from rural agriculture to urban manufacturing and services, where new jobs have been located in urban areas with higher earning potential (Michaels, Rauch, and Redding 2012; Packard and Nguyen 2014).

The region is projected to maintain this path of high growth. Estimates indicate that only a modest reduction in growth is expected, from 6.5 percent in 2015, to 6.3 percent in 2016, and 6.2 percent in 2017–18 (World Bank 2016). Almost two-fifths of 2015 global economic growth occurred in EAP—or twice the contribution of all other developing countries combined. The trajectory for the next two years also appears positive; for example, the Philippines and Vietnam are expected to have the highest growth potential, over 6 percent in 2016 alone (World Bank 2016).

Within the region, Malaysia has been hailed as an example of a country that has managed high economic growth while simultaneously reducing poverty and inequality.[12] In Malaysia, the share of households living in poverty dropped from more than 50 percent in the 1960s, to less than 2 percent in 2012. This development progress has been achieved primarily through social programs that provided immediate support to the urban poor in the short term and supported infrastructure and human capital development in the long term (UN Habitat 2008). If managed well, positive economic growth in other EAP countries can help facilitate further poverty reduction.

In general, urban areas demonstrate lower poverty levels (World Development Indicators 2015), though the hidden pockets of vulnerable populations are difficult to account for and data are often scant at the intra city level (UN Habitat 2015). There are also multidimensional aspects of poverty that are not captured through the standard poverty measures that typically reflect income poverty. Unlike the rural poor who produce much of what they use and consume, the urban poor are reliant on the cash-based economy of urban areas and must pay for the food they consume (Tacoli 2012). Expenses for shelter and other basic services put further strain on poor households, perpetuating their vulnerability and hindering upward mobility (boxes 1.2 and 1.3). Noting these caveats on the challenges of measuring urban poverty, table 1.2, below, presents the most recently available urban poverty estimates based on country-specific surveys using US$3.10/day 2011 purchasing power parity (PPP) estimates, which account for spatial price differentials, as well as the percentage of urban population below national poverty lines for urban areas. The table shows relatively higher levels of urban poverty in a

Box 1.2   **Challenges in Measuring Urban Poverty**

Measuring poverty, particularly in cities, is fraught with problems, including the following:

 (i) Difficulties in capturing income and expenditure accurately
 (ii) Multidimensional aspects of poverty that account for the nonmonetary aspects of deprivation;
 (iii) Establishing where to set the poverty line, which represents a common threshold across countries and time
 (iv) How to account in national-level poverty lines for the higher cost of living in urban areas;
 (v) Inconsistent approaches to defining urban areas
 (vi) The fact that most household surveys are conducted at the national level with representation of urban/rural areas, but not at the intra-city level.

Concerns also arise as poverty measures do not take into account the social effects on welfare such as relative deprivation, shame, and social exclusion.

The most commonly used methodology relies on welfare estimates using consumption data from national household-level surveys and defines poverty at two levels: an extreme poverty line of US\$190 per day and a higher poverty line of US\$3.10 per day (in 2011 purchasing power parity [PPP] dollars). These data include spatial price adjustments to account for cost of living differences in urban and rural areas.[a]

In 2015, Vietnam announced the countrywide integration of a multidimensional[b] poverty measurement alongside the traditional income-based approach to monitor urban livability across a range of settlement sizes. The new measure captures information along dimensions of health, education, housing, water and sanitation, and information, in addition to an income threshold. Recent estimates highlight significant regional differences in the level of multidimensional poverty, particularly driven by lack of access to basic services and infrastructure, with the Mekong Delta Region demonstrating the highest level of multidimensional deprivation.[c]

a. Ravallion 2008.
b. See http://vpcp.chinhphu.vn/Home/Ban-hanh-chuan-ngheo-tiep-can-da-chieu/201511/17556.vgp.
c. Le, Nguyen, and Phung 2015.

Box 1.3   **Multidimensional Poverty in Metro Manila**

Income poverty alone does not provide a sufficient understanding of the extent of deprivations faced by residents of Metro Manila's slums. Multidimensional poverty is a better measure, taking into account the effect that variables such as access to municipal services or tenure security can have on the experience of poverty. In the case of Metro Manila, access to clean water, education, and employment are the top three factors that contribute to multidimensional poverty as shown in figure B1.3.1, below.

Relative contributions of the variables differ across slums. For example, lack of access to clean water is much more pronounced in its contribution to multidimensional poverty in "pocket" and "wet" slums[a] than in mixed settlements, while household assets and access to health services remain consistent across the board. This information feeds into the larger narrative that all slums are not the same.

(Box continues on next page)

Box 1.3   Multidimensional Poverty in Metro Manila *(continued)*

How important exactly are the nonmonetary dimensions of poverty? A transitional matrix approach was used to estimate the probability of being multidimensional poor, given income poverty status as shown in table B1.3.1, below.

Importantly, nearly one-quarter of nonpoor individuals (23.36 percent) are considered multidimensional poor. This result suggests that multidimensional deprivations are highly prevalent within slum communities and that income over the poverty threshold is not sufficient to ensure a standard of living without significant deficits.

Figure B1.3.1   **Relative Contribution to Multidimensional Poverty, Metro Manila, 2016**

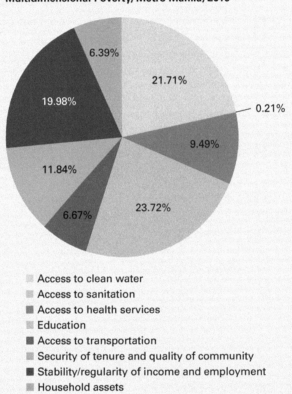

- Access to clean water
- Access to sanitation
- Access to health services
- Education
- Access to transportation
- Security of tenure and quality of community
- Stability/regularity of income and employment
- Household assets

Table B1.3.1   **Comparing Income versus Multidimensional Poor Individuals Based on Income Status**

		Multidimensional poverty (k = 40%)	
		Poor (%)	Nonpoor (%)
Income (nonfood poverty threshold, 2015)	Nonpoor	23.36	76.64
	Poor	34.45	65.55

Source: World Bank 2017b.
a. Wet slums are prominently situated along, on, and near water bodies. Pocket slums are small and highly dense informal settlements in vacant spaces. See Metro Manila Case Study for full details.

Table 1.2   **Urban Poverty and Inequality across the EAP Region**

Country	Year	Data source	Poverty rate ($3.10/day 2011PPP)	Number of urban poor ($3.10/day 2011 PPP)	Poverty gap ($3.10/day 2011PPP)	Poverty rate using national poverty lines	National Gini coefficient
Cambodia	2012	CSES	6.96	207,879	0.94	6.4	28.6
China	2013	EAPTSD	3.44	24,826,200	0.72	3.44	36.7
Fiji	2008	HIES	11.07	47,700	2.61	26.2	43.1
Indonesia	2014	SUSENAS	28.97	40,100,300	8.05	8.3	41.0
Kiribati	2006	HIES	37.40	15,400	11.29	—	33.2
Lao PDR	2012	LECS	26.09	597,300	6.76	10.0	37.9
Malaysia	2012	HIS	0.42	88,400	0.06	1.0	41.8
Micronesia, Fed. Sts.	2013	HIES	35.28	8200	13.05	—	40.3
Mongolia	2014	HSES	2.76	57,200	0.50	18.8	32.9
Papua New Guinea	2009	HIES	51.34	448,000	21.51	29.3	42.4
Philippines	2012	FIES	17.42	7,495,000	4.58	13.0	44.5
Samoa	2008	HIES	7.33	2,760	1.37	—	43.5
Solomon Islands	2005	HIES	21.85	18,300	5.44	—	39.8
Thailand	2013	SES	0.42	135,800	0.05	7.7	36.4
Timor-Leste	2007	TLSLS	72.04	201,200	27.68	45.2	34.4
Tonga	2009	HIES	7.99	1,900	2.29	—	39.2
Vanuatu	2010	HIES	48.17	28,000	16.39	—	35.2
Vietnam	2014	VHLSS	2.64	789,300	0.57	3.8	33.1

Note: — = no observation/no data available. Poverty gap measures the extent to which individuals fall below the poverty line (the poverty gaps) as a proportion of the poverty line. Poverty gap squared, also known as poverty severity, averages the squares of the poverty gaps relative to the poverty line. Poverty rate measures the proportion of the population that is poor. World Bank, Global Poverty Working Group data were compiled from official government sources or computed by World Bank staff using national (that is, country–specific) poverty lines. CSES = Cambodia Socio-Economic Survey; EAPTSD = East Asia and Pacific Team for Statistical Development based on the following data: China National Bureau of Statistics, the Central Statistics Agency, using the China urban/rural integrated household survey since 2013, and separate China Rural Household and Urban Household surveys for earlier years. FIES = Family Income and Expenditure Survey; HIES = Household Income and Expenditure Survey; HIS = Household Income survey; HSES = Household Socio-Economic Survey; LECS = Lao Expenditure and Consumption Survey; SES = Household Socio-Economic Survey; SUSENAS = Survei Sosial Ekonomi Nasional; TLSLS =Timor-Leste Survey of Living Standards; VHLSS = Vietnam Household Living Standards Survey.

number of the Pacific Islands, in Indonesia and in Lao People's Democratic Republic (PDR).

Poverty reduction trends in EAP cities show notable advances. Despite the progress in poverty reduction, there are still an estimated 75 million urban poor in EAP countries (figures 1.5 and 1.6).[13] There has also been

Figure 1.5   Regional Urban Poverty Rates

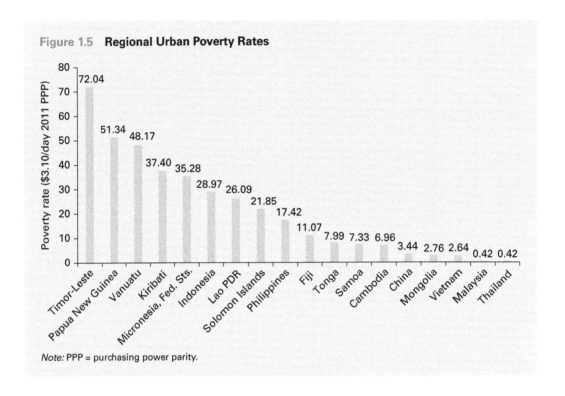

Note: PPP = purchasing power parity.

Figure 1.6   Urban Poverty Rates over Time, in the EAP region

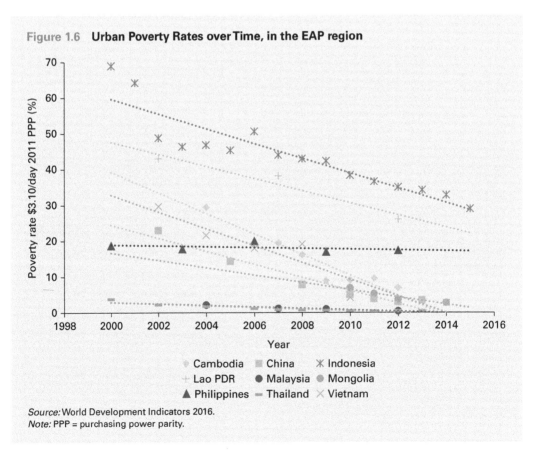

Source: World Development Indicators 2016.
Note: PPP = purchasing power parity.

a slight reversal of the gains in poverty reduction in recent years in Mongolia and the Philippines. In Mongolia, during the 2015–16 period, urban poverty was projected to increase, and World Bank estimates suggest that approximately 6.5 percent of the urban population may have already fallen below the poverty line (World Bank 2017a). In the Philippines, there was a slight increase in the share of urban poor (1 percent) between 2003 and 2012 (World Bank 2016).

Income Inequality in EAP Cities

Rising Income Inequality in Urban Areas

Despite exceptional economic growth, an overall increase in incomes, and a substantial reduction in poverty, income inequality has been increasing in the region, especially in high-growth economies such as China and Vietnam (UN Habitat 2008). Research suggests that East Asia has largely moved from a "growth with equality" model. This model links the rising inequality in the region to increasing income disparities that arise from the shift from a modern urban industrial society to a more services-driven economy.[14] This shift is consistent with rises in income inequality globally.[15] High income inequality levels have been found to: (i) reduce the efficacy of poverty reduction strategies; (ii) hamper economic growth; (iii) negatively impact all aspects of human development; and, (iv) contribute to social tension and conflict (UN Habitat 2008).

Rich EAP countries, such as Japan and Korea, are more urbanized (World Bank 2015a) in part due to their ability to harness the economic potential from urban growth at an early stage. No country has achieved high GDP levels without urbanizing, and those considered high-income have urbanization rates above 70 percent, a situation that demonstrates the correlation between place and welfare (World Bank and IMF 2013). However, urban growth does not reduce income inequality in cities on its own (World Bank 2015b). Instead, policies such as strategic spatial planning promote inclusion in cities by removing the physical barriers of accessing jobs and services (figure 1.7).

The rise in inequality in the region varies substantially by country and can be broken into rural-urban inequality, intra-urban inequality, and intra rural inequality.

Pockets of Urban Income Inequality

Pockets of poverty emerge as a result of intra-urban inequality, which can be especially stark given the proximity of rich and poor populations. There is a correlation between urbanization levels and the incidence of urban-rural inequality. The countries for which intra-urban inequality is greatest—such as Mongolia, Indonesia, and the Philippines—are more urbanized. Regardless, there are noted variations in inequality within EAP cities.

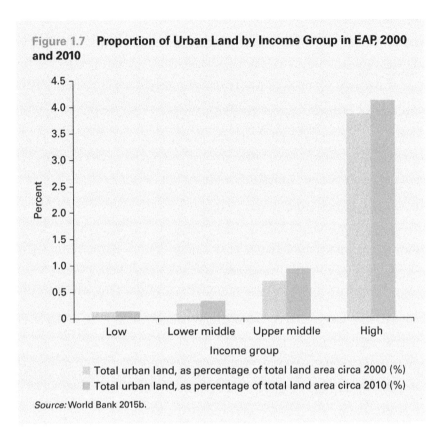

Figure 1.7 **Proportion of Urban Land by Income Group in EAP, 2000 and 2010**

Total urban land, as percentage of total land area circa 2000 (%)
Total urban land, as percentage of total land area circa 2010 (%)

Source: World Bank 2015b.

The most common measure used to understand the range and depth of inequalities is the Gini coefficient.[16] Gini coefficients for cities should be used with some caution as city-level estimations are not standardized across cities. Though data are limited, available Gini coefficient information demonstrates a range of income inequality across select EAP cities, as well as countries in the region (figure 1.8).

Beijing, for example, has the lowest Gini coefficient (0.22) and is therefore indicated by the numbers as the most egalitarian city—not only in EAP, but also in the world,[17] whereas Hong Kong SAR, China, has the highest Gini coefficient among all EAP cities. Other cities in EAP with high inequality (that is, above the 0.4 inequality threshold) include Chiang Mai (0.58), Udonthani (0.56), and Ho Chi Minh City (0.53). These cities also have a high incidence of urban poverty, somewhat indicative of the role inequality has in proliferating the threshold (UN Habitat 2008). It should be noted that cross-country comparisons of urban Gini coefficients are challenging to analyze as some are based on consumption data and other on income data; as a result, they should be cautiously interpreted (Sheng, Yap, and Thuzar 2012).

Figure 1.8   Intra-urban Inequalities (Gini Coefficients)

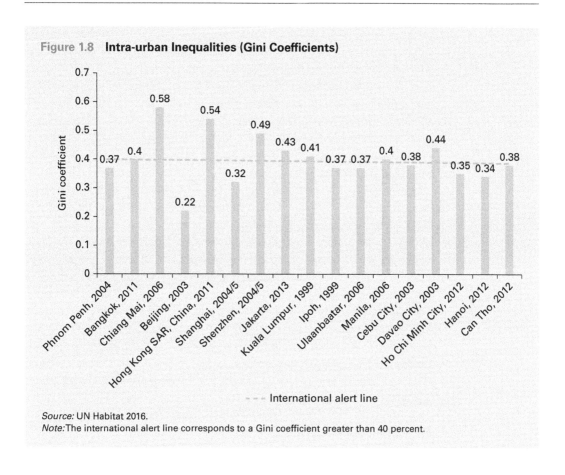

Source: UN Habitat 2016.
Note: The international alert line corresponds to a Gini coefficient greater than 40 percent.

Urban Poverty in Smaller Cities and Towns

The largest share of urban poverty in the EAP region is in smaller cities and towns. In the initial stages of urbanization, large cities and mega cities experience higher economic growth, while medium and small cities grow their economies in the later stages of urbanization. This situation can be explained by that fact that industries such as manufacturing first concentrate in existing cities, where people and services are already available, allowing economies of scale to flourish (World Bank 2009).

In the case of Vietnam, which is rapidly progressing on its development trajectory, Hanoi and Ho Chi Minh City are the two most important cities from an economic as well as a population perspective. Yet there is also a clear trend of the increasing importance of small and medium secondary cities; the proportion of the population in urban areas with more than 100,000 people increased from approximately 18 percent to more than 25 percent from 2000 to 2010. While manufacturing employment is still concentrated in the larger cities, growth in manufacturing employment between 1999 and 2009 was higher in small and medium-sized cities (World Bank 2011).

A study of eight developing countries worldwide showed an "inverse relationship between poverty and city size," where urban poverty was both more severe and widespread in smaller towns versus large cities. [18] In addition, the study found that the majority of the urban poor (both in proportion and in absolute terms) lived in medium, small, or very small towns, and therefore also suffered from severely reduced access to basic infrastructure and services.[19] A complementary issue is the quality of infrastructure, as many urban poor living in these smaller urban centers occupy substandard and dilapidated housing.

In line with the results in eight countries globally, additional studies show that poverty rates are lowest in the megacities and extra-large cities of the EAP region (figure 1.9) (Lozano Garcia et al. 2016). In Vietnam, only about 4.5 percent of those living in extra-large cities in 2009 were poor, while about 12 percent of those living in medium and small cities and more than 26 percent of those living in smaller towns and rural areas fell below the poverty line. In the Philippines, the poverty gradient along settlement sizes looks very similar to that of Vietnam, with the lowest poverty rates found in megacities (3.2 percent) and poverty increasing as city size decreases. Exceptions to this pattern are the medium-size cities in the Philippines. These cities outperform large cities (that is, they have lower poverty rates) by two percentage points, and with a poverty rate just above 7 percent experience half the poverty rate of small cities. Furthermore, in both Vietnam and the Philippines, more than 85 percent of the poor are living in smaller towns and rural areas. Faster reductions in poverty in large cities have led to a steeper poverty gradient, leading to differences in poverty rates of more than 20 percentage points between the largest city class and smaller towns and rural areas.

Indonesia started the 21st century with considerably lower poverty rates than Vietnam and the Philippines, but with a much flatter poverty gradient. In the early 2000s, poverty rates in megacities were 16 percentage points lower than in small towns and rural areas. That difference has declined to less than 10 percentage points or half the difference seen in Vietnam and Philippines. The distribution of the poor along the categories of settlements has remained much the same for the past 10 years, with a slight decrease of the percentage of the poor living in rural areas, from 51 percent in 2020 to 49 percent in 2012. This situation reflects an increase in the proportion of the poor living in megacities. Indonesia's flattening poverty gradient is the result of the fastest decline of poverty rates in smaller towns and rural areas, where poverty rates fell by 10 percentage points. Poverty reduction in Indonesia has been the result of steady economic growth, a reduction of unemployment, increasing incomes, and several poverty alleviation programs.

Such shifts in the transformation of economic geography go hand-in-hand with shifts in rural-urban migration streams to smaller cities. Increased migration, along with growth due to natural increase, puts pressure on the limited carrying capacity of urban infrastructure and services in these

Figure 1.9   Poverty and Place

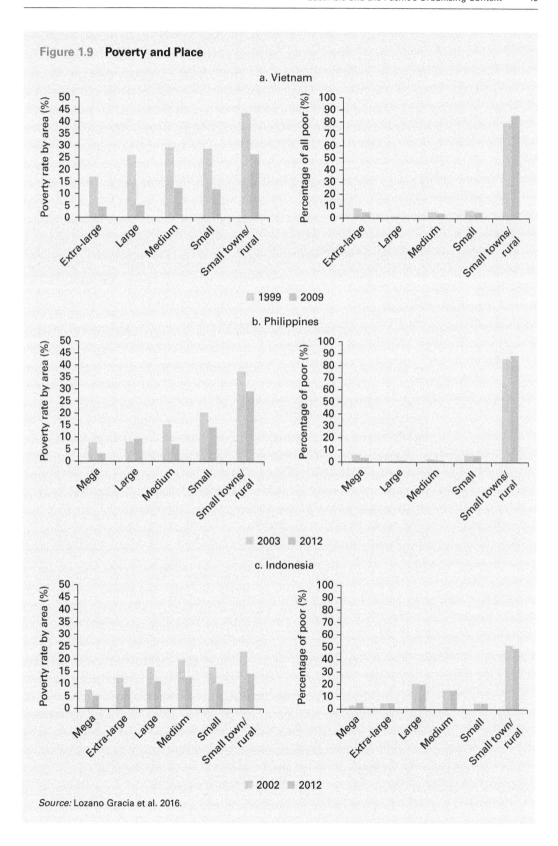

Source: Lozano Gracia et al. 2016.

smaller cities. It also affects the employment rate, if there is more anticipation of economic growth than actual jobs created.

The concentration of poverty in medium and small towns across the region will require a targeted response as these urban areas generally have more constrained resources, poorer service delivery, and less access to opportunities. Spatial unevenness will have to be examined closely in addressing urban poverty and growth patterns.

Characteristics of Urban Poverty in EAP: Large Slum Populations

One of the most visible physical manifestations of inequality and urban poverty is the prevalence of informal settlements or slums.[20] The persistence of slums within EAP cities signals a trend towards the urbanization of poverty and raises concerns that the benefits of urban agglomeration have not accrued to all residents in these cities. While not all urban poor live in slums and not all slum dwellers are income poor, slums nevertheless mark the sites of deprivation and exclusion (monetary, infrastructural, social, and political) within the urban built environment. No city can claim to be livable and prosperous when large population segments live in slums without access to basic services or adequate infrastructure.

Although slums offer the short-term benefits of access to the city, jobs, low-cost services, and markets to support self-employment, there are long-term and cyclical negative impacts. The urban poor reside in substandard housing with unsecure tenure. Without proper land regularization and tenure security, they are unable to access certain services. This situation can result in further exclusion from formal institutions, in a dependency on informal markets for employment, goods, and services, and in identity marginalization as the poor may lack formal proof of urban residency.

Around one-third of the urban population in developing countries, or about 1 billion people, live in slums (figure 1.10). Although the global share of the urban population living in slums has declined from 40 percent (2000) to 33 percent (2012), the absolute number has increased from 760 million (2000) to nearly 881 million (2014) (table 1.3) (UN DESA 2014).

In EAP, the slum population is estimated at 251.5 million (2014), the largest share of slum population in the developing world (UN Habitat, Global Urban Indicators Database). Within the region, Indonesia (29.2 million), the Philippines (17.0 million), and China (191.1 million) have sizeable slum populations[21] (see chapter 3, below). Some of these numbers are conservative estimates as the enumeration process is often under-resourced and lengthy, and households go unreported.

The pervasiveness of substandard living conditions and slums highlights the level of deprivation and of inequality experienced by urban residents across the region. Given its size, China holds the largest number of

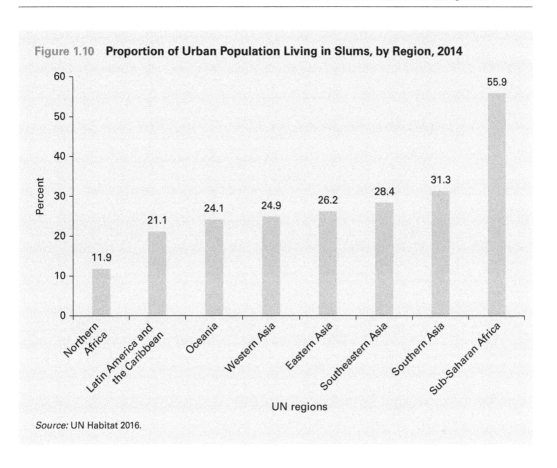

Figure 1.10   **Proportion of Urban Population Living in Slums, by Region, 2014**

Source: UN Habitat 2016.

Table 1.3   **Urban Slum Population by Region, 2014**

Region[a]	Urban slum population (thousands)	Proportion of global urban slum population (%)
Oceania	591	0.07
Northern Africa	11,418	1.30
Western Asia	37,550	4.26
Southeastern Asia	83,528	9.48
Latin America and the Caribbean	104,847	11.90
Southern Asia	190,876	21.66
Eastern Asia	251,593	28.56
Sub-Saharan Africa	200,677	22.78
Total:	**881,080**	**100.0**

Source: UN Habitat 2016.
a. The regional breakdowns used by the UN data that include Southeastern Asia, Eastern Asia, and Oceania, correspond with World Bank EAP countries in the regional definition.

population living in urban villages, at 191 million people. There are sizeable slum populations in Indonesia (29.2 million) and the Philippines (17.0 million). However, in smaller, less-developed countries such as Cambodia and Myanmar, the percentage of urban poor residing in slum areas is highest (table 1.4). Box 1.4 highlights some of the various forms of informal housing across the region.

Table 1.4 **Urban Population Living in Slum Areas in Select EAP Countries, 2014**

Country	Percent of urban population	Urban slum population at mid-year (millions)
Cambodia	55.1	1.7
China	25.2	191.1
Indonesia	21.8	29.2
Lao PDR	31.4	0.8
Mongolia	42.7	0.8
Myanmar	41.0	7.3
Philippines	38.3	17.0
Thailand	25.0	8.2
Vietnam	27.2	8.2

Source: http://mdgs.un.org/unsd/mdg/Data.aspx.

Box 1.4 **Informal Settlements and Slum Communities from across the EAP Region**

Ger Area in Ulaanbaatar, Mongolia. Mongolian citizens registered to live in Ulaanbaatar are entitled to a free plot of land that, combined with rapid rural-urban migration, has resulted in low-density outward spatial development. Without many affordable rental options in the city center, new arrivals are being pushed further and further to the periphery. This *ger* area is a patchwork of plots divided by fences and occupied by detached single-unit homes ranging from traditional *gers* (round, felt-lined tents), to more free-standing, single-level, built houses. These neighborhoods are home to many of the urban poor, whose income poverty is worsened by inadequate infrastructure and service delivery by the municipal government.[a]

Kampungs in Jakarta, Indonesia. Informal settlements, or *kampungs*, are found throughout Jakarta as well as other Indonesian cities. They comprise densely populated, inner-city neighborhoods and are often located in flood-prone areas. Many of Indonesia's poorest households are pushed to land around lakes, canals, and other natural waterways as well as disposal sites and railway tracks, leaving them vulnerable to flooding. An estimated 12.2 percent of urban residents live in slums.[b]

Slums on Stilts in Manila, Philippines. Approximately 100 households live in an informal community near Laguna de Bay. Houses are built on stilts, with unsound wooden bridges connecting the structures. Mobility within the settlement is an issue, particularly for the elderly, the disabled, and pregnant women. There is a common fear of young children falling between the planks into the water below. The community is also susceptible to disease because of the ever-present stagnant water below the settlement. And every major storm, typhoon, and flood puts the community at risk.[c]

(Box continues on next page)

Box 1.4   **Informal Settlements and Slum Communities from across the EAP Region** *(continued)*

Urban Villages or Substandard Housing in China. Chengzhongcun (literally the "village in the city") are found in metropolitan areas throughout China. As cities expanded, local governments developed modern infrastructure and buildings on agricultural land acquired from rural collectives, without incorporating these villages into the urban master plan. As a result, high-rises and skyscrapers in city centers were built around villages that are governed by a village committee, and are excluded from municipal oversight and from municipal services. Consequently, these urban villages or substandard housing are subject to overcrowding and poor sanitary conditions, as residents rent rooms to incoming rural migrants to compensate for lost income opportunities, following the sale of their farmland. In Beijing, an estimated 1,700 urban villages house 3.7 million local residents along with 3.5 million to 4.0 million migrants. Half of China's migrant population lives in about 50,000 urban and suburban villages across the country.[d]

a. World Bank forthcoming b.
b. Anderson 2015.
c. World Bank forthcoming a.
d. World Bank 2014.

Notes

1. This study follows the World Bank's definition of the EAP Region. This diverse region includes Cambodia, China, Fiji, Indonesia, Kiribati, Korea, the People's Democratic Republic of Lao (Lao PDR), Malaysia, Marshall Islands, Federated States of Micronesia, Mongolia, Palau, Papua New Guinea, the Philippines, Samoa, Solomon Islands, Thailand, Timor-Leste, Tonga, Vanuatu, and Vietnam.

2. These cities were selected to coincide with parallel work that benefited greatly from new data on low-income residents.

3. Urban population growth rate describes the rate of growth of the urban population whereas urbanization rate describes the rate of change in urban population as a proportion of total population (World Bank 2015).

4. Urban population growth rates are from 2013. Source: World Development Indicators, "Urban population growth (annual %)." When only developing countries in EAP are considered, the urban population growth rate increases to 2.82. The Sub-Saharan Africa (SSA) urban population growth rate is the same for all countries and developing countries in SSA.

5. According to GeoHIVE 2015, approximately 32 percent of the world's urban population live in EAP (over 1.2 billion people). The second largest urban population lives in Africa (11 percent).

6. Based on World Development Indicators. Note: Comparisons of "urban" and "urbanization" are somewhat limited as the definitions of urban are often vague and vary widely across the region. In the case

of the Philippines, for example, the definition combines "administrative, population, and density criteria," whereas Lao PDR's definition of urban is based on a combination of population and physical characteristics of the city (such as roads, electricity, tap water, and so on) and Vietnam's definition relies on population without mention of population density (World Bank 2015a).

7. Analysis is from the 2016 World Development Indicators.

8. Extreme poverty is defined as living on less than 2005 PPP $1.25 per day.

9. World Development Indicators. The indicator is "Poverty headcount ratio at $1.25 a day (PPP) (percent of population) for EAP (developing countries only); 2010 was most recent figure available.

10. Poverty gap data are for EAP developing countries only for 1990 and 2011, respectively. Source: World Development Indicators.

11. Based on poverty rate (that is, "Poverty headcount ratio at $1.25 a day (PPP) (percent of population) and total population for China for 1990 and 2009. Source: World Development Indicators (WDI).

12. Malaysia's significant reduction of urban poverty from 18.7 percent of the urban population in 1979 to 2.4 percent in 1997 can be largely attributed to its rapid economic growth during this period. The unique feature about this country, however, is that urban income inequalities have also been decreasing since 1978, largely due to social programs.

13. Based on WDI using the US$3.10 (2011 PPP) poverty line.

14. Feng 2011. More specifically, Feng notes that "large-scale manufacturing industries, frequently associated with more equitable wages, were replaced by the expansion of service sectors where pay is much more heterogeneous and unequal. At one end of these service sectors (e.g., finance and information technology) are a small number of extremely well-compensated individuals while at the other end of the spectrum (e.g., temporary hires) are far more numerous lowly paid individuals."

15. Pew Research Center analysis of the World Bank PovcalNet database and the Luxembourg Income Study database, August 2015.

16. The Gini coefficient draws on expenditure and income growth data to rank economic disparities on the range of 0 to 10, with 0 being the most equal, 10 the most unequal, and 0.4 illustrating the international alert line threshold that determines the performance of different areas.

17. However, one study showed that, when migrants are included, the Gini coefficient for Beijing increased to 0.33 (Source: Dai 2005).

18. Ferré et al. 2012. The eight countries include Albania, Brazil, Kazakhstan, Kenya, Mexico, Morocco, Thailand, and Sri Lanka.

19. Ibid. They also found that "in four of the eight (Albania, Brazil, Sri Lanka and Thailand), a majority of the urban poor live in towns smaller than 100,000 people."

20. A slum is defined as a group of slum households based on the UN Habitat definition referring to individuals living under the same roof in an urban area who lack one or more of the following: 1) durable housing of a permanent nature that protects against extreme climate conditions;

2) sufficient living space which means not more than three people sharing the same room; 3) easy access to safe water in sufficient amounts at an affordable price; 4) access to adequate sanitation in the form of a private or public toilet shared by a reasonable number of people; and 5) security of tenure that prevents forced evictions.

21. In China this population lives in urban villages or substandard housing.

References

Anderson, R. P. 2015. "Indonesia - National Affordable Housing Program Project." World Bank, Washington, DC.

Bauer, A., and M. Thant, eds. 2015. *Poverty and Sustainable Development in Asia: Impacts and Responses to the Global Economic Crisis*. Manila: Asian Development Bank.

Dai, E. 2005. "Income Inequality in Urban China: A Case Study of Beijing." The Working Paper Series, Volume 2005-04. International Centre for the Study of East Asian Development, Kitakyushu.

Feng, W. 2011. "The End of Growth with Equity? Economic Growth and Income Inequality in East Asia." East-West Center, Honolulu, Hawaii.

Ferré, C., F. H. G. Ferreira, and P. Lanjouw. 2012 "Is There a Metropolitan Bias? The Relationship between Poverty and City Size in a Selection of Developing Countries." *The World Bank Economic Review* 26 (3): 351–82.

International Organization for Migration (IOM). 2015. *World Migration Report- Migrants and Cities: New Partnerships to Manage Mobility*. Geneva: IOM.

Jha, A., and Z. Stanton-Geddes, eds. 2013. *Strong, Safe, and Resilient: A Strategic Policy Guide for Disaster Risk Management in East Asia and the Pacific*. Washington DC: World Bank.

Hanson, S., et al. 2011. "A Global Ranking of Port Cities with High Exposure to Climate Extremes." *Climatic Change* 104.1: 89–111.

Lozano Gracia, et al. 2016. *Spatial Disparities in East Asia*. Draft.

Michaels, G., F. Rauch, and S. J. Redding. 2012. "Urbanization and Structural Transformation." *The Quarterly Journal of Economics* 127 (2): 535–86 (May).

Packard, T. G., and T. V. Nguyen. 2014. "East Asia Pacific at Work: Employment, Enterprise, and Well-Being." World Bank, Washington, DC.

Satterthwaite, D., M. Montgomery, and H. Reed. 2003. "Diversity and Inequality." In *Cities Transformed. Demographic Change and Its Implications in the Developing World*. National Research Council of the National Academies, Washington DC.

Sheng, Y. K., and M. Thuzar, eds. 2012. "Urbanization in Southeast Asia: Issues and Impacts." Institute of Southeast Asian Studies, Singapore.

Tacoli, C. 2012. "Urbanization, Gender and Urban Poverty: Paid Work and Unpaid Carework in the City." Human Settlements Group, International Institute for Environment and Development, New York.

UN DESA. 2012. *World Urbanization Prospects, 2011 Revision*. New York: UN DESA.

———. 2014. *The Millennium Development Goals Report*. New York: UN DESA.

UN Habitat. 2008. *State of the World's Cities 2008–2009: Harmonious Cities*. Earthscan. London: UN Habitat.

———. 2015. *The State of Asian and Pacific Cities 2015*. London: UN Habitat.

World Bank. 2009. *World Development Report 2009: Reshaping Economic Geography*. Washington, DC: World Bank.

———. 2011. *World Bank East Asia and Pacific Economic Update 2011, Volume 1: Securing the Present, Shaping the Future*. Washington, DC: World Bank.

———. 2015a. "*East Asia's Changing Urban Landscape: Measuring a Decade of Spatial Growth*." Urban Development. World Bank, Washington, DC.

———. 2015b. "World Inclusive Cities Approach Paper." World Bank Report AUS8539. World Bank, Washington, DC, May.

———. 2016. "Growing Challenges." In *East Asia and Pacific Economic Update*. World Bank, Washington DC, April.

———. Forthcoming a. "Navigating Informality: Perils and Prospects in Metro Manila's Slums. Metro Manila Slum Study." World Bank, Washington, DC.

———. Forthcoming b. "Urban Poverty in Ulaanbaatar: Understanding its Dimensions and Addressing the Challenges." World Bank, Washington, DC.

World Bank, and Development Research Center of the State Council, the People's Republic of China. 2014. *Urban China: Toward Efficient, Inclusive, and Sustainable Urbanization*. Washington, DC: World Bank.

World Bank and IMF (International Monetary Fund). 2013. *Global Monitoring Report 2013: Rural-Urban Dynamics and the Millennium Development Goals*. Washington, DC: World Bank.

CHAPTER 2

Economic Inclusion and the Urban Poor

Introduction

Economic inclusion is centered on enabling even the most marginalized to contribute to the economy and share in the benefits of economic growth. Employment and good jobs are critical to poverty reduction and economic inclusion in cities, particularly given the heavy reliance of the urban poor on cash incomes, their vulnerability to job losses and wage reductions in urban-based industries, and the absence of agricultural production to fall back on. External shocks can also impact their economic inclusion, particularly if mechanisms for resilience do not exist, as is typically the case for the urban poor.

In the East Asia and Pacific (EAP) region, employment is characterized by a high degree of informality, which leaves many, particularly the poor, without stable incomes and benefits. Recent estimates show that the informal economy represents 65 percent of total employment in East Asia (excluding China). This situation is comparable to rates seen in Sub-Saharan Africa (66 percent) and is higher than rates in Latin America (51 percent), Eastern Europe (10 percent), and Central Asia (10 percent) (ILO 2014). Within the region, levels of informality vary significantly between countries (figure 2.1).

The EAP region is also particularly vulnerable to shocks, due to its integration with the global economy and to the fact that it experiences over 70 percent of the world's natural disasters. This affects the economic inclusion of the urban poor, as they tend to be more vulnerable to shocks due to their living conditions, limited access to safety nets, and a lack of savings on which to rely. Economic inclusion is unattainable unless the resilience of the urban poor to external shocks can be strengthened.

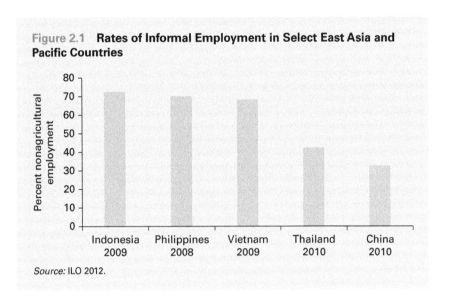

Figure 2.1   **Rates of Informal Employment in Select East Asia and Pacific Countries**

Source: ILO 2012.

Employment Trends in East Asia and the Pacific

Global Economic Integration and Employment Opportunities

For the past two decades, EAP economic activity has been defined by high levels of integration in the global economy. More than any other developing region, EAP has oriented itself towards world trade and export manufacturing, and as a result, has created employment opportunities that have allowed millions of people to rise out of poverty over the past 20 years.

The types of jobs available to those entering labor markets are changing, creating new opportunities, but also new requirements for skills. In China, rising labor costs have resulted in low-cost labor production moving to countries such as Bangladesh, Mexico, Morocco, and Turkey (Packard and Nguyen 2014). In addition, employers in value-added manufacturing and services firms across the region are demanding higher-skilled and more educated workers. In a survey of 473 manufacturing and service firms in Indonesia, 95 percent of respondents expected their demand for skilled labor to rise over the next decade (Packard and Nguyen 2014). The current growth slowdown in most emerging markets and developing economies, and the increase in protectionism may have future impacts on the labor markets in EAP countries.

Labor Earnings and Rising Inequality

The *World Development Report 2013: Jobs* (World Bank 2013b), provides evidence that increasing jobs and employment enables three critical development transformations, namely: productivity gains, improvements in living standards, and greater social cohesion. For much of their recent history, EAP countries were able to achieve all three transformations at a similar rate, which is common for countries in the early stages of urbanization.

Now, however, countries such as China, Indonesia, and Vietnam that have already achieved significant urbanization levels are experiencing more moderate growth rates, and a subsequent slowdown in productivity gains. This situation, in turn, has led to slower gains in living standards, and a focus of public attention on rising inequality.

Inequality is, in part, linked to jobs and the differences in labor earning, as well as to the increasing returns experienced by skilled labor. Among salaried workers in Indonesia, nonpoor workers saw an annual wage increase of 9.3 percent from 1999 to 2003, while poor and near-poor workers saw an increase of only 6 percent in the same time period. In Vietnam, there was a modest rise in income inequality from 2004 to 2010. In recent years, perceived inequality has given rise to employment-related protests throughout the region. In Indonesia, mining unions have organized strikes of thousands of workers, and in Vietnam there has been a notable increase in the number of illegal "wildcat" strikes, without the support of union leadership. In the context of rising inequality, working class and emerging middle class populations are voicing their demands for inclusive and equitable growth.

Growing Prevalence of Informality among the Urban Poor

Informal employment is particularly important for the urban poor, as it provides opportunities to workers who might not otherwise have jobs. Although the impact of the informal sector is difficult to quantify, available estimates suggest that the informal economy's contribution to GDP ranges from 30 to 70 percent in developing countries worldwide (ILO 2014). Urban informal workers are typically engaged in four broad categories of work, namely: domestic work (maids, housekeepers, nannies, care providers); home-based work (subcontractors for factories); street vending (food stalls, retail kiosks); and waste picking (ILO 2013b). Another category particular to EAP cities is the fishing of urban waterways by small entrepreneurs. Informal workers might also be employed illegally in formal enterprises. All these are sources of low-wage labor.

There is a strong association between informality and poverty in most countries. For example, in Indonesia significant wage differentials were found between formal and informal workers (table 2.1).

Informal work is also associated with a lack of labor regulations and social protections, lower wages, and an increased vulnerability to external shocks and exploitation (box 2.1).

Significant Female Labor Force Participation Creates Opportunity for Poverty Reduction

Women's labor force participation rate in the region is higher than any other region (table 2.2) and provides opportunities for both urban and rural households to rise out of poverty. Participation in the labor force is also increasing among young women (Packard and Nguyen 2014), suggesting that this trend will continue. Women are

Table 2.1   Average Wage Earnings by Employment Status in Urban Areas in Indonesia, 2011

	Formal (US$)	Informal (US$)	Ratio of formal: informal
Yogyakarta (Province)			
Employees	216	82	2.62
Self-employed	—	106	—
Average earnings	216	93	2.33
Banten (Province)			
Employees	193	144	1.35
Self-employed	246	118	2.08
Average earnings	194	134	1.45

Source: ADB 2011.
Note: — = not available.

Box 2.1   Informality in the Global Economic Crisis

Economies throughout East Asia and the Pacific not only withstood the global financial crisis and economic contraction of 2008–10, some also generated additional employment opportunities. This situation was managed, however, through a downwards adjustment in earnings, with workers shifting from formal to informal employment. Regionally, workers who had previously enjoyed full-time, registered, and regulated work, opted or were encouraged into part-time, unregistered, and informal contracts.[a] While "labor market flexibilization" or informal work was already common throughout the region, there were firms who used the economic crisis to accelerate the trend.

A direct result was the deterioration of labor conditions for workers. The garment industry was particularly hard hit by the financial downturn, and a survey of 2,000 Cambodian garment factory workers (90 percent female and 95 percent migrant) reported the following changes in their workplaces in the span of three months:

- Reduced overtime and a reduction in income
- Reduced regular working hours through compulsory paid leave, suspensions, shorter work weeks, or compulsory unpaid leave
- Delays in salary payment or fewer/no bonuses
- Unsafe working environment (such as fewer functional bathrooms, worse ventilation, no air conditioning, limited supplies in factory medical clinics)

Of the 1,200 workers still employed at the time of the benchmarking survey, more than half reported that they had insufficient income to meet such basic needs as food expenses, transportation, and healthcare, school fees for their children, or remittances to send home. Tellingly, the majority also had no savings to rely on in the event that they too were laid off.

Source: ILO 2011.
a. Packard and Nguyen 2014.

Table 2.2   **Female Labor Force Participation Rate by Region, 2014**

Region	Female labor force participation rate (%)
Global	50.293
East Asia and Pacific	61.345
Europe and Central Asia	50.784
Latin America and the Caribbean	53.757
Middle East and North Africa	21.853
North America	56.828
South Asia	30.548
Sub-Saharan Africa	63.774

Source: Labor force participation rate, female (% of female population ages 15+) (modeled ILO estimate). International Labour Organization, Key Indicators of the Labour Market database.

increasingly moving out of household work and family-owned enterprises and into nonagricultural employment.

The flow of migrants to several cities in the region has become increasingly female, and women comprise a significant proportion of the international migration in the region at large. The annual proportion of women migrating, of all Indonesian workers, reached approximately 80 percent in 2007, an increase from about 70 percent in 2000, while in Vietnam, women constituted 57 percent of individuals who had migrated internally or who were international migrants in the preceding five years (World Bank 2012, 186). There are also higher rates of female participation in the informal sector; working in this sector allows them the flexibility to assume the greater burden of household responsibilities that gender norms demand.

Key Challenges to Employment for the Urban Poor

A number of dynamics in urban labor markets create challenges for the urban poor in finding gainful employment and pathways out of poverty. Significant barriers are presented inter alia by the following:

* constraints in educational opportunities, skills and social networks
* social network gaps in accessing formal employment
* inadequate infrastructure to enhance job accessibility and working conditions
* a lack of financial inclusion

These barriers affect some subgroups of urban poor, such as migrants, youth, and women, to a greater extent.

Constraints in Education, Skills, and Social Networks

Educational and skills constraints: There is a clear link between urban poverty and educational attainment, and as markets across the region shift towards more skilled labor, it will be harder for workers with no higher education or skills training to secure jobs that pay living wages (box 2.2). For example, in Ho Chi Minh City and Hanoi, Vietnam, the proportion of workers without professional qualifications is much higher among the poorest quintile than among the richest quintile (table 2.3). Perhaps most telling is the difference in levels of higher education—in 2010, only 2 percent of workers among the poorest quintile had college or university education, compared to 46 percent of those in the richest quintile (UNDP 2010).

Low-income rural migrants remain at an additional disadvantage given the disparities in education quality between rural and urban areas. In addition, in several countries, including China and Vietnam, the children of rural migrants may be excluded from urban education systems due to capacity constraints, legal and regulatory barriers related to residency, and high costs. With what is essentially an unfunded mandate, municipalities have struggled to extend social services, including education, to migrants and their children. However, without access to good schools, these children are unprepared for a labor force requiring skilled and educated workers.

As a result, rural migrants are overrepresented in informal sectors, and the generational transfer of disadvantage is likely to continue as cities cannot meet the needs of the children of migrants. While barriers to educational attainment are key constraining job opportunities for migrants, these challenges are also coupled with the inability of migrants to be recognized

---

Box 2.2   Educational Barriers to Employment in Vietnam

A four-year urban poverty monitoring study was conducted in several peri-urban, low-income districts of Hanoi and Ho Chi Minh City, Vietnam. Below are excerpts of group discussions on the role of education in securing employment.

"Today without good education, business is not good. One is unable to apply for a job if one has not finished high school. For people of 35–40 years of age without education, their lives are very hard now." (Core group in Nhue Hamlet, Hanoi)

"In the past when one finished secondary school one could find a job, just taking into account one's health. Today even working as a factory worker, one has to finish high school. Now poor households are more aware of the importance of education than in the past. Now without education, one can do nothing. In 2008 the qualification was not important; 14-15 year-old boys and girls could be recruited as long as they had some skills. In the past it was easily to apply for a job, today it is more difficult." (Core group, Ho Chi Minh City)

"With primary and lower secondary level of education, one can only apply for jobs at small processing workshops, or work freelance with an unstable income. With an upper secondary level education, one can apply for state-owned companies or joint venture companies with more stable incomes." (Group of young unskilled workers, Ho Chi Minh City)

Source: Oxfam and Action Aid Vietnam 2012.

Table 2.3   Professional Training of Urban Labor Force, by Income Quintile and Percent, Vietnam, 2009

Income quintile	Untrained professional level (%)	Short-term technical worker (%)	Long-term technical worker (%)	Professional secondary and vocational secondary (%)	Colleges and vocational colleges (%)	University or higher (%)
Quintile 1 (poorest)	87.1	4.5	1.5	3.9	1.3	1.7
Quintile 5 (richest)	32.4	6.0	1.0	8.6	5.7	46.3

Source: UNDP 2010.

as legitimate urban residents in many cities in the EAP. In China, for example, more than 60 percent of migrant workers in 2010 had jobs in the informal sector, with limited mobility to formal employment (World Bank 2014). A study of migrants in Vietnam revealed that migrant workers were more likely than residents to be in unskilled labor (67 versus 43 percent), have no professional training (76 versus 60 percent), work an average of 10 hours more/week than residents, and were less likely to have a long-term contract (8 versus 27 percent). While child labor in Vietnam is relatively uncommon, 14.7 percent of migrant children between the ages of 10–14 were working, compared to only 1.1 percent of permanent resident children (UNDP 2010).

Youth unemployment and underemployment: With increased life expectancy in EAP, a key challenge in urban labor markets is to provide adequate jobs for a sizeable and growing youth population. Young people (16–24) in EAP economies are more likely to be working than elsewhere in the world, but youth unemployment across Southeast Asia and the Pacific remains high at 10.6 percent overall, and constrains poverty reduction in cities (Packard and Nguyen 2014). Youth unemployment trends are significant given that early labor market experiences can have ramifications on wages and employment throughout a worker's lifetime (box 2.3).

Fiji, Indonesia, the Philippines, Tuvalu, and Vanuatu have among the highest youth unemployment rates in the world, with more than 30 percent of people ages 15–24 not in employment, education, or training. The youth-to-adult unemployment ratio (5.2) in this region is the highest globally and is nearly double the global average (2.8),[1] meaning that youth in this region are five times more likely to be unemployed than adults. In Vietnam, the urban youth (15-19 years) unemployment rate is 11.5 percent, more than three times the overall urban unemployment rate.[2] This situation is slightly better than in Indonesia, where the unemployment rate (22.5 percent) for urban youth (15–24 years) is nearly five times the adult unemployment rate.[3] The same trend is also seen in Metro Manila where, at 28.1 percent, youth unemployment is more than four times the adult unemployment rate (UNDP 2013).

Box 2.3   **Youth Inactivity and Informal Employment in Indonesia**

Recent evidence from Indonesia has correlated youth unemployment with increased entry into the informal sector (Naidoo et al. 2014). Youth who resort to informal employment early on see very little mobility in their careers and find it especially difficult to transition to formal sector work (Packard and Nguyen 2014).

  Panel data from the Indonesia Family Life Survey from 2000 to 2007 revealed as much by following young men (ages 15–24) who identified as "self-employed sole traders." Essentially informal vendors working alone, these individuals saw the deterioration or stagnation of their own human capital, and zero or negative returns over time. Over the course of the study, only 2.6 percent of workers surveyed were able to transition to "self-employed with staff" and even fewer to formal sector work. In 2007, the median wage for youth working as sole-traders was around Rp 285,000 per month as compared with government work or private sector work with wages of Rp 475,000 and Rp 512,000 per month, respectively (Packard and Nguyen 2014).

Source: World Bank 2014.

Early unemployment pushes youth to enter the labor market through informal work, which then affects earning potential over the course of their working years. Underemployment is a related phenomenon that describes employed persons looking for more or better paying work to meet living expenses, and occurs most commonly among the urban poor.[4] Underemployment can be destabilizing for a society as real wages fail to keep up with the rising cost of living in urban areas.

For example, in the Philippines, underemployment persists at 20 percent, while among the poorest quartile of workers, underemployment is even higher at 33 percent. Paradoxically, of the underemployed, 38 percent (or 8 percent of the total employed population) are already working 40 hours or more per week (Chua et al. 2013). Underemployment is highest among less-educated workers as well as "prime-age" workers (35–44). This situation points to the economic vulnerability of the urban poor, who struggle to meet living expenses with their wages.

Social Networks: Social networks are vital links to larger social systems, and neighborhood networks may have a strong influence on job accessibility for low-income families. However, low-income families who live in predominantly poor areas (including affordable housing clusters) are often isolated from larger and more diverse social and economic opportunities, as they tend to rely on closer and more homogeneous social networks in searching for work (Kleit 2001).

Newly arrived migrants are at a disadvantage in finding job opportunities in markets where these opportunities are shared through social networks. In a multiyear study of urban poverty in Vietnam, respondents highlighted the difficulties that rural migrants faced in understanding urban labor markets due to imperfect information (Oxfam and Action Aid 2012).

These quotations from the young job seekers in Ho Chi Minh City, Vietnam, interviewed summarize the challenges:

"Here, parents seek information about different training institutions many years before their children finish secondary school. It is not like in rural areas, where parents are overloaded with work, so they just tell their children to select whatever training institutions they like. Even if they wanted to, they could not give guidance to their children. From my own experience, they are very disadvantaged compared to those in cities." (Migrant youth group)

"In rural areas, parents with children who have passed university entrance exams are very happy and proud. However, they have not thought about employment and do not know that university diplomas aren't always useful." (Educated youth group)

Similar experiences and perceptions were documented in the case of Myanmar. In addition to information, social networks may also reduce the opportunity cost of the move to cities while job searching (box 2.4).

Impacts of Inadequate Infrastructure and Service Delivery on Employment Opportunities

The urban poor disproportionately suffer from inadequate infrastructure and service delivery, which can affect their employment opportunities. For the urban poor living in peri-urban areas, access to the urban labor market can be seriously impaired unless the city provides adequate and affordable public transportation. The urban poor who choose to live in the city center are often concentrated in slums, where overcrowding and poor living conditions can create a host of other concerns. While in general, access to jobs is better for the poor living in the city center, barriers to mobility still exist

---

Box 2.4   Importance of Social Networks in the Job Search in Myanmar

Risk management, shock response, and upward mobility are the three primary drivers of Myanmar's growing rural-urban migration trend. For households in the first two categories, the threat or experience of an external shock (a natural disaster, medical illness, and so on) pushes families to send one or more members to the city in search of an alternate source of income. However, even those in already desperate financial situations are hesitant to make the move without first securing employment or assurances from other migrants as seen by survey responses below:

"There should be someone you know in the receiving community; only then you can get a job easily and you're more likely to succeed in your migration attempt." (Female, Magway)

"If I hadn't had a friend who secured a job for me and was willing to let me live with her, my family wouldn't have let me go to Yangon, even if we didn't really have any other option." (Female, Labutta Township, Ayeywarwady)

"I would like to go but if I go to Yangon while looking for a job it would be very difficult [financially] for my family left in the village. It is also difficult to find an affordable lodging in Yangon." (Male, Kyaunggon Township, Ayeywarwady)

Source: LIFT and World Bank 2016.

in the form of low spatial integration with the rest of the city, such as poor street connectivity, which effectively isolates the poor within slum areas (see chapter 3). These barriers may also serve to nudge the urban poor towards informal work if they are unable to easily access jobs in formal urban labor markets (Huitfeldt and Jüttin 2009).

For informal home-based workers, inadequate infrastructure and service delivery affect not only their living environment, but also their ability to work. For example, a small survey of home-based workers in Phnom Penh and Siem Reap, Cambodia, revealed that 74 percent lived in an unhealthy environment. None of the 60 workers in Siem Reap had access to water connections, adequate drainage, or garbage disposal. Workers also cited health hazards resulting from the use of unregulated materials and processes at the household level (Shalini 2013). While other residents might leave slums for work during the day, home-based workers are exposed to poor environmental conditions both day and night.

In addition to unsafe working conditions, home-based workers are generally required to cover all overhead costs for their work such as rent, equipment, and electricity. With inadequate service provision, home-based workers might unexpectedly see their earnings drop due to nonexistent or unreliable household electricity connections, as well as frequent power cuts. Common workaround measures, such as the reliance on private generators, create higher overhead costs. In both Cambodia and Thailand, home-based workers complained of the high cost of electricity, saying that despite working in dark, windowless rooms and in high temperatures, they chose not to use lights or fans to keep electricity costs low (Sinha 2013).

Lack of adequate services, such as affordable childcare services, can present specific impediments to women's labor force participation, especially when gender norms dictate their status as the primary caregivers. Women face several challenges, including greater time constraints due to a higher burden of domestic responsibilities. This situation is exacerbated by living conditions with low access to basic infrastructure; the uncertainty of work and income; low earnings and a gender gap in wages; and vulnerability to exploitation. Women's access to formal employment is often limited, and informal employment is a larger source of employment for women than men (Chen et al. 2006). Data on wages across the region suggest a significant and increasing gender gap. In Bangkok, men earned nearly 16 percent more than women in 2012, and in Cambodia, the male-female differentials in earnings in urban areas increased from 14.3 percent in 2004 to 32.8 percent in 2009 (UNDP and UN Habitat 2013).

Observations from a focus group in Ulaanbaatar indicate that young women, especially those who are married, are less employable due to perceptions among employers that they might exit the workforce to care for children. Young mothers often drop out of the labor force due to lack of child daycare centers and kindergartens, and limited social support systems. This situation compounds the barriers that poor women face in accessing employment in the city (box 2.5).

Box 2.5   **Employment Constraints for Young Women in Ulaanbaatar**

All women in the focus groups in Ulaanbaatar (2014) agreed that prospective employers demonstrate negative attitudes towards mothers, who are perceived as unemployable due to their childrearing responsibilities. Others recounted instances of employers explicitly asking about their plans to have children or asking women outright to delay pregnancies.

"I went to one place to get a job. I was asked whether I have husband and I said, 'Yes.' Then I was told that I should not have a baby for some years in near future. So I thought that a child was a barrier." (Female, unemployment focus group discussion)

When working, women with children also face difficulties in accessing childcare options. This predicament is particularly true for migrants who live in the very peripheral *ger* areas. There are a number of settlements in the far north and west of Songonokhairkhan, and the north and pockets of Khan-Uul where there is either no kindergarten or the kindergarten is located is more than 40 minutes' walking distance. This is a significant impediment for low-income women needing to work.

Source: World Bank 2016c.

Risk and Resilience among the Urban Poor

The impacts of natural hazards and economic shocks have been shown to negatively impact economic inclusion and to slow poverty reduction efforts. It is estimated that over 110 million people in Asia were prevented from escaping poverty (ADB 2013) and that the incidence of urban poverty increased by more than 1.5 percentage point in East Asia as a result of natural hazards and economic shocks (Baker 2008a). Communities have resisted, absorbed, and accommodated the effects of such disruptions in a variety of ways. In the following sections, the impacts of natural hazards and larger economic crises, the coping mechanisms adopted by the urban poor, and their overall levels of resilience are examined.[5]

Exposure to Natural Hazards and the Impacts on the Urban Poor

Natural disasters introduce an element of volatility to the economic growth of the EAP region and have proven to be quite costly. In 2011, one of the most expensive years on record, losses in EAP due to natural disasters totaled US $259 billion. These costs accrued in the first nine months of the year, and accounted for 80 percent of global losses due to natural disaster that year (Jha and Stanton-Geddes 2013). Because they disrupt work and production, natural disasters have a disproportionate effect on the urban poor, who rely on cash incomes from work to stay afloat in the urban economy. Table 2.4 and box 2.6 provide examples.

Due to the lack of affordable housing and land, the urban poor often live in less desirable and higher-risk locations such as hillsides and flood-prone areas at the banks of rivers or canals (either in slums or at the city periphery). In Jakarta, Indonesia, the poor are more likely to concentrate in flood-prone informal settlements in the north and northeast sides of the city,

Table 2.4   **Impacts of Flooding on Residents in Tham Luong–Ben Cat Subcatchment, Ho Chi Minh City, Vietnam**

Indicator	Poor	Nonpoor	Total
% households whose health was affected	86	64	68
% households whose employment was affected	69	56	58
% households whose income was affected	67	40	44

Source: World Bank and AUS AID 2014.

Box 2.6   Disruption of Home-based Work Due to Flooding in Thailand

The Informal Economy Monitoring Study is a current longitudinal study by WIEGO on the urban informal economy of 10 global cities. As part of the study, focus groups meetings were conducted with home-based workers in Bangkok, Thailand. Focus group participants spoke of the sustained impact on their livelihoods of severe flooding in Bangkok from July 2011–January 2012.

Mobility constraints: As a consequence of flooding, roads were damaged and communities isolated, a particularly devastating situation for home-based workers who had no alternative workspace and were unable to collect supplies or deliver final products. One group of workers who recycled waste plastic described how they had no space to dry plastic and that their employer was unable to pick it up. Another snack food seller reported: "During the big floods last year, my house was underwater and we could not work for more than two months. We had no money to repair the flood damage and no money to restart our business and had to borrow from the moneylender by using our house as collateral."

Limited incomes: The loss of work and wages had immediate impacts on household expenditures. The dramatic change in quality of life demonstrates how vulnerable the urban poor remain to external shocks and how fluctuations in cash incomes are more consequential in urban areas than in rural areas. One worker described her efforts to cut back on spending as follows: "I used to cook two dishes to have with the rice, but when I had no job, I cooked only one dish. I couldn't share my food with my neighbors, which is our normal practice." Another woman reported asking relatives in her home village to send food. "They are farmers, they grow rice for their own consumption, so they shared rice with us," she said. She noted that her experience was not unique, and that others also "got food support such as rice and fermented fish from their relatives in the rural area."

No guaranteed return to employment: Once the floods had receded, workers had mixed experiences going back to work. Some worked overtime to make up for lost production during the floods. Five workers who made brand name shirts for a factory reported that "the factory gave us a lot of work, to catch up on orders and get back into business." Others had the opposite experience, such as two women who were subcontracted to embroider garments. "We have always for a long time received work from this owner but since the flood problem last year, we have received less work; and for the last two to three months, we have no work. Fortunately, we were supported by our husbands and children."

Source: Chen 2014.

in areas such as Waduk Pluit, which is said to be house more than 70,000 people (World Bank 2011d). Many of the urban poor also live without secure tenure and are under threat of eviction, leaving little incentive or ability to invest in their housing. As a result, their housing is typically small, overcrowded, of substandard quality, in poor structural condition, and located in highly dense areas with haphazard or irregular layouts that lack basic services (Baker 2012). Living in these tenuous structures further increases their vulnerability to natural disasters.

In addition to unfavorable locations, limited access to basic services and infrastructure puts residents at risk. In the event of heavy rainfall and high tides, areas with poor drainage and sanitation often experience severe flooding, water contamination, and the spread of water-borne diseases, while relief and recovery efforts are inhibited by poor road networks.

Poor sanitation also means a higher risk of water contamination, water-borne diseases, and subsequent disabilities. A study of informal settlements in Jakarta reported the incidence of diarrhea at 342 episodes per 1,000 inhabitants, an infection rate of 43 percent in children with at least one type of intestinal worm, and an increase in the incidence of dengue (Baker 2012). These ailments can lead to the loss of livelihoods and to poverty. All these impacts were also captured and reflected in a study on the impacts of flooding on residents of Ho Chi Minh City, Vietnam, with several case studies detailing a chain of events, beginning with frequent flooding, that eventually pushes a number of residents into poverty.

There is also substantial evidence that poor women and girls remain particularly vulnerable to natural hazards. A 2007 study of 141 natural disasters between 1981 and 2002 found that more women than men died in disasters. Women also represented an estimated 61 percent of fatalities in Myanmar after Cyclone Nargis in 2008, and 70 percent of fatalities during the 2004 Indian Ocean tsunami in Banda Aceh, Indonesia (World Bank 2011a). Existing socioeconomic inequalities, such as restricted mobility education, decision-making and economic opportunities, further increase women's vulnerability to natural hazards (World Bank 2013a). More than half of all those affected by disasters worldwide are children (UNISDR 2011), however, girl infants are at a particular risk. Recent research on how typhoons in the past 25 years affected the Philippines shows that for up to 2 years after the disaster, "post-typhoon mortality among baby girls is approximately 15 times higher than average typhoon exposure, likely due to the indirect poverty-worsening effects of the storm" (University of San Francisco 2014; UC Berkeley 2013). Factors include the reduction of health-related expenditures, including nutrition and medical visits, with infants inadvertently bearing the brunt of the economic devastation as families cut spending.[6]

Impacts of Economic Shocks on the Urban Poor

The impacts of economic shocks on the urban poor can be significant. For example, in the aftermath of the Asian financial crisis, Indonesia saw a significant increase of urban poverty from 5.0 percent in 1996 to 8.3 percent in 1998 (Atinc and Walton 1998). During economic shocks, higher costs directly hit the poor's consumption budget—especially when an average poor household spends about 60 percent of income on food. Price increases temporarily reduce a household's disposable income and may lead to the selling of household assets to compensate for cash shortages.

The impacts on the near poor, especially those who are close to the poverty threshold, are of significant concern. A shock can quickly move households from near poor into poverty. Lagging social safety nets may not be available in time to provide the needed support for near-poor households in times of emergency, and there is a high incidence of these households falling back into poverty. One study estimated that in Asia, a 10 percent increase in domestic food prices could push 64 million more people into poverty (based on the $1.25 per person per day poverty line at 2005 purchasing power parity [PPP]) (ADB 2013). Another study of the impact of the 2008 financial crisis found that the crisis resulted in an additional 1.4 million people living under the poverty line in the Philippines, primarily due to labor income losses of a much larger magnitude than average households (25–50 percent versus 3–5 percent). These near-poor or "crisis-vulnerable" households are found mostly in urban areas and tend to be less skilled than the general population (Habib et al. 2010).

In times of economic hardship there is a well-documented tendency of urban-based industries to reduce jobs or wages, further affecting the employment of the urban poor. A study of informal workers in Indonesia showed 80 percent did not have any social security or formal insurance, which is mandatory for formal workers. Facing economic shock, the most common coping strategies include borrowing from moneylenders or from family or neighbors, selling or pawning belongings, reducing the number or quality of meals, and working odd jobs (Baker et al. 2013).

A comparative study on the impacts of the 2008–2009 economic crisis in five Asian countries (Cambodia, Lao PDR, Mongolia, Thailand, and Vietnam) found layoffs in urban-based industrial zones, with laid-off workers resorting to underemployment, informal work, or reduced working hours in sectors where there are high costs of recruitment and retraining. In the informal sector, noted price increases and erratic work opportunities (reductions in days worked by 50–70 percent and in real daily earnings by 17 percent or higher in select sectors) made livelihoods extremely fragile (Turk and Mason 2010).

The impacts on women are particularly significant. Women tend to lose their jobs first as they work in sectors which are hit first, such as garments and textiles. There is a tendency to discontinue schooling for daughters before doing the same, if needed, for sons. Moreover, compared to boys, girls rarely recommence schooling (Atinc and Walton 1998). When food is scarce. it is often a custom for mothers to forgo their own meals and in many countries in the region, boys receive preference over girls for food provision (Baker 2008a).

Urban Poor Coping Mechanisms

Numerous examples demonstrate that the urban poor are resourceful and adaptive in responding to and surviving natural disasters and other shocks. At the individual and community levels, they are taking the initiative to improve their own resilience to natural disasters by building stronger building foundations, heightening floors, digging trenches, clearing drainage and ditches, planting trees, and even proactively evacuating during disaster-prone periods.

A survey in Ho Chi Minh City, Vietnam, found that many households borrowed money from different sources to raise the floor of the home or to build a preventive wall outside of their home to prevent flood damage (World Bank and AUS AID 2014). In Jakarta, communities self-organize under *gotongroyong* (traditional communal projects or activities that benefit the community at large or specific members), adapting to flooding and extreme weather with strong community spirit and organization. People help one another through community savings programs and early warning systems, join informal professional unions for women artisans, and undertake small-scale environmental cleanups like clearing smaller drains (World Bank 2011d). Another example in Jakarta is Kampung Melayu, where residents have developed an early-warning system for floods using the minaret of the local mosque upon receiving SMS warnings from the floodgate area upstream (Baker 2012). These initiatives show that where social capital is strong, the poor can find some level of security and support, and hence increased resilience, through their community.

Facing economic shocks, the urban poor find different ways to maintain their livelihoods through temporary hardship. There is strong evidence from the monitoring studies of five Asian countries following the 2008–2009 financial crisis that laid-off workers mostly remain in urban areas and look for temporary work in the informal sector, even if they are underemployed or with reduced earnings. There were also examples of people organizing themselves to cope with hardships through the following initiatives: job-sharing arrangements in the informal construction sector in Vietnam; informal savings and credit groups in Cambodia and Laos; community-organized distribution of food or expenses in Cambodia and Vietnam; and food credits in Mongolia (Turk and Mason 2010). These initiatives help the poor to help themselves to stay resilient through the shocks.

However, it is clear that many of the resources needed to reduce risks and vulnerabilities to natural and economic shocks are still unavailable to the poor, including infrastructure and social services that the poor cannot provide themselves. The need for investments in crucial infrastructure at the primary, secondary, and even tertiary levels in storm and surface drainage, road and path networks, water connections, and sanitation services requires special skills and carries a billion-dollar price tag that communities cannot self-finance. Formal social safety net coverage is also missing for the urban poor because they may be living in hard-to-reach, informal settlements and tend to be more transient in urban areas (Baker 2008a). This gap forces the poor to rely entirely on informal support networks of family and friends, who may equally be affected during hard times. Without formal interventions through appropriate policies, the urban poor will only have these above-mentioned measures to rely on, which is not enough.

Economic Inclusion: Increasing Jobs and Resilience

At the policy level, there is much evidence that investing in better access to and quality of/access to quality education for the poor improves their lifetime economic opportunities. Improvements in housing quality, infrastructure, and basic services in cities are key to strengthening the resilience of the urban poor. Beyond these critical investments, a number of programs across EAP have effectively contributed to the economic inclusion of the poor and are particularly relevant for many countries in the region. Many of these programs could be transferable to other city or country settings and be considered for replicability and scaling up.

Increasing Access to Job Opportunities

As countries across the region continue to urbanize, the numbers of people coming to cities in search of opportunities will continue to increase. Creating good jobs is critical to economic growth, and creating good jobs that are accessible to the urban poor helps to ensure sustainable, inclusive growth. A number of tested strategies promote economic inclusion. They largely fall into the following four categories:

  (i)   connecting people and jobs
  (ii) building skills
  (iii) access to credit and finance
  (iv) pro-poor economic development strategies (Shah et al. 2015)

The following section highlights successful interventions from the EAP region in each of the four categories.

Connecting the Urban Poor to Jobs
Integration of peri-urban villages through road networks in Hanoi, Vietnam. As Hanoi experienced rapid urbanization, it facilitated the densification of surrounding peri-urban villages by modernizing road networks just outside of the city. The demolition of old housing stock was avoided except in instances of road widening. This not only allowed formal developers access to new land, but also improved connections to the urban center from peri-urban areas. Coupling this with housing policies that promoted the upgrading of older homes, Hanoi was able to prevent the development of slums by ensuring a ready supply of affordable and conveniently located housing for low-income populations (World Bank 2011e).

Using online outsourcing and microwork to target unemployed youth.
Much of Asia (particularly China, India, and the Philippines) has benefited
from the outsourcing and offshoring of business processing jobs such as
bookkeeping and customer service call centers. Similar opportunities are
being extended to vulnerable populations through impact-outsourcing. Still
in its relatively early stages of development, impact-outsourcing involves
breaking up tasks into lower-skilled microwork. For example, managed
service platforms such as Samasource specifically target and train disadvantaged youth to complete web-based tasks such as image recognition, tran-
scription, and data enrichment that can be completed on inexpensive
devices. Such platforms have gained a foothold in India, Kenya, and South
Africa, and impact-outsourcing currently employs an estimated 150,000
workers (World Bank 2016b). This emerging industry can help to address
regional youth unemployment, although it has already been criticized for
the informal nature of the work and the vulnerability of workers to changes
in demand for services (Kuek et al. 2015).

Building Skills and Access to Education among the Urban Poor
*Supporting street-vendors through private sector-led trainings in Ho Chi
Minh City, Vietnam.* In 2013, Bel Access launched a pilot aimed at introduc-
ing processed food products, such as Laughing Cow cheese, to low-income
consumers in Vietnam. Initially, Bel Access tried to create a system of door-
to-door sales using recruits through local women's associations. However,
the initiative failed, leading Bel Access to look to street vendors and their
existing sales networks. Bel Access recognized the market opportunity, given
that low-income consumers use street vendors as their primary source of
groceries.[7] In dialogue with vendor associations, Bel Access created a comprehensive program complete with technical training, optional uniforms, distribution at wholesale sites, assistance integrating into the formal sector, and
partnerships with microcredit institutions to assist street vendors with testing
their product. Less than a year into the program's launch, 240 vendors had
been recruited, with each vendor contacting 100–150 households per week.
The 70 vendors who completed the skills training course saw an average
15 percent rise in income after three months (Guesné and Ménascé 2014).

Inclusive urban education in Shanghai, China. In 2010, Shanghai declared
that it had achieved the provision of universal compulsory education for
migrant children. This achievement was accomplished through a program
of building new schools as well as paying for the enrollment of migrant
children into private schools. In Shanghai, private schools are generally of
lesser quality than public schools; however, the government of Shanghai
actively audited private schools to determine that could accommodate
migrant children. The government created a three-year, school-upgrading
plan, complete with district financial and administrative support, and at the
end of the upgrading period, 162 private schools had been approved for
enrolling migrant students. These schools receive financial support based on
enrollment figures (World Bank 2014).

Pro-poor Economic Development in the EAP

Formalizing spaces for street vendors in Surakarta, Indonesia. In 2005, the newly-elected mayor of Surakarta (and current Indonesian president Joko Widodo) approached the street vendors in and around the popular Banjansari park about relocation. Without legally designated spaces to work or permits to operate, the vendors had long been subjected by criminal groups and officials to threats of eviction and extortion in the form of bribes. The then-mayor had 54 meetings with vendors, and over time he gained their trust and developed a working relationship with them. Together, both parties agreed that the vendors would move to Khitilan Semanggi, a location that was easy for customers to reach and where the city would provide facilities, including permanent shelters and connections to municipal water and electricity grids. The relocation day was marked by a citywide celebration, as 989 street vendors moved to Khitilan Semanggi. Relocated vendors also had access to trainings on food safety, sanitation, business development, and management. Tests by public health officials showed lower incidences of harmful bacteria in food sold by relocated vendors. By 2014, nearly 77 percent (4,455) vendors had been successfully moved to city-designated spaces (Natawidjaja et al. 2015).

Organizing informal workers to protect livelihoods in Cebu City, Philippines. By organizing under the Cebu City United Vendors Association, informal vendors were able to create a platform to lobby city authorities for the security of their livelihoods and reduce harassment. In 2000, the mayor created a working committee to study the conditions of street vendors and the implications of legalized trading in some parts of the city. In addition, the city administration agreed to a policy that any demolitions of vendor stalls could not occur without a consultation with the vendor, allowing them time to arrange for a relocation site. Previously, vendors were subject to unannounced demolitions. While there are still clashes with the city administration over informal vending, by organizing under common associations, vendors are able to gain clout with the media and government. As a result, the urban poor have more active participation in governance (Etemadi 2004).

Urban Poor Access to Credit and Finance

Integrated finance and social services for waste-pickers in Quezon City, the Philippines. The Payatas dumpsite in Quezon City has become a source of livelihood for approximately 5,000 informal workers, around 2,000 of whom are engaged in waste-picking and another 3,000 in recycling and trading found materials. A rehabilitation program of the dumpsite from 2004–08 resulted in the reduction of waste materials brought to Payatas, and to a subsequent reduction of income for households in the surrounding communities. The city government, recognizing the economic and environmental contribution of waste-pickers, created an alternative livelihood project whereby formal trading areas were established near the dumpsite and waste-pickers were organized into groups that were then assigned to

specific dump trucks. This process led to a more orderly and equitable distribution of waste materials. Workers were also encouraged to act as a
cooperative, through which they could collectively receive assistance in the
form of education, skills training, and access to finance. Some groups working out of junkshops were able to borrow money to buy trucks and collect
garbage from nearby communities, thus increasing incomes. Joint financing
and skills training was also available to workers seeking to develop minor
business ventures and find alternative livelihoods. Financing was presented
within a complete package of assistance, making it more likely that multiple
concerns of the community would be addressed simultaneously (Casanova-
Dorotan 2012). Mobile banking (for example, M-Pesa, CellBazar) initiatives provide urban workers a way to transfer money directly to their
families in rural areas through mobile phones, thereby making money
transfer easier and more affordable than the traditional method of going
through an intermediary.

Building Resilience among the Urban Poor

The vulnerability of the poor to natural and economic risks may be
addressed through measures that improve their access to employment
opportunities, housing, infrastructure, and services. Some regional programs that have strengthened the resilience of the poor in response to disasters and shocks can be broadly arranged into two categories: preventive
measures and responsive measures, which focus on longer term recovery.

Creating Insurance and Catastrophic Risk Pools

Insurance plays an important role for cities and countries when disasters
occur but the existing instruments are generally not accessible for the urban
poor, who do not have credits or collateral. To protect this vulnerable
group, individual insurance or catastrophic risk pools may be established to
spread the cost of risk or damages across a population or over time.

Natural disasters represent a significant contingent liability for EAP
countries, some more than others. Due to insufficient urban planning strategies and heightened socioeconomic vulnerability, a person in the Philippines
is up to 17 times more likely to be killed in a natural disaster than someone
in Japan, despite the higher risk of exposure in the latter country (IFRC
2010). Pacific Islands, such as Tonga and Vanuatu, face average annual
losses due to natural hazards in the sum of 6.6 and 4.4 percent of national
GDP, respectively. Furthermore, if affected by a 1 in 200-year event,
Cambodia, Lao PDR, and the Philippines would expend 18 percent or more
of total public budget on recovery (Jha and Stanton-Geddes 2013).

To address these potential challenges, the government of the Philippines
took out two World Bank Disaster Risk Management Development Policy
Loans with a Catastrophe Deferred Drawdown Option (CAT-DDO). This
attention to disaster risk financing and insurance strategies, along with
strengthening institutional capacity was pivotal in ensuring that disaster
risk reduction mechanisms were in place on the systemic and local levels in

the wake of typhoons Pablo and Yolanda, and Tropical Storm Sendong (Washi) (World Bank 2015a). Comprehensive financial planning was established under the first CAT-DDO, to offer the Philippines an opportunity to draw down on insurance options. These loans benefitted communities by providing liquidity for local government to support homeowners and businesses, to make post-disaster conditional cash transfers, and to run cash for work programs (World Bank 2015b).

Building-back-better Workfare Programs

After natural disaster with significant infrastructure destruction, reconstruction efforts provide a good opportunity to involve the poor and provide them with financial transfer in exchange for their labor work. In addition to providing income support and employment for the poor, workfare programs can also provide on-the-job training for unskilled workers, setting them up for future employment opportunities once the program ends. An example is the Community-based Settlements Rehabilitation and Reconstruction project in Aceh, Indonesia that was developed after the 2006 Java earthquake. Under this program, community and local workers were trained and employed for reconstruction works (Baker 2012). The project was designed using a community-based approach to ensure that all the affected persons were involved in the reconstruction process. In implementing this participatory strategy, forms of community mobilization, technical assistance, and training for incremental housing construction were used to ensure that the community members had a low-cost solution for building back better. These self-help programs went so far as to provide advice in preparing and submitting proposals, identifying priority reconstruction subprojects to benefit the neighborhood, and manage the entire rebuilding process (World Bank 2011b). Community contracting was used as a tool for rehabilitation and reconstruction in post-disaster conditions and created a sense of ownership for the community, including the urban poor.

Strengthening Disaster Planning and Early Warning Systems in Urban Areas

EAP countries have become better at streamlining early warning systems to ensure there are adequate communication channels. There are, however, major information gaps such as the location of the urban poor; housing data; subsidence maps and data on climate hazards; and measurement of risk and potential losses. The urban poor are less likely to abandon their assets during a disaster and therefore the functioning of these systems are critical in conveying messages and updates (Jha and Brecht 2011). Investing in building up information systems and the development of city-level action plans can help cities plan for shocks and mitigate the impacts on the population. Such programs can also take into account the specific needs of groups most affected, such as the urban poor and women.

For instance, in Vietnam, three cities (Hanoi, Dong Hoi, and Can Tho) have developed local resilience action plans (LRAP) and in Can Tho, a city resilience action plan was followed by a project to improve resilience through infrastructure investments and capacity building. The China Meteorological Administration Weather Alert System uses SMS to provide comprehensive forecasting and warning information (Zhenlin 2010). Similarly, the Jakarta Flood Early Warning System has been used to coordinate standard operating procedures and build local capacities to manage disaster risk. Much of this capacity-building occurred on the community level, with trainings for representatives in urban neighborhoods most vulnerable to flooding (UNISDR 2010). The participatory planning approach ensured urban residents were being included, regardless of income and community status.

Other Social Safety Net Programs for the Urban Poor

Well-designed safety nets can be extended during crises to protect the affected population and reduce the toll of human suffering. Emerging evidence from recent crises demonstrated the effectiveness of social safety nets in avoiding long-term damages to human lives, livelihoods and capital. Among the popular safety net programs are conditional cash transfers (CCTs); fee waivers; and targeted cash or in-kind transfer schemes such as food distribution, food stamps, or vouchers. These programs are particularly relevant in times of financial crisis when children may be pulled out of school to work and support their family (Baker 2012). In recent times, governments in EAP have been making the effort to extend social programs to address the increasing vulnerability of urban poor communities, post-disaster. Some examples are highlighted in table 2.5, below.

Table 2.5   Regional Examples of Social Safety Net Programs for Disaster Relief

Country	Social protection for disaster relief	Program description
Philippines	Disaster Risk Management Development Policy Loan with a Catastrophe Deferred Drawdown Option (CAT-DDO) (First and Second)	As part of the disaster financing and protection of public assets, social safety nets have been built into the two CAT-DDOs in the Philippines. Acknowledging the impact the disasters had on poverty levels in affected communities, the program offered targeted social protection interventions for the poor and most vulnerable.
Philippines	Pantawid Pamilya modified conditional cash transfer (CCT)	One of the identified target groups for the modified urban CCT program is evacuees and households displaced as a result of a disaster or conflict. The program offers cash transfers to vulnerable persons and provides social welfare programs that offer disaster preparation activities to protect against future impacts.
China	Urban Di Bao: minimum livelihood guarantee system	The Urban Di Bao social protection program in China ensures that the poor have access to basic needs, including disaster relief. In times of disaster, the program funds emergency supply items such as water, food, heat, medication, and clothing, and makes provision for temporary shelter or resettlement.

(Table continues on next page)

Table 2.5   **Regional Examples of Social Safety Net Programs for Disaster Relief**
(continued)

Country	Social protection for disaster relief	Program description
Indonesia	Indonesia Social Protection Policy	The Ministry of Social Welfare has implemented social assistance in the form of disaster relief in Surakarta and Makassar cities to combat the adverse impacts of hazards faced particularly by the urban poor. Furthermore, Indonesia builds the financing of basic safety nets into the post-disaster recovery process.[a]
Fiji	Post-Cyclone Winston Emergency Recovery Development Policy Operation	For the Cyclone Winston Recovery efforts, Fiji is utilizing USD$50 million in World Bank financing to implement disaster recovery that will a focus on robust social protection programs. The most vulnerable will be protected through targeted cash transfer programs alongside the physical risk reduction measures.[b]

a. World Bank/ GFDRR/ Indonesia 2011.
b. World Bank 2016a.

Notes

1. Rates are for 2012 (ILO 2013).
2. 2013 figures. (Viet Nam General Statistics Office 2013).
3. 2012 figures (UNDP 2013).
4. Visible underemployment includes persons working less than 40 hours per week, whereas invisible underemployment includes persons working 40 hours or more per week.
5. Resilience is the ability of a system, community, or society that is exposed to hazards to resist, absorb, accommodate to, and recover from the effects of a hazard in a timely and efficient manner (Jha and Stanton-Geddes 2013).
6. "The study found that in an average year, the income of Filipino households in typhoon-hit areas is depressed 6.6 percent due to typhoons that occurred the year before, leading to a 7.1 percent reduction in average household spending. However, when particularly strong storms strike, incomes may fall more than 15 percent the following year—compounding loss from damage to a family's home and belongings" (UC Berkeley 2013).
7. An estimated 80 percent of food expenditures for low-income households are made from street vendors in Hanoi, while 37 percent of meals are bought from street vendors across Vietnam.

References

ADB (Asian Development Bank) and BPS Statistics Indonesia. 2011. "The Informal Sector and Informal Employment in Indonesia." ADB, Mandaluyong City, Philippines.

———. 2013. "Food Security in Asia and the Pacific." ADB, Mandaluyong City, the Philippines.

ADB, ESCAP (United Nations Economic and Social Commission for Asia and the Pacific), and UNDP (United Nations Development Programme). 2013. "Asia-Pacific Aspirations: Perspectives for a Post-2015 Development Agenda." ADB, Manila.

Atinc, T. M., and M. Walton. 1998. *Responding to the Global Financial Crisis: Social Consequences of the East Asian Financial Crisis.* Washington, DC: World Bank.

Baker, J. 2008a. *Impacts of Financial, Food, and Fuel Crisis on the Urban Poor.* Directions in Urban Development. World Bank: Washington, DC.

———. 2008b. "Urban Poverty: A Global View." Urban Papers, No. UP-5. World Bank, Washington, DC.

———. 2012. *Climate Change, Disaster Risk, and the Urban Poor: Cities Building Resilience for a Changing World.* Urban Development. Washington, DC: World Bank.

Baker, J. L., et al. 2013. *Indonesia - Urban Poverty and Program Review.* Washington, DC: World Bank.

Casanova-Dorotan, F. 2012. "Informal Economy Budget Analysis in Philippines and Quezon City." WIEGO Working Paper No. 12. WEIGO, Cambridge.

Chen, M. 2014. "Informal Economy Monitoring Study Sector Report: Home-based Workers." WIEGO, Cambridge.

Chen, M., J. Vanek, and J. Heintz. 2006. "Informality, Gender and Poverty: A Global Picture." *Economic and Political Weekly* 41 (21): 2131–39.

Chua, K. K., et al. 2013. *Philippine Development Report: Creating More and Better Jobs.* Washington, DC: World Bank.

Etemadi, F. 2004. "The Politics of Engagement: Gains and Challenges of the NGO Coalition in Cebu City." *Environment and Urbanization* 16 (1): 79–94.

Guesné, J.-M., and D. Ménascé. 2014. "Sharing Cities: An Innovative Partnership between the Bel Group and Street Vendors." Field Actions Science Reports, Special Issue 12: 2014. http://factsreports.revues.org/3694.

Habib, B., et al. 2010. "The Impact of the Financial Crisis on Poverty and Income Distribution: Insights from Simulations in Selected Countries." *Economic Premise* No. 7. World Bank, Washington, DC.

Huitfeldt, H. and J. Jüttin. 2009. "Informality and Informal Employment." In *Promoting Pro-Poor Growth: Employment*, 95–108. OECD, OECD Development Centre.

IFRC (The International Federation of Red Cross and Red Crescent Societies) 2010. *World Disasters Report 2010 - Urban Risk.* Geneva: IFRC.

ILO (International Labor Organization). 2011. "Women and Labour Markets in Asia: Rebalancing for Gender Equality." ILO, Bangkok.

———. 2012. *Statistical Update on Employment in the Informal Economy*. Geneva: ILO.

———. 2013a. *Global Employment Trends for Youth 2013: A Generation at Risk*. Geneva: ILO.

———. 2013b. *Women and Men in the Informal Economy: A Statistical Picture* (Second Edn.). Geneva: ILO.

———. 2014. *Transitioning from Informality to the Formal Economy: Realizing Decent Work for All*. Geneva: ILO.

Jha, A., and H. Brecht. 2011. "An Eye on East Asia and Pacific." *Building Urban Resilience in East Asia*, Issue 8. World Bank, Washington, DC.

Jha, A., and Z. Stanton-Geddes. 2013. *Strong, Safe, and Resilient: A Strategic Policy Guide for Disaster Risk Management in East Asia and the Pacific*. Washington, DC: World Bank.

Kleit, R. G. 2001. "The Role of Neighborhood Social Network in Scattered-Site Public Housing Residents' Search for Jobs." *Housing Policy Debate*, 12 (3): 541–73.

Kuek, S. C., et al. 2015. *The Global Opportunity in Online Outsourcing*. Washington, DC: World Bank.

LIFT (Livelihoods and Food Security Trust Fund), and World Bank. 2016. "A Country on the Move: Domestic Migration in Two Regions of Myanmar." World Bank, Yangon.

Naidoo, D., T. Packard, and I. Auwalin. 2014. "Mobility, Scarring, and Job Quality in the Indonesian Labor Market." Draft, World Bank, Washington, DC.

Natawidjaja, R. S., et al. 2015. "Inclusive Governance of Informal Markets: The Street Vendors of Surakarta." IIED, London.

NBS (National Bureau of Statistics of China). 2012. *China Statistical Yearbook 2012*. Beijing: NBS.

Oxfam, and ActionAid Vietnam. 2012. "Participatory Monitoring of Urban Poverty in Vietnam," the Fifth Round Synthesis Report. Oxfam and ActionAid, Hanoi.

Packard, T., and T. V. Nguyen. 2014. *East Asia Pacific at Work: Employment, Enterprise, and Well-being*. Washington, DC: World Bank.

Shah, P., et al. 2015. *World - Inclusive Cities Approach Paper*. Washington, DC: World Bank.

Sinha, S. 2013. "Housing and Urban Service Needs of Home-Based Workers: Findings from a Seven-Country Study." *WIEGO Policy Brief* (Urban Policies) No. 15. WIEGO, Cambridge.

Turk, C., and A. Mason. 2010. "Impacts of the Economic Crisis in East Asia: Findings from Qualitative Monitoring in Five Countries." In *Poverty and Sustainable Development in Asia: Impacts and Responses to the*

Global Economic Crisis, 51–76. Mandaluyong City, Philippines: Asian Development Bank.

UC Berkeley. 2013. "Report Details High Costs of Philippine Typhoons for Families, Baby Girls." https://newscenter.berkeley.edu/2013/11/19/report-details-high-costs-of-philippine-typhoons-for-families-baby-girls/.

UNDP (United Nations Development Programme). 2010. "Urban Poverty Assessment in Ho Chi Minh City and Hanoi." UNDP, Hanoi.

———. 2013. "Addressing Urban Poverty, Inequality, Vulnerability in a Warming World." UNDP, Bangkok.

UN Habitat. 2015. "The State of Asian and Pacific Cities 2015." UN Habitat. Nairobi.

UNISDR (United Nations International Strategy for Disaster Reduction). n.d. "Disaster through a Different Lens." http://www.unisdr.org/files/20108_mediabook.pdf.

———. 2011. Official Press Release. https://www.unisdr.org/archive/22742.

———. 2010. "Many Partners, One System: An Integrated Flood Early Warning System (FEWS) for Jakarta." *Local Governments and Disaster Risk Reduction: Good Practices and Lessons Learned.* UNISDR, Geneva.

University of San Francisco. 2014. http://www.usfca.edu/Magazine/Summer_2014/news/USF_Research.

Viet Nam General Statistics Office. 2013. "Labour Force Survey: Quarter 3, 2013." Viet Nam GSO, Hanoi.

World Bank. 2011a. *Gender and Climate Change: Three Things You Should Know.* Washington DC: World Bank.

———. 2011b. "Implementation Completion Report. Community Recovery Project through the Urban Poverty Program in Earthquake-Tsunami Affected Areas of Nanggroe Aceh Darussalam and North Sumatra." World Bank, Washington, DC.

———. 2011c. *Indonesia: Advancing a National Disaster Risk Financing Strategy—Options for Consideration.* Washington, DC: World Bank.

———. 2011d. *Jakarta - Urban Challenges in a Changing Climate.* Washington, DC: World Bank.

———. 2011e. "Vietnam Urbanization Review: Technical Assistance Report." World Bank, Washington, DC.

———. 2012. "Towards Gender Equality in East Asia and the Pacific." World Bank, Washington, DC.

———. 2013a. "Improving Women's Odds in Disasters." http://www.worldbank.org/en/news/feature/2013/12/12/improving-women-disasters.

———. 2013b. *World Development Report 2013: Jobs.* World Bank: Washington, DC.

————. 2014. *East Asia Pacific at Work: Employment, Enterprise, and Well-being.* World Bank: Washington, DC.

————. 2015a. "Philippines - Disaster Risk Management Development Policy Loan with a Catastrophe Deferred Drawdown Option (CAT-DDO)." World Bank, Washington, DC.

————. 2015b. "Press Release. Philippines: New Initiative to Boost Resilience Against Natural Disasters." December. http://www.worldbank .org/en/news/press-release/2015/12/22/philippines-new-initiative -to-boost-resilience-against-natural-disasters.

————. 2016a. "World Bank Commits $50 Million to Support Fiji's Long-term Cyclone Winston Recovery." http://www.worldbank.org/en/news /press-release/2016/06/30/world-bank-commits-50m-to-support-fijis -long-term-cyclone-winston-recovery. June 29.

————. 2016b. *World Development Report 2016: Digital Dividends.* Washington, DC: World Bank.

————. forthcoming. "Urban Poverty in Ulaanbaatar: Understanding its Dimensions and Addressing the Challenges" World Bank, Washington, DC.

World Bank and Australian Agency for International Development (AUS AID) 2014. "'Where Are We during Flooding?' A Qualitative Assessment of Poverty and Social Impacts of Flooding in Selected Neighborhoods of HCMC."

World Bank, and Development Research Center of the State Council, the People's Republic of China. 2014. *Urban China: Toward Efficient, Inclusive, and Sustainable Urbanization.* Washington, DC: World Bank.

World Bank/ GFDRR/ Indonesia. 2011. "Advancing a Natural Disaster Risk Financing Strategy – Options for Consideration." World Bank, Washington, DC. October.

Zhenlin, C. 2010. "Public Meteorological Service Delivery and Disaster Risk Management for the Farming Community of China." http://www .wamis.org/agm/meetings/walcs10/S2-Chen.pdf.

CHAPTER 3

Spatial Inclusion and the Urban Poor

Introduction

As countries develop, not all regions or areas develop at the same rate. This geographic variation in economic development increases at early development stages and then diminishes as countries reach high-income status.[1] One reason for this spatial unevenness is regional specialization and the growth of agglomeration industries that allow economies of scale in production. For example, certain industries may leverage locational proximity to each other to develop economies of scale or situate themselves in areas with easy access to raw materials and large markets. To the extent that such specialization and the positive effects of agglomeration are correlated with increases in productivity, spatial unevenness in development is necessary and even desirable (Kim 2008). However, persistent patterns of spatial inequality, with wide differences in standards of living and socioeconomic mobility, can hamper the benefits of economic development, exacerbate social exclusion, and ripen the conditions for social instability. This situation is particularly acute within cities, given the density where inequality is very evident within close proximity.

Most often, regional and national discussions of spatial inequality are focused on differences in development between rural and urban areas. As discussed in chapter 1, the breakdown of poverty figures between rural and urban areas shows substantial differences. Yet these numbers often mask the complexity and heterogeneity of urban poverty. As chapter 1 notes, intra-urban inequality is on the rise, resulting in a hierarchy of urban neighborhoods where poor populations are relegated to locations with low-quality living conditions. Such locational patterns of inequality within cities often coincide with dimensions of social hierarchy, class, caste, or community-based segregation, which can perpetuate social exclusion.

This section focuses on intra-urban spatial disparities in the context of urbanization in EAP countries. It includes a discussion of key nonmonetary dimensions of urban inequality that manifest spatially across neighborhoods, specifically the challenges of:

- access to affordable housing
- infrastructure and service delivery
- mobility and access to the city

Housing, Informality, and the Urban Poor

With continued urbanization, cities across the EAP region face the challenge of providing affordable and adequate housing options to growing populations. City planners and policy makers must balance their efforts between two general development approaches: high-density, mixed-use, and infill development; and low-density fringe development. The former approach has clear benefits. It requires high initial investment, but allows for the more manageable and cost-effective maintenance of infrastructure and transportation systems in the long-term, as well as the close proximity to nearby economic opportunities.

Limited budgets and capacity, however, might push cities towards the latter approach. The long-term effects of low-density peripheral development include increased traffic, decreased mobility, and high costs for extending services. The result is a less sustainable overall pattern of development. In both instances, there is the potential for the emergence of slums or growth of existing slum communities; the development choices and housing policies promoted by cities have very real consequences for the urban poor.

Urban poverty and quality of life are directly influenced by the location, cost, and quality of housing. The urban poor often have to negotiate the trade-off between easy access to employment, and secure and affordable housing. Settlements that are affordable for the urban poor in both the city center and at the periphery are often informal and exhibit the UN-defined characteristics of slums, namely inadequate access to safe water, sanitation, and infrastructure; poor structural quality of housing; overcrowding; and insecure residential status (UN Habitat 2015).

The level of housing deprivation for the urban poor varies across countries and is dependent to some extent on the geography and spatial development of a given urban center. Frequently, the poor resort to settling in high-risk areas to maintain proximity to employment opportunities. These areas vary and might include dilapidated blocks in the inner city, low-lying flood plains, or hard-to-reach settlements in the hillsides on a city's outskirts (box 3.1). For cities where the urban center is already developed, such as Beijing, it is common for low-income households to be situated as many as two hours away from workplaces. In some cities, informal settlements are not always concentrated, and therefore not always visible.

Slum and squatter settlements develop and grow when the urban poor are prevented from accessing even the most minimal housing provided by formal markets, either due to price or other legal and social barriers. Across the region, urban populations are growing faster than housing stock can be added. For example, a housing survey conducted in 2013 by Indonesia's National Statistics Agency (BPS) estimated a housing backlog of 11.8 million units nationwide, with 820,000 to 920,000 new units required in urban areas annually. Currently, the private sector constructs about 400,000 units per year, while public sector programs provide an additional 200,000. Still, a gap of approximately 220,000–370,000 units remains, creating the conditions for informal housing development and overcrowding in existing housing infrastructure (Anderson 2015).

Informal rental markets have emerged in response to the shortage of affordable urban housing, particularly for new migrants or temporary workers. This housing provides flexibility and affordability, regardless of one's registration status. However, rental arrangements can also serve as a reminder of disparities among the urban poor, and the relative privileges enjoyed by more established residents (box 3.2).

To generate additional revenue for households, apartments or settlements in poor neighborhoods are subdivided to accommodate renters,

---

Box 3.1   All Slums Are Not Equal—Slum Development in Metro Manila, the Philippines

The Philippines is home to an estimated 1.5 million informal settler families (ISF) across the country, with nearly 40 percent (600,000 families) residing in Metro Manila, or the equivalent of 3 million people. One out of every four Metro Manila residents living informally. For these people, the experience of poverty is deepened by the deprivations that accompany informal housing, including limited mobility, increased vulnerability to natural disasters, and inadequate access to infrastructure and services.

Traditional poverty alleviation and slum upgrading programs have typically approached slums as a monolithic entity. One reason for this is a lack of comprehensive and up-to-date data on the locations, characteristics, and risk exposure of slums, which becomes a barrier to proper planning and an impediment to addressing the needs of the urban poor.

In the case of Metro Manila, with the application of satellite imagery and GIS mapping techniques, researchers were able to identify and delineate slums and create a new database of 2,500 informal settlements (figure B3.1.1). This was a unique exercise and a first successful attempt in classifying slums based on the built environment type at the city scale and resulted in the creation of a slum typology.

Analysis of slums by typologies indicates that not all slums are equal—there are differing poverty levels within the various typologies as shown in table B3.1.1, below. Access to infrastructure and services also varies—for example, results from a household level survey of informal settler families showed that households in mixed settlements have higher instances of metered electricity connections compared with residents of both wet (frequently flooded) and high dense settlements.

(Box continues on next page)

Box 3.1   All Slums Are Not Equal—Slum Development in Metro Manila, the Philippines *(continued)*

Figure B3.1.1   **Informal Settlements by Type, Metro Manila, the Philippines**

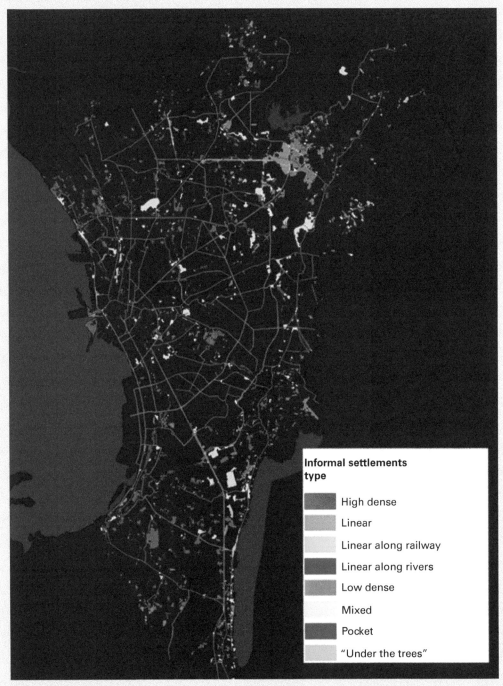

Informal settlements type

- High dense
- Linear
- Linear along railway
- Linear along rivers
- Low dense
- Mixed
- Pocket
- "Under the trees"

Source: World Bank forthcoming a.

(Box continues on next page)

Box 3.1 **All Slums Are Not Equal—Slum Development in Metro Manila, the Philippines** *(continued)*

Table B3.1.1 **Poverty Levels by Slum Typology**

Typology	Bottom 40%	Income poverty rate	Multidimensional poverty rate
High dense	0.50	0.23	0.29
Linear	0.52	0.25	0.24
Mixed	0.54	0.27	0.22
Pockets	0.57	0.31	0.30
Wet	0.51	0.26	0.30
Overall	**0.52**	**0.26**	**0.26**

Similarly, piped water connections were available at a much higher rate in mixed settlements compared with pockets and high dense settlements.

Given the differences in the availability of services, it is not surprising that employment and income levels also varied across typologies. Regression results show that residents of pocket slums— small and highly dense informal settlements in vacant spaces—are significantly poorer than those in high dense and linear settlements. By understanding how the urban poor's experiences might differ depending which type of informal settlement they inhabit, policy makers may be better positioned to target the areas of most need and to customize interventions at a granular level.

Source: World Bank forthcoming a.

Box 3.2 **Housing for Migrant Workers**

Surveys of workers in informal rental accommodations reveal an acute awareness of the disparities in housing and land tenure enjoyed by local residents as compared with migrants. Young migrant workers participating in an urban poverty survey in Vietnam spoke to this point:

"It's difficult for those migrating from rural areas to get richer. The rent for our rooms is half of our income. People here live an easier life and they have enough to eat, they have land to build rooms for rent. Even poor people here can rent part of their rooms for a few million a month." (Quarter 25 – Ward 6, Go Vap, Ho Chi Minh City)

Source: Oxfam and Action Aid Vietnam 2012.

often incoming rural-urban migrants. For example, there were 67,000 subdivided housing units accommodating 171,300 persons in 2013 in Hong Kong SAR, China. Each subdivided unit provided individual living quarters for at least two separate households, with an average area per capita of 6.3 m^2 (UN Habitat 2015). In Vietnam, studies have found pervasive overcrowding among workers' housing, where four persons reside in one 10 m^2 unit in Hai Phong, Can Tho, and Ho Chi Minh City (World Bank 2014b).

These sorts of housing situations raise serious concerns about overcrowding, health risks, and safety hazards. However, resource-constrained local governments might turn a blind eye to their development, given that these settlements achieve high density and are able to absorb growing populations while preserving the façade of adequate housing (UN Habitat 2015).

In addition to cramped quarters and overcrowding, tenants of informal housing are often subject to higher service costs. Given their lack of connection to municipal supplies of water and electricity, tenants turn to private service vendors who charge higher fees for similar or lower quality services (see below for further discussion).

Limited Access to Affordable Housing Programs

Numerous attempts have been made to provide low-income housing through subsidy programs or the government-sponsored construction of apartment buildings. However, limited budgets and growing urban populations almost always ensure that supply will fail to meet demand. Furthermore, subsidized urban housing is often captured by lower-middle-class or middle-class households who are better informed and connected than the urban poor and thus more able to access subsidies (UN Habitat 2015). Take for example, the Public Rental Housing Program in China, which is explicitly open to migrants without urban *hukou* (a system of housing registration). In practice, the program is often used to attract talented professionals rather than benefiting the urban poor and low-income wage earners (World Bank 2014).

Another example is found in Indonesia, where the Ministry of Housing funds a variety of programs designed to support the provision of housing. Budget allocations favor programs targeting middle-class and upper-middle-class households, such as the subsidy for fixed mortgage interest rates (FLPP), which accounts for 43.4 percent of the budget. With more than 60 percent of Indonesians out of the formal workforce, it is unlikely that poor households or even lower-middle-class households would meet the minimum qualifications for a mortgage or access the subsidy. The remainder of the ministry's budget is divided between programs targeting lower-income households such as the BSPS incremental home improvement subsidy program (19.3 percent), the *Rusunawa* rental housing program (15.3 percent of annual budget), and other neighborhood upgrading and titling programs. The amount of subsidy available per household is larger in programs targeting higher-income households, so that a household accessing FLPP might receive an effective government subsidy of IDR 126 million compared to the IDR 10–20 million BSPS subsidy for lower-income beneficiaries (Anderson 2015).

Evictions and Forced Relocations

Given the prevalence of informal housing, the urban poor face a constant threat of eviction. Evictions tend to increase in times of economic growth, as people and investments flow into cities, and land available for development near the city center grows scarce. Informal settlements that were once tolerated are now viewed as a hindrance to formal development.

In China, municipal public rental units that are unsuitable for privatization due to deterioration, are instead rented out informally. Located on prime real estate near city centers, these buildings are commonly slated for demolition and reconstruction under city urban renewal programs, leaving poor urban tenants in a state of constant uncertainty and vulnerable to eviction (World Bank 2014).

Other common reasons for eviction include large infrastructure projects and city beautification schemes (UN Habitat and UN ESCAP 2008). Relocation sites often fail to address the criteria for housing valued by evicted residents, namely proximity to workspace for home-based work, affordability, and an environment that fosters community. This situation is illustrated in the accounts of evictions that have been documented in a number of EAP countries. The experience of eviction with its subsequent dislocation and loss of livelihoods is an extreme example of how living conditions can result in increased poverty and risk.

Key Challenges to Providing Secure Housing

Continued urbanization in EAP has led to the scarcity of urban land and subsequent exorbitant increases in land prices. The poor are priced out of formal land markets, and forced out of informal settlements. There are three challenges to the provision of housing for the urban poor, namely:

  i) *access* in the form of land tenure
 ii) *affordability* and lack of financing and credit mechanisms
iii) *availability* with the limited development of new low-income housing units

These challenges are detailed below.

Land Availability and Land Tenure

Security of land tenure remains a major constraint for low-income households in cities throughout EAP. Private houses are often built on illegal sites and are routinely bought and sold without the property being registered with the local government. This lack of legal documents creates a range of problems, as follows: people, in principle, cannot register their residency, have utilities installed, or obtain access to credit. In addition, they will receive little or no compensation if relocated, or might face outright eviction.[2] As a result of this informality and uncertainty, the urban poor are hesitant to make investments to improve their houses and neighborhoods.

A number of challenges related to securing land tenure vary across countries. In Cambodia, for example, the Khmer Rouge destroyed all records of land ownership, making the process of securing land tenure almost impossible for everyone.[3] In Vietnam, some of the regulatory and administrative requirements governing construction standards—such as the minimum plot size and the prohibitively costly infrastructure requirements—push households into informality. Even in countries with clear land tenure systems, securing land tenure for informal settlements and slums comes with challenges. In some instances, the regularization of informal settlements has led to the displacement of the urban poor as developers or other residents vie for the recently titled land (Payne et al. 2008). At other times, city officials might discourage formalization to prevent the development of additional informal settlements (Smolka and Biderman 2012).

High Prices and Limited Credit

With high land prices and development costs, formal housing is largely unattainable for the urban poor. Throughout EAP, the price-to-income ratio (PIR), which is used to measure the affordability of homeownership, indicates high levels of unaffordable housing. The ratio is 9.2 in Bangkok, 20.5 in Manila, 23.5 in Jakarta, and 31.1 in Shanghai[4]—all well above the indicative affordable level of 3 to 5. Meanwhile, access to formal housing finance is a major constraint for the urban poor, as formal finance largely fails to extend to low-income households.

Poor urban households also lack the regular incomes necessary to secure a mortgage. Of the poorest 40 percent of the population across the region, only 39 percent have an account with a financial institution (Brhane et al. 2014). Unsurprisingly, savings or down-payment capacity is extremely limited for low-income households. In Vietnam, for example, a standard 20 percent down payment is required for a housing loan. However, the lowest two income quintiles often have a savings rate close to zero or have higher expenditures than household income. In the case of detached houses in the *ger* areas outside Ulaanbaatar, Mongolia, for instance, only 2 to 9 percent of total costs are financed through formal loans (Kamata et al. 2010).

While some formal housing finance institutions have sought to go down-market through networks of microfinance agencies, local nongovernmental organizations (NGOs) or mass organizations, the reach of these programs is limited due to high operating costs (UN Habitat 2010). In addition, pockets of the poor in urban areas do not have the same community ties that enable collective efforts and exert peer pressure for the timely repayment of group-based micro-lending for home improvement in the same way that rural communities do.

The urban poor must therefore rely on other finance mechanisms, such as personal savings or informal loans from friends and family, to purchase or make improvements to their homes. For cash-strapped households or migrant households without strong community ties, this situation means that much needed expenditures for housing are continually deferred.

Land Use and Regulatory Environment

In cities experiencing rapid development, the existing housing stock might not be sufficient to meet the needs of a growing population. Given the limited payment capacities of low-income households, developers tend to focus on catering to middle- and high-income earners to maximize their profits. Without pro-poor policy interventions, market-driven growth can exacerbate many of the trends regarding inadequate housing, displacement, and eviction, leading to further poverty highlighted above. However, governments looking to create stronger revenue bases often welcome urban real estate development targeting middle- and high-income households.

Some cities have established frameworks to develop partnerships with private developers and stimulate the construction of affordable housing for the poor. In most cases, commercial development rights are granted to private sector enterprises with the condition that they must build affordable housing units on a specified percentage of the total land under development. One example of this is Indonesia's "1:3:6" housing policy, where private developers must build a minimum of three middle-class houses and six basic or very basic units for every high-cost house (UN Habitat 2010).

However, lack of enforcement often leads to social housing delivery failures. In Vietnam, for example, a formal decree requires that all residential development set aside 20 percent of the total plot size for the construction of social housing for the poor. However, lower profits and negative biases associated with social housing discourage many private developers from fulfilling their obligations. Lessons from these land-for-infrastructure arrangements in Vietnam show that without strong contractual arrangements and the systemic tracking of land allocation, pro-poor housing policies face significant implementation challenges.

Basic Infrastructure and Services in Low-Income Urban Areas

With the rapid expansion of urban areas through informal settlements, there are significant and increasing gaps in basic service delivery and the provision of infrastructure such as sanitation, electricity, and solid waste collection, particularly for the urban poor. The EAP countries have largely met their Millennium Development Goals (MDGs) in delivering safe water and are keeping pace with rapidly growing populations in urban areas, while Southeastern Asia remains one of five developing regions that has yet to meet its target for providing sanitation services.[5] At the country level, the largest deficiencies in urban areas for access to safe water are in Lao PDR and Mongolia, and for improved sanitation, Indonesia, Mongolia, and the Philippines lag the most[6] (figure 3.1 and table 3.1).

Unequal Access between Cities and within Urban Areas

As a whole, the EAP region has seen incredible progress in access to improved water sources and sanitation. Countries such as Malaysia and Cambodia have achieved 100 percent access to safe water for their urban populations. However, a closer look at how these improvements are measured reveals significant disparities in access to piped water infrastructure or running water within households. For example, in Cambodia, urban piped water infrastructure covers nearly 90 percent of the population of Phnom Penh. Elsewhere, urban piped water coverage ranges from zero (in the Kep province) to 62 percent (in the Takeo province) (World Bank 2012b, 7).

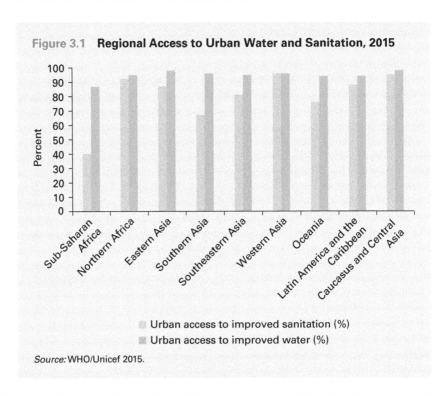

Figure 3.1   Regional Access to Urban Water and Sanitation, 2015

■ Urban access to improved sanitation (%)
■ Urban access to improved water (%)

Source: WHO/Unicef 2015.

Table 3.1   Access and Individual Urban Water Coverage, and Access and Sewerage Connection Coverage, 2015

Country	Urban access to safe water (%)	Urban share piped on premises (%)	Urban share other improved sources[a] (%)	Urban access to sanitation facilities (%)	Urban share practicing open defecation (%)
Cambodia	100	75	25	88	0
China	98	87	11	87	0
Indonesia	94	33	61	72	13
Lao PDR	86	64	22	94	1
Malaysia	100	100	0	96	0
Mongolia	66	33	33	66	1
Philippines	94	59	35	78	3
Thailand	98	76	22	90	0
Vietnam	99	61	38	94	0

Source: WHO/Unicef 2015.
a. Other improved sources include public taps or standpipes, tube wells or boreholes, protected dug wells, protected springs, and rainwater collection.

In Vietnam, piped water coverage varies widely based on the size of the city—larger cities such as Ho Chi Minh and Hanoi enjoy nearly 100 percent coverage, whereas smaller cities and towns have less than 60 percent coverage. Notably, while Hanoi and Ho Chi Minh account for 30 percent of urban residents, they are home to only 10 percent of the urban poor, while the 634 smallest Vietnamese towns (with an average population of 10,000) account for 55 percent of the urban poor (World Bank 2012b, 7). Looking at access according to income distribution, only 43.3 percent of the urban poor in Ho Chi Minh and Hanoi have access to private tap water, compared with 75.0 percent of the city's richest urban residents (UNDP 2010).

Similarly, despite significant gains in sanitation across the region, major gaps in services persist. In Indonesia, the Philippines, and Vietnam, 27 percent, 21 percent, and 7 percent, respectively, of the urban populations still do not have access to improved facilities (World Bank 2013). Of these, 5 percent, 5 percent, and 3 percent, respectively, are considered urban poor. In Indonesia, an estimated 13 percent of urban residents, most of whom are poor, still defecate in the open (WHO/Unicef 2015).

As an example of intra-city spatial disparities, the map of Ulaanbaatar (figure 3.2) represents the probability of access to sanitation measures based on access to flush toilets. Overall, only parts around downtown are more than 70 percent likely to have access to sanitation. The spatial pattern of access to sanitation also follows the spatial distribution of poverty, emphasizing that the level of access to sanitation positively correlates with level of income. With respect to urban poor, 77 percent of household in the poorest income quintile lack access to improved sanitation, as compared to 43 percent of the richest quintile.

Figure 3.2   **Access to Sanitation Services in Ulaanbaatar, Mongolia, 2014**

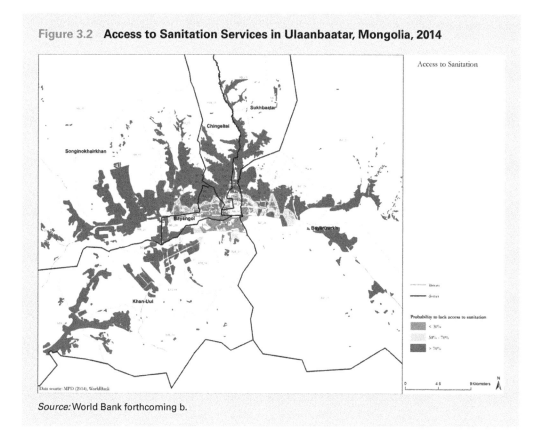

Source: World Bank forthcoming b.

Excluded from Citywide Subsidies

In the case of piped water, many EAP countries, including Indonesia, the Philippines, and Vietnam, structure their water delivery payment structure around block tariffs, where water consumption under a certain amount is significantly less expensive than water consumption at higher levels (World Bank 2012b). Revenues from higher water consumption essentially offset water consumed by the poor; this process, in theory, ensures that even the lowest income households can afford piped water to meet their basic needs. However, in settlements with a shared water kiosk, a number of households might be using the same water point and thus paying the higher tariff rate (Tacoli 2012). Furthermore, in areas with limited access to piped water infrastructure, the poor are unable to make use of the favorable tariff structure and are instead forced to rely on other sources, both improved and unimproved.

For services such as solid waste management, which are essential to public health, cities will often cover costs to compensate for nonpayers. Various fee structures are in place throughout the region, ranging from no fees for waste disposal charged to households in Quezon City, the Philippines, to low fees and no punitive measures for nonpayers in Kunming, China (Wilson et al. 2012). Despite waste management being partially subsidized and the fact that that the urban poor tend to produce much less solid waste than other urban residents and less than their counterparts in higher income countries,[7] they usually have much more limited access to solid waste management systems. Once again, the poor are unable to take advantage of available subsidies.

Only 60 percent and 70 percent of urban solid waste is collected in China and the Philippines, respectively (UN Habitat 2010, 10). Solid waste collection is higher in Ho Chi Minh City and Hanoi, Vietnam, but collection rates vary. For example, the solid waste collection rate is 99.1 percent for those in the highest quintile, but only 80.7 percent for those in the lowest quintile in the two cities (UNDP 2010, 82). Reasons for this include the following: (i) the difficulty of extending these services into congested slums and settlements; (ii) the reluctance of private business and informal garbage pickers to collect waste of the urban poor because it is predominantly organic material and usually does not contain anything of high value (for example, bottles, cans, and so on) (World Bank 1999); and (iii) the inability of the urban poor to pay for this service.

Lacking in Quality, Adequate Coverage, and Sufficient Standards

In areas where service delivery and infrastructure are available, concerns remain over its quality and challenges regarding its reliability. For example, in Vientiane, Lao PDR, many households—even those with access to piped water infrastructure—must still rely on private wells and water tanks to compensate for low pressure and intermittent water supply (World Bank 2012b, 10). Options such as these may not be available to the urban poor, who are forced instead to turn to groundwater, surface water (rivers, streams, canals, lakes, and so on), and private vendors (see below).

With regards to sanitation, although access is relatively high, rates of sewerage disposal are low throughout most of the region.[8] Of the countries covered in the World Bank's 2012 regional urban water supply and sanitation sector review (World Bank 2012b), only China and Vietnam had greater than 50 percent urban coverage with sewer connections. Countries such as Cambodia and Lao PDR as well as more urbanized countries such as Indonesia and the Philippines all had limited sewerage networks.

Limited sewerage disposal also results in a gap with regards to the collection, treatment, and disposal of wastewater (World Bank 2013a, 12). In Vietnam, where an estimated 60 percent of urban households have sewer connections, only 10 percent of the wastewater is treated (World Bank 2013a, 10), and in Indonesia and the Philippines, these numbers dip down even further, to 1 percent and 4 percent, respectively.

In addition, even with relatively high use of septic tanks in the region, poor regulation of septic tank construction and maintenance, combined with extremely low levels of wastewater collection and treatment, increases the water pollution risk. In Indonesia more than 60 percent of the urban population has flush toilets connected to septic tanks; however, only 4 percent of septage is treated (World Bank 2013b). Septic tanks are often poorly designed or constructed and not de-sludged regularly (World Bank 2012b, 12). In many cases they are open-bottom pits that empty directly into waterways or they lack absorption trenches and lead straight into the storm water drainage system (World Bank 2013b, 10). As mentioned above, the urban poor rely more on groundwater and open water sources, and poor infrastructure construction increases the risk that those sources will be contaminated.

Small-scale Service Providers and Informal Service Provision

Given the gaps in service provision and coverage, many urban residents elect to use small-scale service providers (SPSPs). While usage rates vary by country, significant numbers of the urban poor, in particular, must resort to small-scale providers as their only viable service option. In Jakarta, Indonesia, an estimated 46 percent of slum dwellers use private water vendors, followed by 31 percent in Manila, the Philippines, and 2.5 percent in Hanoi, Vietnam (Asian Trends Monitoring 2012; Pocock and Indrakesuma 2013). The urban poor who elect to use private water vendors pay comparatively more[9] for the same services and are potentially vulnerable to direct health risks and crime related to service provision.[10,11] Residents of Jakarta's northern Muara Angke coastal region, many of whom live on less than US$2 per day, pay up to US$1 every day to buy clean water (IRIN 2010). This willingness to pay higher prices reveals that private water vendors are fulfilling an unmet demand left unaddressed by local governments and utility providers.

In fact, SPSPs, a term that encompasses a range of businesses that are independently financed, developed, and managed,[12] are uniquely positioned to reach the urban poor and fill existing gaps in service provision. SPSPs are generally managed by residents of informal settlements, and their proximity to their customer base and flexibility in navigating available local technology allows them to deliver decentralized services more efficiently than utilities. They are also able to circumvent the high entry cost associated with connecting untenured households with municipal water systems. A survey of private water vendors in selected countries in Africa and Asia, including Cambodia and the Philippines, showed that the majority of water vendors held some type of operating license and that, on the whole, their customers were satisfied with the services they were receiving. These vendors self-reported that 50–60 percent of their clientele were poor (Baker 2009).

Informal service provision also extends to solid waste disposal, with waste-pickers helping to fill an essential gap in basic service provision. Integrating informal waste-pickers into municipal solid waste management has its benefits—in Hanoi, Vietnam, for example, waste-pickers profit off collecting and selling 18 to 22 percent of solid waste, saving the city US$2.5 to US$3.1 million a year (UN Habitat 2010; Virginia, Islam, and Shafi 2007, 197–223). Those who are employed in collecting, sorting, and disposal of solid waste often work on, or near, landfills. In the absence of support, these waste-pickers are at greater risk from personal injury (during waste collection and sorting), air pollution (from burning waste), and water pollution (from leachate into the soil and groundwater), and may be at even greater physical risk. In 2005, a landslide at Leuwigajah landfill near Bandung, Indonesia, resulted in the death of 140 people and the destruction of nearly 70 homes (IDRC and CRDI 2009).

Given the informal nature of small-scale service provision, infrastructure and regulations designed to protect businesses are limited. Though SPSPs provide essential services, these barriers often prevent them from expanding their scope and serving more customers, particularly in low-income communities. Furthermore, given their capital constraints and without access to external financing or government support, SPSPs don't necessarily have the budget to implement certain safety standards, as in the example of private water vendors in Cambodia (box 3.3).

Environmental and Socioeconomic Consequences of Inadequate Infrastructure and Service Delivery

As noted above, the urban poor experience greater exposure to health and safety risks as a consequence of limited service provision. And given the proximity of some informal settlements to landfills, as well as the lack of adequate wastewater treatment and solid waste disposal, open water sources might also be exposed to fecal contamination and pollution (World Bank 2012b, 12).

In Jakarta, Indonesia, for example, where only 2 percent of the city is connected to a sewer system, residents of urban slums and *kampungs* are particularly vulnerable to the effects of environmental pollution due to

Box 3.3   Informality Contributes to Public Health Hazards in Cambodia

A survey of small-scale service providers (SSSPs) in Cambodia included 75 piped network operators (PNOs) who supplied water through a fixed connection sourced from wells, springs, and rivers, then sold it to households. These vendors reported that poor households comprised around 40 percent of their clientele. Though prices charged by PNOs were higher than those charged by utilities, low-income customers still considered them to be affordable. However, there was a significant difference in water quality, stemming from lack of water treatment by PNOs.

Despite more than 70 percent of PNOs sourcing water from rivers and lakes, only one-third reported treating the water, with only half following the recommended sequence for water treatment (aeration-coagulation-flocculation-sedimentation-sand filtration-chlorination). Most consumers purchased water from PNOs due to cost and convenience, and there was limited public awareness of the health hazard posed by untreated water.

To improve water quality, financial support is a requirement. Even if the government were to mandate water treatment standards and was in a position to monitor compliance, the low profit margins of PNOs are, for the most part, not adequate for the self-financing of water treatment systems. Indeed, the majority of SSSPs surveyed financed business investments with their own funds or those of family and friends. Only the largest were able to obtain loans from microfinance institutions or banks, given that most banks require 150–300 percent collateral for loans.

Source: Baker 2009.

inadequate sewerage collection and treatment. As most of these settlements are located near riverbanks and canals, often in flood zones, they are especially vulnerable to contamination of ground and surface water, and the spread of water-borne diseases (such as typhoid) from frequent flooding (World Bank 2013c). In addition, the over-extraction of groundwater has also exacerbated the problem of land subsidence,[13] especially in Indonesia and the Philippines. About 40 percent of Jakarta is now below sea level (and therefore prone to flooding) due to land subsidence (World Bank 2012b). In Cambodia, the lack of quality standards for private service providers contributes to health risks.

Aside from its detrimental effects on health and the environment, poor service delivery also has significant negative economic impacts. Economic costs of poor sanitation were calculated based on the cost of health care; productivity loss; premature mortality; water resource and fishery loss; declining land value; time loss; absence from work or school; and negative impacts on tourism (WSP 2008). As a percentage of GDP, the costs of inadequate sanitation are estimated to be 1.3 percent for Vietnam, 2.3 percent for Indonesia, 1.5 percent for the Philippines, 5.6 percent for Lao PDR, and 7.2 percent for Cambodia (World Bank 2012b, 2–3). Poor water and sanitation supply, as well as difficult road access, affect the ability of home-based workers to fulfill contracts and deliver finished products (see the employment section for more information).

Women are affected by inadequate service delivery to a greater extent than men, as they are often responsible for household management and suffer a greater time burden as they attempt to secure basic services for their households (see chapter 4). Women's safety is also placed at risk through inadequate sanitation infrastructure. Open defecation, which often takes place at night for the sake of privacy, subjects women and girls to greater risk of violent attack. Even when shared sanitation facilities are available, studies have shown that gender-based violence is more likely to occur at toilets that are located away from homes (Tacoli 2012).

Key Challenges in Infrastructure and Service Provision

Legality and cost remain the two primary barriers to affordable and accessible infrastructure for the urban poor. However, limited service delivery to areas inhabited by the urban poor can also be explained by certain characteristics of EAP urbanization, such as dense development and narrow roads that make it difficult to provide large-scale infrastructure (UN Habitat 2010, 20). It is also the case that some governments hesitate to provide basic services and adequate infrastructure due to concerns about promoting further informal settlements.

Legality of Homes and Settlements

Legality plays a significant role in determining whether or not an individual household or an entire settlement receives basic municipal services. Illegality can be related to the absence of a house (for example, in the case of squatters) or of land title. In the case of housing titles, many urban dwellers are unable to show formal proof of residence, and are therefore ineligible for municipally-provided basic services (World Bank 2013d). For example, many newer urban settlements and informal settlements in Indonesia (for example, *kampungs*) do not have full legal land title and are therefore not registered with the National Land Board (World Bank 2013c, 11). In Jakarta alone, more than half of the city's land parcels are unregistered and do not have titles (World Bank 2011). In addition, any settlement that is located along railways, right of ways, riverbanks, under bridges, and along green paths and parks is considered illegal (World Bank 2013c, 11). By law, residents of these settlements cannot be granted citizenship rights and are denied access to basic infrastructure and services. This situation is common across the region, as municipal authorities equate provision of services and infrastructure with recognition of a settlement's legitimacy.

Access to infrastructure and services also varies widely based on the subcategory of urban poor. Migrants and seasonal workers, for example, are sometimes among the most vulnerable of the urban poor because, among other reasons, they are often unable to show the proof of residence needed to access basic services (World Bank 2013d, 111). The government of Vietnam provides a range of services (for example, subsidies and free healthcare) to the poor. However, migrants and seasonal workers in Hanoi are excluded from the list of beneficiaries because they lack an official residence (Asian Trends Monitoring Bulletin 2012) (box 3.4).

Cost

Given that informal settlements populated by the urban poor are often situated in high-risk areas (for example, on steep hillsides, flood-prone areas, and rights-of-ways near railways and highways), some municipal authorities avoid extending infrastructure and services to discourage additional informal settlements. Even where authorities are willing to provide services, they are often unable to extend the necessary physical infrastructure (for example, water pipes) due to the high initial costs and the ongoing cost of maintenance (World Bank 2013d). Authorities may also be attempting to protect their own investments, as low-income settlements are perceived as unprofitable (box 3.5).

Box 3.4   Migrant Workers Lack Permits, Access to Services in Vietnam

A study of migrant workers in Vietnam highlights some of the challenges through individual stories from Hanoi, as follows:

Linh, a migrant worker employed at the Long Bien night market in Hanoi, lives with her children in a boathouse. "We hardly get permanent residence permits and have little access to basic services. My children do not have identification cards nor can they attend public schools."[a]

It is often the case that migrants pay more for services such as electricity and water even if they are renting from residents with household connections to municipal utilities. Hai Phong, a migrant worker in Lam Ha Ward, explains: "We feel unequal compared to locals. We have to pay for rent, and electricity and water tariffs are higher for us than locals, since they enjoy the published price."[b]

a. UN Women 2013.
b. Oxfam and Action Aid Vietnam 2012.

Box 3.5   Costs Accrued in Extending Services to the Urban Periphery in Ulaanbaatar, Mongolia, 2005–10

A pilot project to extend water supply and sewer connections to households in the *ger* areas of Ulaanbaatar, Mongolia, was designed to connect 120 households (about 600 people) and eight public institutions to the city's water supply and sewerage systems. Project components included (i) installation of 4.6 km of water pipe; (ii) installation of 2.4 km of sewerage pipe; and (iii) construction of a standalone activated sludge wastewater treatment plant. The project failed due to extreme weather conditions combined with inaccurate estimates of service demand usage patterns among the urban poor.

Though the main water and sewage pipes were able to withstand the winter climate, household connections froze. Inquiries revealed that poor households were unable or unwilling to use adequate heating and insulation to protect the new infrastructure due to high electricity costs. Consequently, some household connections remained frozen for nearly six months in the pilot's first year of operation.

The project also failed to account for vacant homes (20 of the 120) and water consumption patterns, which differed from rates of households in the city center. Ultimately, water consumption and wastewater tariffs failed to match even operation costs, let alone offset the cost of the initial investment.

Source: World Bank 2012e.

Mobility and Access to the City

As EAP countries experience rapid urbanization, the influx of people and motor vehicles is overwhelming existing infrastructure and raising the urgency of transportation and mobility challenges. While urban populations at large are confronted by issues such as traffic congestion, insufficient public transit, and air pollution, the urban poor must also contend with issues of affordability, accessibility, and safety.

In urban areas across the region, the poor are negotiating the tradeoff between costly commutes to jobs and services in the city center and affordable housing in low-connectivity areas. For example, in Ulaanbaatar, Mongolia, there is a clear spatial distribution of the urban poor; pricier *khoroos*, or neighborhoods, in the city center are home to less than 6 percent of the urban poor, compared with some peripheral districts where the urban poor account for 35–45 percent of the *khoroo* populations (World Bank forthcoming b). Commutes from the periphery to the city center are longer, with more indirect routes, and costlier, and the overall percentage of household income spent on commuting is higher for the urban poor.

As the rural–urban migration continues, newer migrants who cannot find affordable housing in the inner city often make their homes in temporary settlements in the city's outskirts. In places where transportation is prohibitively expensive, this situation can contribute to the physical and social isolation of the urban poor in slums or at the urban periphery. Research has shown that spatial division exacerbates inequality and perpetuates further marginalization of the poor (UN Habitat 2013). The lack of affordable transportation restricts the mobility of the urban poor, who are unwilling or unable to complete non-essential trips.[14] When considering poverty in a multidimensional manner, restricted mobility translates to a constraint on the development of human capacity as the urban poor have access to fewer jobs and fewer social services, such as better healthcare or schools.

Urban transportation has the potential to reduce poverty either directly, by meeting the needs of the urban poor, or indirectly, by impacting positively on a city's economy and contributing to overall economic growth (Carruthers et al. 2005). However, to capture these positive effects, there must be a concerted policy effort to promote an inclusive and affordable transit system that incorporate travel modes that the poor use. Market forces, rather than policy, have thus far determined the pace and shape of urbanization throughout the region, leaving transit systems open to inefficient development that is potentially inaccessible to the poor (World Bank 2015b).

Motorization, Sprawl, and Congestion

Increased motorization is the first visible outcome of these market forces. A high regional economic growth rate has allowed for larger swaths of the population to purchase private vehicles. China, in particular, has seen a dramatic rise in private vehicle ownership, from 56 million in 2000 to 240 million in 2012 (World Bank 2014). In Vietnam's two main urban centers, Ho Chi Minh City and Hanoi, a combined 14 million residents generate approximately 20 million passenger trips a day, 90 percent of which use private vehicles (ADB 2012). A second outcome is urban sprawl, which is both driven by and promotes motorization. As more urban residents rely on private vehicles as a primary mode of transportation, cities grow in a way that encourages and necessitates private vehicle use, which may not be affordable for the urban poor.

Motorization and sprawl lead to a third outcome—increased traffic congestion and commute times (figure 3.3). Average commute times are nearing an hour in megacities such as Beijing, China, and Manila, the Philippines. While congestion is an issue in urban centers worldwide, its economic consequences are far more detrimental/negative in megacities in the developing world, where congestion levels tend to be higher and one or two main urban centers are the primary GDP drivers of a country. The Asian Development Bank estimates that traffic congestion costs Asian economies 2–5 percent of their GDP annually, given higher transportation costs and lost productivity. A study on traffic congestion in Metro Manila, the Philippines, calculates the cost of lost productivity at 3.4 billion pesos (approx. 73 million USD) per year (JICA 2013).

Car-oriented Transportation Policies

To accommodate the increasing use of private vehicles, urban leaders have pursued strategies to facilitate improved motor traffic flow, irrespective of their effects on other transportation modes. Further returns from road network expansions are limited, as cities face urban road networks that are too dense to continue to develop and construction costs

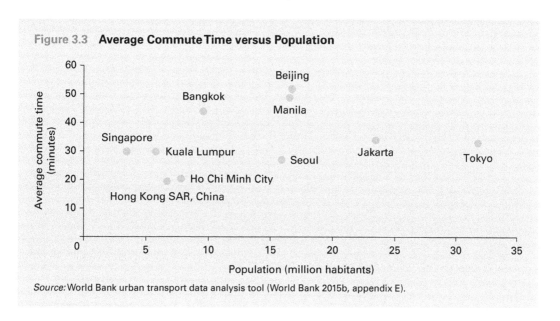

Figure 3.3   **Average Commute Time versus Population**

Source: World Bank urban transport data analysis tool (World Bank 2015b, appendix E).

are high. Such investments divert resources from other city investments and are typically regressive, favoring the nonpoor. For example, in China, from the 1990s to early 2000s, city planners pursued a "build" strategy, opting for road construction and road widening, often at the expense of nonmotorized transportation (World Bank 2013d). In Indonesia, the private vehicle fleet has more than tripled since 2001. Despite allocating 1.6 percent of GDP annually to road network expansion, however, Indonesia's road system has failed to accommodate increasing traffic (World Bank 2012c).

In addition to diverting city resources towards roads and car infrastructure, various cities are banning transportation modes that are favored by the urban poor in attempts to open up more roads to cars. For example, in 2007 Jakarta saw a widespread seizure of *becak* (cycle rickshaws), which provide both mobility and jobs for the urban poor. The city enforced a long-held (but generally overlooked) ban on the cycles to relieve congestion in the city center and promote "modernity" (Tiwari 2005). A similar ban on *mamus* or trishaws (both motorized and nonmotorized) was imposed in Wuhan, China. With over 18,000 registered trishaws prior to the ban, there were widespread consequences on livelihoods for the urban poor, not only for drivers but also their customers. One urban resident commented, "I used to ride a *mamu* to a bus stop on my way to work every day. But this is no longer possible. So people take some of these microbuses instead— but the fare for those is at least Y3, and more on rainy days—more expensive than *mamus*. My commute now costs me Y7 or 8 a day. That's why so many people can't take jobs far away from where they [live]" (Economic Research Institute, Wuhan University 2003). Similarly, a bicycle and motorcycle ban in Yangon, which began in 2003, has impeded low- and middle-income residents from ease of mobility (box 3.6).

East Asia still maintains lower rates of vehicle ownership than other more economically advanced regions (figure 3.4), though those rates are

Box 3.6 Gridlock and Bike Bans in Yangon, Myanmar

In an attempt to improve road safety and avoid congestion, Yangon has enforced a bicycle and motorcycle ban in its central districts since 2003. The direct result of the ban, seen in table B3.6.1, below, is that Myanmar's most populous city has relatively low rates of vehicle ownership, particularly motorcycle ownership, compared to other urban areas in the country.

Nevertheless, traffic speeds in Yangon have been steadily dropping as more cars come on-road. Incidences of traffic accidents and fatalities have been increasing, with police reporting 506 traffic-related fatalities from 3,000 vehicle collisions in 2013, up from 475 fatalities from 2,100 collisions the year before.[a]

(Box continues on next page)

Box 3.6   **Gridlock and Bike Bans in Yangon, Myanmar** *(continued)*

Table B3.6.1   **Registered Vehicles by State/division in Myanmar, 2010**

State/division	Registered vehicles	Registered motorcycles	Registered motorcycles (%)	Registered vehicles/1,000 population
Kayah state	16,711	14,752	88.3	48
Yangon	**253,904**	**50,401**	**19.8**	**36.5**
Taninthayi	70,323	64,787	92.1	41.6
Kachin state	80,953	70,016	86.5	51.8
Shan state	346,073	305,894	88.4	61.2
Mandalay Division	626,202	549,338	87.7	75

Sources: JICA 2014; Government of the Republic of the Union of Myanmar.

Yangon's urban transit system lacks such basic measures as traffic signals or straight railway tracks for the city's commuter railway; cars still present a more reliable way to move around the city. The bike ban has effectively prevented middle-and lower-income urban residents in Yangon from purchasing a private vehicle, holding them captive to a decaying and increasingly inefficient transit system.

Source: JICA 2014.
a. http://www.aljazeera.com/indepth/features/2014/04/strangled-traffic-yangon-201441082132744464.html.

Figure 3.4   **Four-wheeler Motorization Rate Relative to Per-Capita Income**

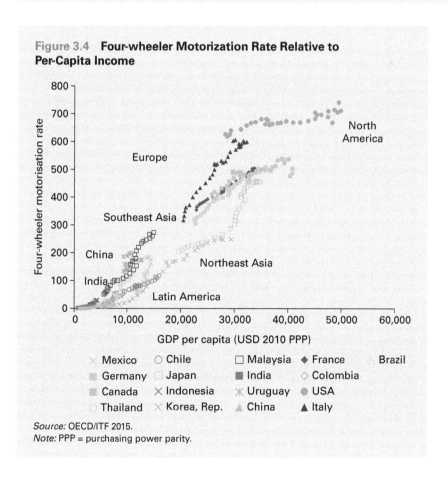

Source: OECD/ITF 2015.
Note: PPP = purchasing power parity.

rising rapidly. For many cities in the region, urban form, or spatial layout, is still taking shape and has not yet fully developed or "locked in," meaning there is still time for policy makers to ensure a "spatial match" between available urban transportation and housing, jobs, and services, particularly in a way that benefits the urban poor (World Bank 2015b). To do so effectively, however, better data collection and analysis of how the urban poor move through cities are needed.

Reliance on Nonmotorized Transportation (NMT) and Walking

High-density urbanization, an EAP characteristic, has lent itself to the development of "door-to-door" transportation services provided through NMT and shared vehicles. *Tuk tuks, becaks, jeepneys*, and minibuses have long dominated the EAP streets and together with pedestrians, cyclists, and street vendors, have defined how public roadways are used. These vehicles generally have low carrying capacity, speed, and energy requirements and operate within a relatively small area of coverage (Ieda 2010). However, within a given area, these vehicles can access small lanes and roadways unavailable to larger cars and buses, thus increasing mobility.

NMT vehicles provide a cheap and flexible mode of transportation, suited to the urban poor, who are often employed in informal sectors with frequent changes in job location. Furthermore, operating NMT vehicles provides job opportunities for the urban poor and recent rural-urban migrants who might not have official documents or the education and skills necessary for more skilled labor (UN Habitat 2013). A report on the commuting habits of the urban poor in Metro Manila, the Philippines, identifies three main reasons for the use of NMT: budget constraints; a preference for staying within a neighborhood or small network to identify employment opportunities; and relatively higher priced public transportation services (Ieda 2010).

The mobility patterns of pedestrians are often overlooked by city planners, including among the urban poor who are "captive walkers," or unable to afford alternate modes of transportation. Though data on pedestrian habits are difficult to collect, there are broad estimates that in low-income developing economies, over half of all trips are undertaken on foot (Gwilliam 2002). In Shanghai and Beijing, China, the urban poor who rely on walking or cycling as their primary mode of transportation spend less than 5 percent of their income on transportation costs; similar travel by bus would cost them 40 percent of their income (Vabdycke and Lloyd 2012). Given cost considerations, captive walkers tend to take fewer "nonessential trips," and are thus even further limited in the range of services to which they have access. Box 3.7, below, presents an example of the commuting habits of the urban poor in Guangzhou, China.

Box 3.7   **Commuting and Employment in Guangzhou, China**

A 2012 survey of the commuting patterns of 220 working residents of Xiguan, an inner-city neighbor-hood of Guangzhou, revealed that commuting choices and employment locations were dependent on respondents' incomes. The average income of the respondents was 2,960 yuan per month, or about 60 percent of the city average. The modal split and travel times for all respondents are shown in table B3.7.1, below.

Table B3.7.1   **Mode Choice and Travel Times of all Respondents**

	Modal split (%)	Average travel time (min)
Walking	18.6	14.9
Bicycle	3.2	19.3
Public bus	55	34.5
Guangzhou metro	19.5	30
Private car	3.6	35

Among low-income residents (earning less than 2,500 yuan per month) the share of pedestrians was higher than in the group average, with 24.4 percent walking to work. None of the low-income respondents commuted by car. A further analysis of income and commuting time revealed that the lower the respondents' income, the likelier they were to use a slower mode of transportation. The study concluded that lower monthly incomes prevented residents from seeking distant employment opportunities.

Source: Lau 2013, 119–127.

Key Mobility Challenges for the Urban Poor

Accessibility among the Urban Poor

Access to jobs, services, and city resources is the underlying goal of a well-functioning urban transit system, and remains a critical factor in the decision-making of the urban poor, particularly about housing (box 3.8). A number of factors limit the access of these essentials by the urban poor, beginning with poor transportation design and maintenance. Narrow roads in slums are without sidewalks, pushing pedestrians into the street. As walking is a preferred and sometimes the only available mode of transportation among the urban poor, poor street quality becomes a major impediment to mobility. Roads that do extend to the urban periphery are often too small or too littered with potholes to accommodate larger public transportation vehicles. For example, in Mongolia, not only do a limited number of roads reach the *ger* areas, or periphery settlements, on the outskirts of Ulaanbaatar, but official records also show that only 10 percent of these roads are paved (World Bank forthcoming b). For residents of both slums and the periphery, basic road infrastructure lies at the heart of accessibility.

Box 3.8   **Accessibility of Informal Urban Settlements in the Philippines**

Focus group discussions were conducted with residents of four informal settlement communities in the Philippines. Two of the communities were located in "danger zones" that are susceptible to flooding. The importance of the location of slums and access to transportation were among the issues raised. Discussants offered the following observations:

Proximity to services and transit increased the desirability of the informal settlement location. "While the men would usually have to commute or bike to their work areas (some as far as Cubao), the participants agree that the settlement is near areas which they consider important: the malls, the public market, school for their children (walking distance) and the highway, to get around to other areas of Metro Manila. Proximity to malls indicates better access to transport." (Community Franville 4, Caloocan City)

Accessibility of community services compensates for commuting times and related expenses. "Most [residents] would need to commute to work and do several transfers to get to their place of employment. The participants said that they are willing to commute because it is more expensive for them to stop work to look for employment nearer their place of residence (it is harder for them to lose work). The settlement is accessible to the malls and other areas such as the public market, which makes it also beneficial to the community because they believe that since they are near the 'busy centers,' there is more work for them (for example, for a tricycle driver, the transportation hub at SM offers more passengers), and the mall serves as a community center as well." (Community Sto. Nino, Caloocan City)

Relocation to safer/upgraded living quarters was associated with new household expenditures directly related to availability and affordability of transportation. "For the participant who was relocated, she said that the relocation site in Bulacan is accessible to the road and to the school (one jeepney ride away), but the public market is too far from the site and there are no butcher shops or sari-sari stores in the relocation site, while the nearest shops to the site are more expensive than those at the public market. This adds to the expenses of the family as they have to make several trips to the public market since they cannot store food in the house (lack of electricity). Also because the relocation site is far from the place of work of the participant's husband, the husband has to stay in at work and just go home during weekends." (Community Bistekville 2, Barangay Culiat Quezon City)

Source: World Bank forthcoming a.

Mobility constraints can also exacerbate the economic, social, and personal isolation of the elderly and people with disabilities. These groups have more limited access to physical environments such as roads, housing, public buildings and spaces; to basic urban services, emergency response and resilience programs; and to information and communications. While principles of "universal design" are increasingly incorporated in urban planning, challenges remain (World Bank 2012a). The general lack of reliable, disaggregated data on disability and disability-inclusive transportation is also a major constraint on efforts to influence policy.

Affordability of Transportation Expenses

Transportation expenses are high for the urban poor, especially in relation to their household incomes. For residents of the urban periphery, trips into the city can often only be made using multiple modes of transportation.

Box 3.9 illustrates the transportation expenses of the urban poor in Ulaanbaatar, Mongolia. In many countries, including Mongolia, even if each segment of the trip is completed on public transportation, there is no integrated fee system, and a flat fee must be paid for each segment of the trip regardless of distance travelled.

This situation is due in part to administrative fragmentation, where various forms of public transit (and other public services) fall under the jurisdiction of separate administrative units. Administrators of peri-urban areas, particularly areas with informal settlements, might not always have the resources to develop or ability to coordinate efficient travel options with the administrators of the city center, leading to the uneven provision of infrastructure services. For example, Metro Manila, the Philippines, includes 85 municipalities and cities in seven provinces, while Jakarta's urban area covers 1,600 square kilometers across 12 jurisdictions. Across the EAP region, there are 350 multi-jurisdictional urban areas, with 135 that have no dominant local jurisdiction (World Bank 2015b).

The direct result of such administrative fragmentation is visible in urban China, where different agencies are responsible for metros, buses, road construction, traffic management, and land use. Poor planning and service integration has resulted in inefficient "door-to-door" trips by public transportation due to excessive transfer distances, mismatched schedules, separate ticketing systems, and lack of easily accessible transfer facilities (World Bank 2014). To get to jobs, both formal and informal, in the city center, the urban poor spend significantly more of their time, as well as a higher percentage of their income, on commuting than other income groups (Suzuki et al. 2013).

Box 3.9   Household Expenditures on Transportation in Ulaanbaatar, Mongolia

Public transportation provides an affordable transit option for most city residents, given the flat fare of MNT 500 (US$ 0.27) charged to adults and MNT 200 (US$ 0.11) for children. Full-fare subsidies are provided for students, people with disabilities, and the elderly, who collectively constitute 40 percent of the ridership. Based on assumptions about transit routines and incomes, the World Bank estimates that monthly household expenditures on transportation range from 9–18 percent of average city household expenditures.

However, among poorer households at the urban periphery, this estimate increases to 24–36 percent of monthly household expenditures. This increase is due not only to the fact that the urban poor have lower incomes than the city average, but also to inefficient public transit route planning. Commuters from the urban periphery must make one or more transfers involving formal buses, informal transport, or both. Fares are not integrated, even between formal buses, and without any transfer discount, total costs can double or triple, regardless of distance travelled. As a result, residents living in the urban periphery are restricted in their general mobility and constrained in their ability to access jobs that could supplement their household incomes and livelihoods.

Source: World Bank 2016a.

Though high transportation costs themselves are seen as a symptom, not a cause of urban poverty, they nevertheless act as a deterrent to making "unnecessary trips," even when pursuing employment activities. This situation is a particular issue for women. Women generally engage in activities such as childcare, household management, and informal employment, which often require multi-segmented trips at off-peak hours or to locations not on main routes. In general, these trips are shorter and more frequent than commuting trips undertaken by men, making them relatively more expensive for public transit systems to accommodate (Gwilliam 2002).

Gentrification is a final cost concern. Interventions targeting the urban poor, such as those that improve walkability of a neighborhood or extend public transit services to an underserved area, might function to drive up surrounding property values. The urban poor, particularly those in informal settlements or without secure land tenure, are thus vulnerable to displacement as a result of forced relocation or housing prices increasing beyond their means (Suzuki et al. 2013).

Safety of the Urban Poor

When the needs of private vehicle owners are prioritized over the needs of the urban poor, not only are the poor denied accessibility, but must also contend with issues of safety. The diversity of vehicles in the EAP region means that roads might be shared between people using up to 10 different modes of transportation, all traveling at varying speeds. Traffic accidents tend to involve nonmotorized vehicles, pedestrians, and motorcycles (table 3.2), leaving the urban poor disproportionately subject to injury or death. As a region, EAP led globally in traffic fatalities in 2010 with 313,317, followed by South Asia with 275,569, then Africa with 248,130 (IEG 2014).

In China the national average for traffic-accident related fatalities was 9.9 deaths per 10,000 motor vehicles. However, in areas with sustained growth in rates of motor vehicle ownership, these rates were significantly higher (table 3.3), with pedestrians and bicyclists being among the most impacted.

In Indonesia, sidewalks are commandeered by parked vehicles, street vendors and markets, forcing pedestrians into the streets. Recent data indicate that around 55 traffic accident-related fatalities occur daily and about 15 percent involve pedestrians (World Bank 2012c). Even in cities with designated lanes for nonmotorized vehicles and pedestrian bridges or walkways, it is not unusual to see people crossing roads directly, indicating poor planning or insufficient stakeholder consultation when designing such facilities. Women face additional safety concerns in the form of harassment at transportation depots or while riding buses (World Bank 2011). Factors contributing to pedestrian mobility and safety include the quality of paths and sidewalks; obstruction; lighting; exposure to crime; and safety of crossings (ADB 2013).

Table 3.2 **Reported Deaths by User Road Category in East Asia, 2010 (percent)**

	Motorized 2- or 3-wheelers	Cyclists	Pedestrians	Drivers (cars)	Passengers (cars)	Heavy trucks	Buses	Other	Total fatalities
Cambodia	67	4	12	3	9	1	—	4	1,186
China	35	10	25	6	17	5	—	2	65,225
Indonesia	36	2	21	1	5	—	35	—	31,234
Lao PDR	74	1	6		15[a]	—	3	1	790
Malaysia	59	3	9	15	11	2	1	—	6,872
Mongolia	19	1	25		40[a]	4	—	11	491
Myanmar	23	9	26	13	13	7	—	9	2,464
Thailand	74	3	8	6	7	1	—	1	13,766
World	23	5	22		31[a]			19	1,240,000

Source: WHO 2013.
Note: — = not available.
a. Statistic provided for occupants (drivers and passengers)

Table 3.3 **Traffic-Accident Fatality Rates, Cities in Northeast China, 2005**

	Benxi	Fushan	Jinzhou	Liaoyang	Panjin
Fatalities/10,000 motor vehicles	34.4	27.9	3.7	14.8	32

Source: World Bank 2006.

Spatial Inclusion: Strategies for Housing, Infrastructure and Service Provision, and Connectivity

There is strong evidence on the importance of adequate shelter, basic services and connectivity for the urban poor. Investing in affordable, safe and reliable housing, infrastructure services and transportation services can reduce spatial inequality, open up new employment opportunities, and reduce health and disaster risk. Beyond these critical investments, there are a number of approaches for promoting spatial inclusion that have worked in EAP countries that could be considered for replication. These approaches are summarized below.

Strategies for Housing the Urban Poor

Many governments have moved away from the historical response of slum clearance and forced eviction and towards resettlement and upgrading. In urban areas of Lao PDR, for example, the government provided long-term land leases to low-income squatters to help regularize the communities;

in Vietnam, the government adjusted existing planning strategy to accommodate the need for low-cost housing solutions and incremental construction. Hanoi, Vietnam has a growing urban center with little slum development, as the government has encouraged flexible land market regulations, the densification of former rural zones, and the development of expanded transit network beyond urban areas for increased accessibility to towns on the outskirts of the city (World Bank 2013d). More detailed examples of housing strategies are given below.

Land Banking and "In- City" Relocation in Iloilo City, Philippines. In the small coastal city of Iloilo, with a population of 800,000, nearly one-third of residents live without tenure or in informal housing. In 2002, the city initiated plans for a flood control project that involved the relocation of 3,500 squatters from their homes along canals and low-lying flood prone areas. The relocation was approached in collaboration with the Homeless People's Federation and the Iloilo City Urban Poor Network to ensure that community concerns would be addressed. The result of the collaboration was the development of a progressive housing policy that ensured no eviction without relocation and that all relocation would occur within city limits, no more than 4 to 6 km from the original settlement site. To achieve this, the city has purchased land parcels from private owners and "banked" them to accommodate future relocation and social housing needs. Eventually, the city plans to implement mechanisms allowing relocated households to form associations and pay the city for the land in manageable installments, resulting in land titles for individual plots (ACHR 2009).

Land Titling and Rental Cooperatives in Bangkok, Thailand. Under the Baan Mankong program, the Community Development Organizations Institute (CODI) works with cooperatives within slum and squatter communities to develop collective housing solutions. CODI uses various ownership structures including cooperative land ownership and long-term leases to community cooperatives to allow low-income communities to secure land titles. The collective approach also discourages speculators from purchasing individual housing units from the poor to sell to higher income groups. CODI finances its programs using a mix of its own funding, government subsidies, and pooled savings from residents. These funds may also be used for infrastructure development and upgrading. Following major flooding in 2011, CODI was able to provide funds to 3,000 families across 50 communities for rehabilitation of housing and infrastructure (Peppercorn and Taffin 2013).

Rental Housing Subsidies in China. Initiated in 2004 by the central government, China's Cheap Rental Housing Guarantee Plan (CRH) essentially combines rental subsidies with new rental developments to provide housing units for low-income households. The program is administered through municipal and local governments, which bear the primary program costs. The central government has stipulated that 5 percent of net gains from land conveyance fees be allocated towards the program—though with limited enforcement mechanisms, the program remains perpetually underfunded. Nevertheless, the program has done a good job targeting low-income tenants, rather than allowing higher income households to capture the subsidy. The program has also done well in enforcing strict development standards. In 2009, China set national targets of developing new rental units for 5.6 million urban residents and providing subsidies to an additional 1.9 million households (Deng et al. 2011).

Community Mortgages in the Philippines. The Philippines Community Mortgage Program enables home ownership and tenure security for low-income households by providing loans for purchasing plots and constructing homes. Through the formation of community associations, low-income households can access subsidized mortgages from the state-run Social Housing Finance Corporation. These associations are also charged with collecting loan payments and enforcing sanctions and penalties. Since 2001, the program has provided loans to over 77,000 households, though with a repayment rate of only 75 percent—high for comparable schemes in the region. In recent years, however, the program has faced challenges due to high operating costs and rising land prices (UN Habitat 2011).

Broadening the Reach of Infrastructure and Service Provision

Urban Infrastructure Upgrading in Vietnam. In 2004, a four-city urban upgrading project was initiated with assistance from the World Bank, with the goal of alleviating urban poverty through infrastructure improvements. More than 200 low-income areas (with at least 40 percent of households under the poverty threshold) were identified and communities were asked to evaluate what improvements would be most beneficial. In-situ upgrading of water supply, drainage, road paving, household electricity connections, and sanitation and solid waste management proved ultimately to be less costly than clearing and moving these households to hard-to-access relocation sites. The initiative also included a microfinance component to be used for home upgrades or income-generation purposes, helping to address some of the credit access barriers often experienced by the urban poor. As of 2014, 2.5 million urban poor residents benefited directly from the project, with an additional 5 million befitting from improvements in primary and secondary infrastructure (World Bank 2016b).

Community-Driven Infrastructure Development in Indonesia. Indonesia's community-driven development program, Program Nasional Pemberdayaan Masyarakat (PNPM), provides block grants for community-level infrastructure and extends to all 11,000 urban wards. The program provides both financial and technical support to poor communities, allowing them to address immediate infrastructure needs. To strengthen local participation and networks, community-based organizations spearhead needs assessments and project design. PNPM is successful in small-scale projects, but is not a substitute for government leadership in infrastructure projects requiring wider coordination or relocation (for example, road network development). As of 2013, the program had financed over 31,100 km of small roads, 8,800 km of drainage, 164,8000 units of solid waste and sanitation facilities, and 9,450 health facilities, and the rehabilitation of 126,800 homes (World Bank 2013e).

Partnering with Small-Scale Private Service Providers in Manila, the Philippines. Private sector participation in urban sanitation is relatively uncommon in the region. However, the Philippines provides a rare exception. Water supply and sanitation have been privatized under two concession contracts in Metro Manila, and rather than subsidizing wastewater treatment directly, Manila finances wastewater treatment through cross-subsidies from water user charges (World Bank 2012b). Furthermore, when the concessions are awarded to private companies, there are incentives for them to work with SPSPs, which are accounted for when first assessing urban access to services. A result of the partnership has been the development of innovation in the extension of access to low-income residents without the use of subsidies. Alternative arrangements include paying connection fees in installments or through a higher water tariff; the use of shared meters to reduce connection costs; and establishing connections in informal settlements through the use of hoses and other low-cost mechanisms (Baker 2009).

Using Mobile Phones to Track Water Usage and Availability in India. To ensure that improved access is sustained, utilities and municipal bodies must find a way to monitor the quality and reliability of service provision. NextDrop, a social enterprise launched in 2010 and now active in Hubli-Dharwad and Bangalore, uses a system of SMS notifications to alert utilities about water outages and customers about the timing and availability of water delivery services. From a customer perspective, accurate information helps to reduce wait times and allows households to plan their water usage, while utilities receive real-time information about their distribution system. Importantly, this system uses mobile phone technology that is already widely used among the urban poor. The benefits of this service, however, extend to the wider urban population (Ndaw 2015).

Decentralized Wastewater Treatment Systems (DEWATS) in Indonesia. Community-managed DEWATS allow for rapid improvements in sanitation facilities in high-priority informal settlements. In Indonesia, DEWATS are seen as a way to address inadequate sanitation infrastructure and high rates of open defecation, and between 2003 and 2011, more than 400 sites were created. Three types of systems have been implemented, as follows:

(i)   The most prevalent is the community sanitation center, which offers washing and laundry facilities in addition to toilets and a sewage treatment facility.

(ii) Next is the simplified sewer system that collects and sends wastewater from households to DEWATS treatment facility.

(iii) The final system combines a community sanitation center with a simplified sewer system, accommodating those who are unable to connect to a network while still maintaining privacy for households who can connect.

These systems are most effective when communities and local government share costs and responsibilities for their operations and maintenance (Eales et al. 2013).

Transportation Policies to Connect the Urban Poor

Mapping Public Transit Routes in Metro Manila, the Philippines. Prior to 2012, there was no comprehensive map of Manila's transit system. Manila's 12 million residents (who made 70 percent of all trips using public transit) had no way to look up schedules or routes. Government agencies had no way to evaluate whether transit lines were meeting demand or failing to reach certain segments of the population. In a joint World Bank/Department of Transportation and Communications (DOTC) project, a database was created, using open source tools, to meet the General Transit Feed Specification (GTFS), an internationally recognized standard for mapping transit routes. The database includes bus and jeepney routes, and can be downloaded on smartphones or accessed through web or SMS-based, trip-planning tools. Since going public in July 2013, there have been over 14,000 downloads of the database. Furthermore, the DOTC was able to develop a reorganization plan based on new route information as well as passenger survey and count data collected from database users. Over the next two years, the DOTC will close redundant bus routes, which is anticipated to reduce GHG emissions by 23 percent and significantly relieve traffic congestion (World Bank 2015a).

Engaging Matatu Drivers in Nairobi, Kenya. Similar to the mapping of jeepney and bus routes in the Philippines, mobile apps were used to track *matatu* routes in Nairobi and create a map of the city's informal bus system. The effort was led by researchers from University of Nairobi, Columbia University, and MIT as well as the technology firm, Groupshot. Using data collected through the apps, a stylized route map, similar to those found for transit systems in Paris, London, and New York, was created and distributed in-person and online. The maps proved to be popular and catalyzed conversations about informal transit at various levels of government. Matatu drivers themselves, upon seeing the maps, had suggestions for how routes and traffic circulation could be improved and were brought into a conversation with the larger transit community (Klopp et al. 2015).

Gondolas and Connectivity in Medellín, Colombia. Slum settlements and shanty towns occupied by the urban poor were climbing up into the mountainsides surrounding the city of Medellín. Mobility was understand-ably constrained, and residents of these settlements were reportedly spend-ing up to four hours commuting to the city center in search of work. Working with the city's unique geography, gondolas were introduced in 2004 as a way to connect those at the periphery with main transit lines within the city center. Movement down the mountain became faster and more affordable, and the improved connectivity was found to have a direct effect in lowering crime rates in the area (Cerdá et al. 2012).

Bus Rapid Transit in Curitiba, Brazil. The iconic BRT (bus rapid transit) system in Curitiba, Brazil, was the first in the world to be fully realized and implemented in 1975. Drawing on elements of light rail transportation, BRT systems include larger buses, payment prior to boarding, multiple bus entry points, and designated lanes. All medium and large urban development projects must take place along BRT corridors to ensure land-use that is complimentary to existing urban transit routes. Curitiba now has a fleet of 2,100 buses and transports 2.04 million passengers daily (Prefeitura Municipal de Curtiba 2010).

Linking Nonmotorized Transportation and Bus Rapid Transportation in Guangzhou, China. In 2010, Guangzhou opened a 22.5 km BRT corridor along one of the city's busiest roads, Zhongshan Avenue. Today, this averages 850,000 weekday boardings, making it Asia's busiest bus corridor. A greenway was developed alongside the BRT corridor, complete with pedestrian walkways and a bike-sharing system consisting of 5,000 bikes across 109 stations. The BRT lines and bike-sharing stations are integrated, and passengers can use the same smart card to access both. The corridor also extends from some of Guangzhou's most developed areas to peripheral neighborhoods where future development is anticipated. The BRT system is estimated to reduce travel times for bus passengers by 29 percent, reducing emissions from improved traffic congestion by 86,000 tons of CO_2 per year, and particulate matter by 4 tons (Suzuki et al. 2013).

Improving Pedestrian Facilities in Northeast China. As part of a World Bank-funded project to improve public transportation and road infrastructure in the "rust belt" of China, the views of low-income residents, especially those with mobility challenges due to disability, were solicited through targeted public consultations. Disabled residents were asked to field test the design of bus stops, intersections, and sidewalks to ensure accessibility. Multiple consultations during the project design and implementation phases allowed city planners not only to incorporate many of the suggested improvements, but also show low-income residents that their ideas regarding traffic management, road safety, and pedestrian mobility were taken into consideration (World Bank 2006).

Notes

1. Theoretical models support the inverted-u pattern of geographic concentration where regional inequality first rises and then falls (see for example, Krugman, Fujita, and Venables [1999]) (World Bank 2009).
2. The practice of evictions and forced relocations of urban poor, especially slum dwellers, without proper legal process has been recognized as the one of the most visible violation of housing rights of urban poor (Millennium Development Goals Report 2012; UN-Habitat 2010).
3. Although Cambodia is an extreme case of inadequate land tenure and management systems in the EAP region, it is representative of the additional challenges faced by many conflict-affected countries.
4. Price to Income Ratios (PIRs) calculated for 2006 (Cruz 2008). See "Housing Sales and Rental Markets in Asia," http://www .globalpropertyguide.com/investment-analysis/Housing-Sales-and -Rental-Markets-in-Asia. These are the most recent PIRs available for major cities in this region. The only other PIRs collected for cities in this

region are from 1998: 8.9 for Phnom Penh; 14.6 Jakarta; 3.4 in Surabaya; 13.3 in Cebu; 8.8 in Bangkok; and 6.8 in Chiang Mai.

5. The countries of EAP include Eastern Asia, Southeastern Asia, and Oceania, as per UN definitions.

6. Service coverage denoted in tables 3.1 and 3.2 is based on the Joint Monitoring Program's definitions for "improved drinking-water source" and "improved sanitation," where improved-drinking water source is "one that, by nature of its construction, adequately protects the source from outside contamination, particularly fecal matter," and "improved sanitation facility" is one that is "likely to ensure hygienic separation of human excrete from human contact."

7. The urban poor in Asia consume less nonfood items and collect, reuse, recover and recycle as much of their waste as possible. Approximately 20 to 30 percent of their waste is recyclable. (UN Habitat 2012, 16).

8. The Joint Monitoring Program's definition of improved sanitation is a facility that separates human excreta from human contact. Sewerage refers to the management of human waste and measures whether these facilities are connected to a piped sewer system, septic tank, or managed latrine.

9. Slum dwellers in large cities pay from 5 to 10 times more for a liter of water than residents of wealthy neighborhoods (http://www.asianews.it/news-en/UN-discusses-water,-a-fundamental-human-right-18951.html).

10. Health risks of lower quality water include malnutrition, diarrhea, and infant and child mortality.

11. In the absence of adequate government provision of services, service provision in informal settlements often falls into the hands of local mafias and other power groups (World Bank 2013c).

12. Private network operators supply water using fixed piped connections sourced primarily from rivers, springs, and wells. Point source vendors operate water kiosks and standpipes sourced from private wells or utilities with customers filling their own containers. Mobile water vendors provide private delivery to households on motorized or nonmotorized forms of transportation. Value-added water vendors operate water treatment systems to sell "purified" water to higher income clients.

13. The urban poor's overreliance on groundwater, combined with poor municipal regulation against over-extraction, have contributed to land subsidence in cities such as Jakarta and Manila.

14. Essential trips include those made to jobs, school, and for day-to-day household management.

References

ACHR (Asian Coalition for Housing Rights). 2009. "Thinking City-Wide in Iloilo City, Philippines." ACHR, Bangkok, Thailand.

ADB (Asian Development Bank). 2012. "Viet Nam Socialist Republic: Transport Sector Assessment, Strategy, and Road Map." ADB, Manila.

———. 2013. "Improving Road Safety in Asia and the Pacific." ADB, Manila.

Amnesty International. 2011. "Eviction and Resistance in Cambodia: Five Women Tell Their Stories." Amnesty International Secretariat, London.

Anderson, R. P. 2015. "Indonesia - National Affordable Housing Program Project." World Bank, Washington, DC.

Asian Trends Monitoring Bulletin. 2012. Lee Kuan Yew School of Public Policy, National University of Singapore, Singapore.

Baker, J., et al. 2005. "Urban Poverty and Transport: The Case of Mumbai." World Bank Working Paper 3693, World Bank, Washington, DC.

Baker, J. L. 2009. "Opportunities and Challenges for Small-Scale Private Service Providers in Electricity and Water Supply: Evidence from Bangladesh, Cambodia, Kenya, and the Philippines." World Bank, Washington, DC.

Brhane, M., et al. 2014. "Access to Affordable and Low-Income Housing in East Asia and the Pacific." World Bank, Washington, DC.

Carruthers, R. C., M. C. Dick, and A. Saurkar. 2005. "Affordability of Public Transport in Developing Countries." Transport Papers; No. TP-3. World Bank, Washington, DC.

Cerdá, M. et al. 2012. "Reducing Violence by Transforming Neighborhoods: A Natural Experiment in Medellín, Colombia." *American Journal of Epidemiology* 175: 10 (2012): 1045–53.

Cruz, P. C. 2008. "Global Property Guide."

Deng, L., Q. Shen, and L. Wang. 2011. "The Emerging Housing Policy Framework in China." *Journal of Planning Literature* 26 (2): 168–83.

Eales, K., et al. 2013. "Review of Community-managed Decentralized Wastewater Treatment Systems in Indonesia." Water and Sanitation Program Technical Paper, WSP. World Bank, Washington, DC.

Economic Research Institute, Wuhan University. 2003. "A Lifetime of Walking: Poverty and Transportation in Wuhan." World Bank, Washington, DC.

Gwilliam, K. M. 2002. "Cities on the Move: A World Bank Urban Transport Strategy Review." World Bank, Washington, DC.

IDRC and CRDI. 2009. "Community Solutions for Indonesia's Waste." IDRC and CRDI, Ottawa.

Ieda, H. 2010. "Sustainable Urban Transport in an Asian Context." Springer, Tokyo.

IEG. 2014. "Making Roads Safer: Learning from the World Bank's Experience." IEG Learning Note. World Bank, Washington, DC.

IRIN News, 2010. "Indonesia: Jakarta's Slums Struggle with Sanitation." IRIN News, Jakarta.

JICA (Japan International Cooperation Agency). 2013. "Roadmap for Transport Infrastructure Development for Metro Manila and Its Surrounding Areas." JICA, Manila.

———. 2014. "Presentation: Major Findings on Yangon Urban Transport and Short-Term Actions." JICA, Yangon

Kamata, T., et al. 2010. "Managing Urban Expansion in Mongolia: Best Practices in Scenario-Based Urban Planning." World Bank, Washington, DC.

Klopp, J. et al. 2015. "Leveraging Cellphones for Wayfinding and Journey Planning in Semi-formal Bus Systems: Lessons from Digital Matatus in Nairobi." In *Planning Support Systems and Smart Cities*, 227–41. Cham, Switzerland: Springer International Publishing.

Krugman, P., M. Fujita, and A. J. Venables. 1999. *The Spatial Economy – Cities, Regions and International Trade*. Cambridge, Massachusetts: MIT Press.

Kyaw, Kyaw Phone. 2015. "Yangon Roads to Grind to Halt without Huge Investment: JICA." *Myanmar Times*. January 23.

Lau, JCY. 2013. "Sustainable Urban Transport Planning and the Commuting Patterns of Poor Workers in a Historic Inner City in Guangzhou, China." *Habitat Int.* 39 (2013): 119–27.

Morichi, S., and S. R. Acharya. 2013. *Transport Development in Asian Megacities: A New Perspective*. Heidelberg: Springer.

Ndaw, M. F. 2015. "Unlocking the Potential of Information Communications Technology to Improve Water and Sanitation Services: Summary of Findings and Recommendations." Water and Sanitation Program report. World Bank, Washington, DC.

OECD. ITF Transport Outlook 2015. OECD Publishing/ITF. http://www.keepeek.com/Digital-Asset-Management/oecd/transport/itf-transport-outlook-2015_9789282107782-en#.WNqdGU3fM6Y#page11.

Oxfam and Action Aid Vietnam. 2012. "Participatory Monitoring of Urban Poverty in Vietnam, the Fifth Round Synthesis Report (2008–2012)." http://www.oxfamblogs.org.

Payne, G., A. Durand-Lasserve, and C. Rakodi. 2008. "Social and Economic Impacts of Land Titling Programmes in Urban and Peri-Urban Areas: International Experience and Case Studies of Senegal and South Africa." Report submitted to Ministry of Foreign Affairs, Government of Norway, Swedish International Development Agency (SIDA), Global Land Tools Network, UN-Habitat.

Peppercorn, I. G., and C. Taffin. 2013. "Rental Housing: Lessons from International Experience and Policies for Emerging Markets." World Bank, Washington, DC.

Pocock, N., and T. Indrakesuma. 2013. "The Unhealthy Impacts of Poor Water and Sanitation." *Asia Trends Monitoring* (2013), Bulletin 22: *Urban Poverty & Health in Asia*, 12–13. Lee Kuan Yew School of Public Policy, Singapore.

Prefeitura Municipal de Curtiba. 2010. "Here Progress Travels by Bus." http://www.curitiba.pr.gov.br/idioma/ingles/progressoonibu.

Smolka, M. O., and C. Biderman. 2012. "Housing Informality: An Economist's Perspective on Urban Planning." In *The Oxford Handbook of Urban Economics and Planning*, edited by N. Brooks, K. Donaghy, and G.-J. Knaap, (July) (September 18): 1–15.

Suzuki, H., R. Cervero, and K. Iuchi. 2013. *Transforming Cities with Transit: Transit and Land-Use Integration for Sustainable Urban Development*. Washington, DC: World Bank.

Tacoli, Cecilia. 2012. "Urbanization, Gender and Urban Poverty: Paid Work and Unpaid Carework in the City." Human Settlements Group, International Institute for Environment and Development, London.

Tiwari, G. 2005. "Self-organizing Systems and Innovations in Asian Cities." In *Urban Transport Development*, 144–57. Berlin and Heidelberg: Springer.

UN DESA. 2012. "Millennium Development Goals Report 2012." United Nations, New York.

UNDP 2010. "Urban Poverty Assessment in Hanoi and Ho Chi Minh City." Draft, UNDP, Hanoi.

UN Habitat. 2003. Global Urban Indicators Database 2 (1998 data). "The Challenge of Slums" UN Habitat, Nairobi.

_____. 2010. "The State of Asian Cities 2010/11." UN Habitat, Fukuoka, Japan.

———. 2011. "Affordable Land and Housing in Asia: Adequate Housing Series." UN Habitat, Nairobi, Kenya.

———. 2012. "State of the World's Cities 2012/2013, Prosperity of Cities." UN Habitat, Nairobi, Kenya.

———. 2013. "State of the World's Cities 2012/2013: Prosperity of Cities." Taylor and Francis, Florence.

———. 2015. "The State of Asian and Pacific Cities 2015: Urban Transformations Shifting from Quantity to Quality." UN Habitat, Nairobi.

UN Habitat and UN ESCAP. 2008. "Housing the Poor in Asian Cities, Quick Guide 4, Eviction." UN Habitat and UN ESCAP, Bangkok.

United Nations. 2014. *World Urbanization Prospects: The 2014 Revision*. New York: United Nations.

UN Women. 2013. "Women Migrant Workers in Viet Nam Take Steps towards Better Rights and Services." 17 December; Web 07 March 2016.

Virginia, M., N. Islam, and S. A. Shafi. 2007. "Solid Waste Management in Asian Cities: Implications for the Urban Poor." In *The Inclusive City: Infrastructure and Public Services for the Urban Poor in Asia*, edited by A. Laquian, V. Tewari, and L. Hanley, 197–223. Baltimore: Johns Hopkins University Press.

WHO (World Health Organization). 2013. "Global Status Report on Road Safety." WHO, Geneva.

WHO/Unicef. 2015. "Progress on Sanitation and Drinking Water – 2015 Update and MDGs Assessment." WHO/Unicef Joint Monitoring Programme. UNICEF, New York.

Wilson et al. 2012. "Comparative Analysis of Solid Waste Management in 20 Cities." In *Waste Management and Research*. London: Sage Publications.

World Bank. 1999. "What a Waste: Solid Waste Management in Asia." World Bank, Washington, DC.

———. 2006. "China - Liaoning Medium Cities Infrastructure Project." World Bank, Washington, DC.

———. 2009. *World Development Report*. Washington, DC: World Bank.

———. 2011. "Jakarta: Urban Challenges in a Changing Climate." World Bank, Washington, DC.

———. 2012a, "Accessibility of Urban Transport for People with Disabilities: Lessons from East Asia and the Pacific." World Bank, Washington, DC.

———. 2012b. "East Asia and Pacific Region: Regional Urban Water Supply and Sanitation Sector Review." World Bank, Washington, DC.

———. 2012c. "Investing in Indonesia's Roads: Improving Efficiency and Closing the Financing Gap." *Road Sector Public Expenditure Review 2012*; Public expenditure review (PER). Washington, DC: World Bank.

———. 2012d. "Implementation Completion Report, Mongolia." Second Ulaanbaatar Services Improvement Project. World Bank, Washington, DC.

———. 2012e. "Urban Mass Transport Infrastructure in Medium and Large Cities in Developing Countries." World Bank, Washington, DC.

———. 2013a. "East Asia Pacific Region: Urban Sanitation Review: A Call for Action." World Bank, Washington, DC.

———. 2013b. "EAP Urban Sanitation Review Indonesia Country Study." World Bank, Washington, DC.

———. 2013c. "Indonesia Urban Poverty and Program Review Policy Note." World Bank, Washington, DC.

———. 2013d. *Global Monitoring Report 2013: Rural-urban Dynamics and the Millennium Development Goals*. Washington, DC: World Bank.

———. 2013e. "Indonesia - Evaluation of the Urban Community Driven Development Program: Program Nasional Pemberdayaan Masyarakat

Mandiri Perkotaan (PNPM-Urban)." Indonesia Policy Note. World Bank, Washington, DC.

———. 2014b. "Qualitative Study on Self-Provided Housing." World Bank, Washington, DC.

———. 2015a. "Asia Urban Transport and ICT Capacity Building." World Bank, Washington, DC.

———. 2015b. "East Asia's Changing Urban Landscape: Measuring a Decade of Spatial Growth." World Bank, Washington, DC.

———. 2016a. "Toward Inclusive Urban Service Delivery in Ulaanbaatar, Mongolia." World Bank, Washington, DC.

———. 2016b, "IEG Review Team; IEG Review Team. 2016." Vietnam - Urban Upgrading Project. World Bank, Washington, DC.

———. Forthcoming a. "Navigating Informality: Perils and Prospects in Metro Manila's Slums Metro Manila Slum Study." World Bank, Washington, DC.

_____. Forthcoming b. "Urban Poverty in Ulaanbaatar: Understanding its Dimensions and Addressing the Challenges" World Bank, Washington, DC.

World Bank, and the Development Research Center of the State Council, the People's Republic of China. 2014. "Urban China: Toward Efficient, Inclusive, and Sustainable Urbanization." World Bank, Washington, DC.

WSP (Water and Sanitation Program). 2008. "Economic Impacts of Sanitation in Southeast Asia." Research Report, World Bank, Jakarta.

CHAPTER 4

Social Inclusion and the Urban Poor

Introduction

Fostering inclusion in cities is essential in improving development outcomes and reducing poverty to ensure that all individuals and groups are integrated into the fabric of the urban environment. The social dimension of inclusion embraces the fundamental principles of inequality in rights, dignity, opportunity, and security regardless of identity.[1] For the purposes of this study, aspects of social inclusion in cities refer specifically to the urban poor, particularly those living in slums. This study recognizes the disparities in the recognition of the urban poor's rights and weak participation in decision making. There are also groups among the urban poor who face additional marginalization and for whom urban poverty can be intensified due to their identity or place in society for various reasons. Social inclusion can manifest among these subgroups in different ways. The specific aspects of social inclusion for the elderly, women, and migrants are explored in this chapter, given their large numbers and visible forms of social exclusion.

Key Challenges in Social Inclusion for the Urban Poor

The key aspects of social inclusion in many EAP countries include the following:

  (i) equitable rights to land and property ownership
  (ii) registration and identity affecting rights to urban amenities
 (iii) equitable access to governance and participation
 (iv) access to social protection programs

These aspects are discussed below.

Land Distribution and Property Ownership Rights

The unequal individual and collective rights to land acquisition, tenure, and housing has perpetuated vulnerability among particular groups in EAP. The urban poor, especially in informal settlements, are frequently without land titles and legal registration. Figure 4.1 illustrates the Gini coefficients for the distribution of land ownership in the EAP region (1 indicates complete inequality and 0 complete equality). As figure 4.1 shows, the land ownership distribution is least equitable in Cambodia and Indonesia, where land titles have historically been left undocumented and vulnerable groups, such as women and indigenous peoples, have limited access to tenure. In parts of Indonesia, Malaysia, the Philippines, and Singapore, poor urban women in particular face constraints in legally attaining land and housing, as a result of inheritance laws. These legal systems favor men; women without land titles face additional limitations in service delivery (see below).

In China, the right to land is contentious/uncertain for migrants in large urban areas. A condition for the purchase of property in Beijing is the payment of at least five years of local tax, which bars newcomers in the city from accessing land and property. This process is specific to the larger metropolis, as smaller cities like Wuhan are more lenient, allowing anyone purchasing property over the market value of $0.5 million Renminbi (RMB) to gain registration. At the town level, there are even fewer restrictions on migrants, and some towns even offer subsidies to rural migrants moving to urban areas (World Bank and Development Research Center of the State Council, the People's Republic of China 2014). In Mongolia, where land titling is tied to urban residency status and often social networks, it is harder

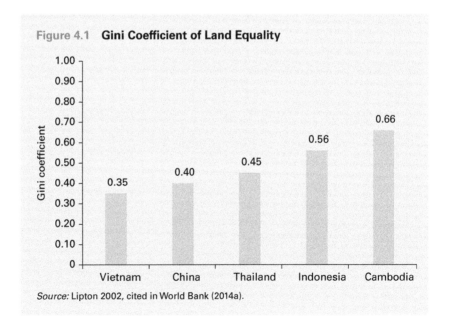

Figure 4.1   Gini Coefficient of Land Equality

Source: Lipton 2002, cited in World Bank (2014a).

Box 4.1   Land-titling and Access based on Identity in Mongolia

Urban residency is key in obtaining eligibility for land titling in Ulaanbaatar. Migrants into the city from rural areas rely on their social networks and apply for residency using plots owned by friends and relatives already living in urban areas. This process is often complicated, and many rural-urban migrants face corruption in attaining registration, such as duplicate land allocation, demands for cash and in-kind bribes, and false information on the availability of the vacant plots and future land development. While the process is tedious, however, migrants are able to achieve ownership as this is encouraged by the Mongolian government—90 percent of *ger* area residents own their land. However, with overcrowding in the city and lack of affordable rentals, this land is mostly located in less desirable areas—for example, in the hills or on the outskirts—with more limited access to services.

Two rural-urban migrant households shared their experiences obtaining land titles in the city, as follows:

- A young married woman, Uranbaigali, aged 31, has two small children, aged four years and nine months, respectively. She migrated from Dornod province to Ulaanbaatar, when her family lost all their herds during *zud* (severe winter) in 2000. She has neither a birth certificate nor an ID document. For this reason, she could not receive any welfare assistance, including allowances for children and pregnancy. She says that she struggles to find good jobs—the only job she has found is as a dishwasher, with a daily wage of MNT 7000.
- Navchaale, aged 45, lives with her auto-technician husband and their children. They migrated to Ulaanbaatar from Tuv province in 1996, obtaining their own plot in 2011, after residing on her sister's plot nearby. She says that her household was without electricity for three years and that the *khoroo* (subdistrict) activities targeted at vulnerable groups have not had much effect on their lives. "There are many people who are not registered to the khoroo and are fighting to make ends meet on the Ulaanchuluut landfill site."

Source: World Bank 2016c.

---

for rural-urban migrants to obtain (see box 4.1 and more details below) (World Bank forthcoming). In Vietnam, legislation ignores customary land rights (box 4.2).

Registration and Identity among the Urban Poor

With the heterogeneity among city and urban dwellers, identity and formal registration as a "right to the city" are important factors in determining social cohesion. The urban poor can often become invisible in the city where they do not have formal title or registration as a resident. Their lack of identification prevents them from gaining equitable access to the opportunities offered in urban areas. This situation is particularly true for migrants and unregistered youth. In some countries, identification cards are essential for accessing opportunities in cities and in some cases have reinforced the exclusion of the poor. For instance, in China, the *hukou* is a household registration that proves residency (box 4.3).

Street Children. Children make up a large percentage of the invisible urban poor population and are adversely affected by how their identity is

Box 4.2   **Vietnam's Legislation Ignores Customary Land Rights**

In Vietnam, formal land legislation continues to ignore the customary land rights and management practices which are particularly influential in many ethnic minority villages. Although the 2003 Land Law allows land allocation to communities, there is evidence that customary land use and management practices are not taken into account under the government's land allocation and land management practices, respectively. Thus, ethnic minorities still exercise limited powers to make decisions over their land. While they can receive collective land certificates, they often they cannot make decisions about the use and assignment of land within their communities or on the effective allocation of the areas for economic development. This runs counter to the customary role of community-based institutions and village leaders in land governance in many ethnic minority villages.

Source: Bell 2014.

Box 4.3   **Hukou System in China: Evolving Reforms over Time**

The hukou system, or household registration system, was instituted in the late 1950s to help manage the flow of people between rural and urban areas. Individuals were presented with a "rural" or "urban" hukou based on their place of birth. An estimated 260 million urban residents (migrants) currently lack urban hukou and therefore are at a substantial disadvantage in accessing basic urban infrastructure and services, as well as urban employment opportunities. This disparity between migrants and urban residents contributed to China's rising urban inequality. Although migrants were increasingly paid wages comparable to those of urban residents, their lack of access to education (due to their lack of urban hukou) prevented them from accessing higher-skill/higher-wage work.

The need for reform was recognized with the potential positive outcomes to include:

 (i) higher productivity and wages by enabling greater mobility of workers in China;
 (ii) reduction of the rural-urban income disparity by enabling greater mobility, which would then reduce the labor supply in rural areas and increase rural wages; and
(iii) higher inclusivity by equalizing access to social services by migrants and urban hukou holders.

One of the main concerns with hukou system reform was that rural-to-urban migration may accelerate and put additional stress on already overstretched and inadequate urban infrastructure and services. A reduction in the quality of or access to services could, in turn, create additional tension between migrants and urban residents. A second concern was that migrants might move into cities in pursuit of improved access to infrastructure and services, rather than for employment opportunities. This situation would lead to increased congestion and unemployment.

As a result, system reforms began in the early 1980s. One of the most notable effects was the elimination of physical mobility restrictions by the end of the 1980s. The State Council also created a policy framework in 2006 to promote the integration of migrants into urban areas by improving their access to social services (for example, in education, training, health, housing, social insurance, employment, and family planning services). In 2011, the State Council encouraged the registration of temporary populations in cities, the adoption of a residence permit system, and formulated hukou reform policy that was linked to the city's administrative level.

(Box continues on next page)

> **Box 4.3   Hukou System in China: Evolving Reforms over Time** *(continued)*
>
> In 2014, in a welcome policy shift, China introduced a National New-Type Urbanization Plan with concrete targets for rural-urban residency reform. The plan included increasing the urban population ratio to 60 percent, as well as measures to formally recognize migrants by reforming hukou. Restrictions will be lifted gradually in cities with populations of under 1 million, loosened for cities with 1 to 3 million residents, and will allow for limited registration for those with 3 to 5 million. Migration to megacities will remain strictly controlled. While it is too early to quantify the positive effects of such a move on the wellbeing of migrants, the impact is likely to be positive and reduce the social and economic marginalization of the "floating populations" as well as their children. Positive trends have been seen in the proportion of migrant workers who have been discriminated against in urban areas, but are now included in the new range of health, aging, and other social welfare government systems.
>
> *Source:* World Bank and the Development Research Center of the State Council, the People's Republic of China 2014.

shaped in urban areas. The Southeast Asia subregion has the highest number of unregistered children in the world, at more than 24 million. In China, under the traditional family planning policies of the past, children born after the first were typically unregistered and, as with migrants, experienced challenges accessing services. These policies have recently changed. In the metropolitan Jakarta area of Indonesia there are 7,500 street children, and in Vietnam, a similar number live on the streets of Hanoi, and more than double that in Ho Cho Minh City. In Ulaanbaatar, Mongolia, the issue of the homelessness of children originated from the migration of minors from rural to urban areas to rebuild their livelihoods, and from children escaping alcoholism, domestic violence, and orphanages (World Bank 2016b). Some of these situations develop from the realities migrants typically face when they are socially excluded from the city. For children, this is even more challenging because they experience further spatial and economic exclusion that can result in other forms of exploitation. In Vietnam, for instance, child prostitution, although illegal, has been growing in cities. The number of child prostitutes has grown to approximately 40,000, with a significant percent trafficked to other countries, such as Cambodia, which has documented one-third of all prostitutes coming from Vietnam.[2]

Spatial Location, Community Spaces and Social Cohesion. Apart from the income advantages, the urban poor value the benefits of social cohesion that come from being included in the city, where they are able to harness the city amenities and foster partnerships to leverage upward mobility. As the urban poor lack access to strong social networks, public spaces are essential meeting points that integrate varying identities, income levels, and social capital. For example, ger area residents in Ulaanbaatar identify the lack of community spaces as a significant barrier to social interaction, especially for women. Analysis illustrates the correlation between the location of

Box 4.4   Inclusive Cities: At-Risk Youth in Urban Areas of Malaysia

Malaysia has made great strides in reducing poverty, with the incidence of poverty in urban areas down to one percent. Inequality, however, remains a challenge. Some of the inequality is linked to the rural-to-urban migration, much of it being by young people in search of better opportunities. Not everyone, however, has benefitted from these opportunities, which can result in divisions in society and lead to social problems, particularly for young people who may have dropped out of school or be unemployed.

A qualitative study of at-risk youth in urban areas of Malaysia found key dynamics contributing to vulnerability and a sense of exclusion among youth that included youth unemployment; poverty and rising costs of living; irregular work patterns; dysfunctional families; difficulties in accessing the education system; and lack of a voice to influence decision making.

Among the recommendations for fostering social inclusion based on international good practice for Malaysia are the following:

(i)   strengthening programs for at-risk youth to help prevent school dropouts
(ii) encouraging entry to the labor market and better spatial integration through housing and transportation
(iii) supporting policies to keep children in school as a critical preventive investment for at-risk youth
(iv) scaling up targeted programs for vulnerable groups
(v)   investing in safe neighborhood programs

Source: World Bank 2015a.

urban dwellers and their collective capacity, through involvement in civil groups and local decision making. As a result, it is unsurprising that only 10 percent of the urban poor living in the ger fringes participate in civic engagement, in comparison with 42 percent of apartment dwellers (World Bank forthcoming). Therefore, the location identity of urban dwellers is a crucial determinant in integration and visibility.

In Malaysia, at-risk youth cite a number of factors that contribute to their sense of exclusion, including challenges adjusting to urban life, unemployment, and difficulties in accessing the education system. The lack of spatial integration between jobs, housing and transportation also contributes to exclusion for some (box 4.4).

Quality of Governance and Participation

Social inclusion stems in substantial part from the influence of governance structures in enabling an equitable environment (World Bank 2015b; ADB 2015a). The culture of public participation is generally weak in the EAP region, and the integration of engaged citizens in the urban sphere has traditionally been motivated by external groups, namely multilateral organizations, nongovernmental agencies, and others. Table 4.1 shows the democracy scores of EAP countries. As illustrated, most countries have

Table 4.1   Democracy Rating of EAP Countries, 2016

Country	Political rights[a]	Civil liberties[a]
Cambodia	6	5
China	7	6
Fiji	3	3
Indonesia	2	4
Kiribati	1	1
Korea, Rep.	2	2
Lao PDR	7	6
Malaysia	4	4
Myanmar	6	5
Mongolia	1	2
Papua New Guinea	4	3
Philippines	3	3
Solomon Islands	3	3
Thailand	6	5
Tonga	2	2
Vanuatu	2	2
Vietnam	7	5

Source: Freedom House, http://freedomhouse.org.
a. Rating 1–7, with 1 representing the highest and 7 the lowest level of freedom.

lower levels of freedom, correlated to their highly centralized governance structures. However, noting that top-down institutional approaches have not been tremendously successful in reducing poverty in urban areas (as demonstrated in countries such as the Philippines, which still has high rates of poverty in its largest cities), some countries in the region have begun to capitalize on innovative strategies, such as citizen engagement tools, to encourage development.

Public participation and approaches to incentivizing citizen engagement have been significant factors in achieving social inclusion. Finding ways to embed social integration in the decision-making process creates a sense of ownership and of the sustainability of the investments being made. The legal frameworks enabling this environment exist in most of the EAP; however, the implementation of participatory planning practices has not been uniform. The Philippines, for example, has a longer history of incorporating social accountability and citizen involvement in local planning than countries such as Cambodia and Vietnam, which have the legal framework but are less successful in implementation.

Across the EAP, the capacity of many national and local governments is weak and highly fragmented, with the challenges of transparency, sustainable management of urban investments, and the need for institutional strengthening (UN Habitat 2003). The decentralization of government structures plays an important role in creating an enabling environment for the enhancement of local voices and equality in the decision-making process. The region has varied patterns of governance; for example, Korea and Myanmar maintain highly centralized planning systems; China and Vietnam have adopted some economic reforms to enable decentralization but still have a long way to go with much of the power residing in subnational governments, while the Philippines and Thailand have a history of devolution to local governments and participatory frameworks (figure 4.2).

Figure 4.2   Country Contexts from Less Participatory to Most Participatory

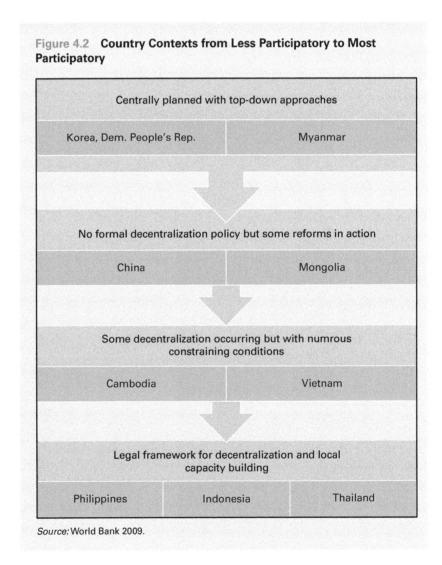

Source: World Bank 2009.

Given the proliferation of slum settlements and the limited services available to pockets of urban dwellers, it seems that more developed regulatory frameworks and rigid master planning practices have been less successful in achieving inclusive urban growth. Analysts have observed that urban planning in China and Vietnam could be less bureaucratic, and more participatory and transparent. On the other end of the spectrum, countries such as Vanuatu lack national or local urban management mechanisms, with is no legislation, oversight and enforcement to ensure planned, inclusionary urban growth (UN Habitat 2009).

Some countries and economies, however, have been pioneering inclusive planning through models of public participation. For example, in Hong Kong SAR, China; Malaysia; and the Philippines, provisions have been made for public input in the preparations of both the draft structure and local plans through various channels.

Overall, there is a growing relevance for the strategic functions of civil society and local institutions in the urban planning process. The co-production of public goods and services ensures that the public's needs are addressed and that the urban populations often excluded from development, such as the elderly, women, youth, and the disabled, are given a voice. In the EAP, the mobilization of local governments to involve the public in the planning process has been prioritized by countries, as encouraging equality is aligned with increased economic development and poverty alleviation for urban areas (World Bank 2015b).

Social Protection Programs

Social safety net programs play an important role in addressing the risks faced by the poor, as noted in chapter 2. These programs, mostly consisting of conditional cash transfers, social assistance, and public works, are substantially designed to alleviate poverty in rural areas. Only 17 percent of the urban poor households typically benefit from social protection due to three main factors (Gentilini 2015), as follows:

   (i) the perception that social safety nets are not necessary in urban areas which have more vibrant labor markets
   (ii) the underestimated urban poverty numbers, especially among migrants and informal workers
   (iii) slum-upgrading and community development programs that often focus on infrastructure improvements and less directly target the beneficiaries

Overall, the case for social protection for the urban poor is more complex because of the perceived higher levels of welfare from residents' spatial relation to the city and its amenities.

To address some of these challenges, countries in the region have implemented specific policy actions and governance reforms that have helped facilitate this process. In the Philippines, the Pantawid Pamilyang Pilipino conditional (and modified) cash transfer program has helped alleviate poverty for millions of households, with targeted interventions for many urban residents. Modified in 2012, the program focuses particularly on the urban poor, including homeless street families, indigenous people, and those displaced by disaster. They receive support in health care, education, case management, housing, employment (cash for work), skills training, psychological counselling, livelihoods assistance, and referral services. Similarly, the Keluarga Harapan Program (PKH) in Indonesia provides social protection opportunities for the urban poor. Although PKH is not modified for urban versus rural contexts—as costs of living are higher in urban areas—there have been some important benefits. For instance, the program has been most impactful in improving the use of and behavior towards health care in urban settings. Also, the blanket program is providing many lessons assisting local government in re-centering service delivery and social integration for the urban poor (Gentilini 2015).

Historically, EAP social protection programs have focused on human capital accumulation through health and education. Direct assistance (cash transfers) or social insurance (in-kind transfers) have for the most part compensated specific categories for their inability to work, such as old age, veterans, people with illness and disability, children, and orphans. More recently, however, there are signs of a growing reliance on income-based cash transfers.

While social assistance spending appears to have increased in most countries in the region over the past years, the spending levels remain low. Economic stress has intensified the demand for social programs and the need to exploit scarce public resources to the fullest. Many poor households still do not receive much-needed social assistance. While in Mongolia and Thailand, coverage of the poorest stands above 90 percent due to the universal nature of the benefits, in Cambodia, Fiji, Malaysia, Indonesia, and Timor-Leste, rates are below 25 percent (World Bank 2013, 1).

It is important for countries in the region to reduce spending on regressive transfers, such as generous pension schemes that benefit a limited number of people, and shift resources towards more progressive, better targeted programs. In China and Vietnam, for example, reforms to urban residency requirements are underway that will allow for better access to social protection.

There is still work to be done in ensuring social protection programs adjust to urban poor groups, especially those who are undocumented. In China and Vietnam, there have been reforms to exclusionary systems allowing for better access to social protection. The hukou in China (mentioned above) and *ho-khau* in Vietnam were designed to base access to services, such as education and health, on legally registered urban residency. These systems are undergoing changes to accommodate the most excluded and vulnerable, but still encounter challenges. The main challenge is that the urban poor require customized interventions, particularly for elderly and migrants, and support programs that capture those outside the formal system

(World Bank 2013). EAP governments are recognizing the importance of addressing these needs for the overall prosperity of cities, signified by the program reforms. Therefore, changes are being made, albeit slowly.

Subgroups among the Urban Poor: Women

Women are often portrayed as the particular beneficiaries of urbanization, gaining economic agency as they engage in paid labor. This is a compelling narrative in EAP, where demand for low-skilled labor in light manufacturing industries has resulted in higher labor force participation among young women relative to young men.[3] However, women's access to the increased job opportunities, service delivery, infrastructure, and social mobility found in cities is determined by income level, environment, and migratory status. Of particular interest in this study is equity in opportunity for the subgroup of women among the urban poor in EAP. A framework for understanding gender inequality identifies three primary areas: endowments, economic opportunity, and agency (World Bank 2012b). When considering how each of these factors manifests itself, it is apparent that there is a strong gendered element to urban poor inclusion.

A related gender issue linked to inclusion of the urban poor is that of lesbian, gay, bisexual, and transgender and/or intersex (LGBTI) people, for which data are lacking across EAP (as well as in other regions). A World Bank study in Thailand is underway which is conducting surveys to understand the following: i) how LGBTI people perceive their experiences in access to finance, housing, education, jobs, and health insurance, and, ii) the general population and their own experience when accessing these services and markets, but also their perceptions and attitudes towards LGBTI people. The goal is to create comparable quantitative data in those sectors. The surveys are complimented by life story interviews with LGBTI people and an extensive literature review. This process will help to provide a better understanding of these issues in Thailand.

The most relevant analysis is from a study in India, which links LGBT people and poverty (World Bank 2014c). The study notes that: "Discrimination and exclusion are likely to lead to increased poverty in the LGBT community in India and elsewhere. Lack of access to jobs, barriers to education and housing, and rejection by families, for example, can put LGBT people in precarious economic positions. While all LGBT people potentially face those barriers, those living in poverty would have fewer financial resources and opportunities with which to mitigate the impact of stigma and discrimination."

Endowments

As a region, EAP has made significant progress in addressing gender gaps in endowments, defined as the human and productive capital that enables opportunities to improve welfare and refers to factors such as education, health, and physical assets contributing to human and productive capital. Yet poor women still face basic issues of health and safety stemming from inadequate housing, infrastructure, and service provision in slums and peri-urban areas.

Health: The issues of access to quality basic services for the urban poor living in informal settlements, slums, and/or at the urban periphery leave many residents vulnerable to water-borne diseases such as cholera and other related illnesses. In Indonesia, rates of diarrhea are 34 percent higher among young children from households using an open well for drinking water as opposed to piped water (UNICEF 2012). Similarly, township-level data from Myanmar indicates that diarrhea remains a major killer of children under the age of five (World Bank 2014a). Women play a primary role in the care of dependents, securing water supply, and disposing of household waste, and shoulder the responsibility of managing the effects of inadequate household service delivery.

Outside of the home, numerous studies have shown that girls who are menstruating are deterred from attending school when sanitation and washing facilities in schools are not provided or not separated by gender. This situation can have long-standing effects on attendance records and overall quality of education (World Bank 2012a). Regionally, coverage disparities are larger between urban and rural areas. However, there are still countries with coverage gaps in urban areas. For example, an estimated 16 percent of urban schools in China remain without adequate water supply and sanitation coverage (UNICEF 2015).

Accessing healthcare services and facilities in urban areas can also be burdensome for poor women. In countries such as Mongolia, most healthcare facilities and family clinics are located in the city center, while the urban poor live in the *ger* areas on the urban fringe (World Bank 2016c). Setting aside spatial barriers, the quality of care extended to the poor is often substandard, with overworked doctors in overcrowded hospitals. In Indonesia, an increase in urban mortality during the neonatal period has been attributed to poor quality of care, overcrowding and lack of sanitation facilities available to the urban poor (UNICEF 2012). Care is sometimes withheld unless women are able to pay a bribe. A woman from a central *ger* area in the Chingeltei district of Mongolia recounted, "I lost my baby while giving birth for the first time in the Maternity Hospital No 1. I heard that pregnant women usually gave 100,000 tugrik for bribe. I didn't give that money directly, so I was neglected. I was in pain continuously for 10 hours and was scolded for screaming" (World Bank 2016c).

Safety: Studies have shown that gender-based violence is more likely to occur in certain locations within low-income urban settlements, including toilets, located away from people's homes. Public transportation depots also register as areas where women are harassed and are targets of physical violence, prohibiting their mobility and access to jobs and services around the city (World Bank 2012b).

In Cambodia, female garment workers share cramped apartments close to the factories on the periphery of Phnom Penh. Poor street lighting and toilet facilities located up to 300 meters from apartments increase the risk of violent attacks, including rape. One garment worker reported "The lights are always turned off at 9:00 pm and I am afraid to go to toilet at night time because there are some men who are not good hanging around near the toilet" (Taylor 2011). For areas without sanitation facilities, open-defecation tends to happen at night in attempts to preserve privacy, but also places women at risk of violence and attacks (Tacoli 2012).

In times of emergency and natural disaster, women also face a higher risk to their physical safety. Women made up an estimated 61 percent of casualties in Myanmar after Cyclone Nargis in 2008, and 70 percent of fatalities during the 2004 Indian Ocean tsunami in Banda Aceh, Indonesia (World Bank 2014b). This difference in rates is attributed to a range of factors including women trying to save children or not ever being taught how to swim or climb trees. Similar issues exist in flood-prone areas or high-risk slum areas.

Economic Opportunity

As discussed in chapter 2, EAP boasts relatively high labor force participation and low rates of unemployment among urban women when compared to other regions. This trend is driven in large part by the reliance of export-oriented manufacturing industries on low-wage female labor (ILO 2011). Growth in manufacturing and the subsequent increase in wage-work among urban women is associated with improved health and education outcomes for women and children (Morton et al. 2014).

Nonagricultural informal work accounts for 64 percent of total female employment across the region and encompasses home-based work, domestic work, and street vending. The flexibility of informal work makes it a particularly attractive option (or indeed the only viable option) for low-income women with dependents and caregiving responsibilities, as well as limited education and skills (Chant 2007). In Mongolia, for instance, the reduced provision of subsidized childcare in urban areas resulted in a reduction in formal female labor force participation, while in Vietnam, insufficient childcare has been shown to be a significant factor in leading mothers to choose informal employment (World Bank 2012a).

In times of economic crises, women typically lose their jobs first, as they are often concentrated in sectors such as garments or textiles that are hit first. While men and women are both employed in manufacturing, export-oriented manufacturing industries such as textiles, apparel, leather, footwear, and electronics employ a 75 percent female workforce (ILO 2011). Women are more likely than men to be employed as temporary workers and are used as a "buffer work force" that can easily be laid off in response to shocks or changes in market demand. This situation was apparent during the global financial crisis, when low-wage female workers faced mass lay-offs across the region. Some notable examples include the following:

- Cambodia: 18 percent of the garment industry workforce (or 63,000 majority female workers) were laid off within the span of eight months.
- Philippines: Layoffs were concentrated in export processing zones, with a 75 percent female work force.
- Thailand: Older women and workers with longer tenure were dis-missed. Younger workers were brought in on flexible work arrange-ments with shorter contracts and lower wages. In total, 125,700 women were either fired or given irregular work hours (ILO 2011).

Occupational segregation is one of the major factors in the persistent gender wage gap, and in countries across Asia women earn one-half to two-thirds of what men earn for the same work (ADB 2015b).

Productivity Constraints: Within the informal sector men are more likely to be employers or paid employees of informal enterprises, while women work as subcontractors or on their own. This situation means that female-led enterprises are usually smaller in size and less productive (World Bank 2012a). For example, with street vending, women are often relegated to insecure or illegal spaces, sell cheaper goods, or work as employees of other vendors, in each case making less than their male counterparts (ILO 2011). In Indonesia women are relatively more likely to run businesses in the food, retail, and garment manufacturing sectors, which rank among the least capital-intensive and least productive sectors. Men, on the other hand, are more likely work in sectors such as transportation, which is more capital intensive and results in higher productivity (World Bank 2012a). These dif-ferences are attributed to general credit constraints on small firms within the informal sector. For women, this is compounded by cultural norms of propriety when interacting with male officials, as well as the tendency for assets to be listed with men, depriving women of available collateral for credit (World Bank 2012a).

Agency for Women

Agency in this study refers to women's ability to make choices and act on preferences in the home, in the workplace, and in wider society. Agency both determines and is determined by control over endowments and access to economic opportunities.

Domestic Agency: The significant role that women play in in managing domestic affairs including waste disposal, water supply, and fuel supply, has translated to some measure of increased agency within the home. Evidence from Indonesia indicates that urban women are more likely than rural women to be the sole decision makers on a number of household matters.

However, women often face societal and, in some cases, legal constraints in asset ownership that undermines their housing security. Plural legal sys-tems based on religion in Indonesia, Malaysia, the Philippines, and

Singapore promote inheritance laws favoring men over women. Though the rest of the region has legislation safeguarding the property and inheritance rights of women, in practice land titles are often listed under the name of the male head of household (World Bank 2012a). This issue has a number of consequences for women. Without legal documentation, women are constrained in their ability to engage with public officials about service delivery to their homes. This situation is exacerbated in times of disaster, when relief assistance (cash or in-kind) is distributed to men holding records, tenant, and bank accounts, despite studies showing that food and other aid is more likely to reach all household members if it is distributed through women (Rex and Trohanis 2012).

Lack of Social Protection: Women engaged in informal work are susceptible to potential abuse. This situation is particularly true for recent migrants, who may lack access to information or be without community support. Among female migrant workers in Hanoi and Ho Chi Minh City in Vietnam, for example, 42 percent work in the informal sectors with jobs like domestic work and street vending. One migrant worker, Huong, said of her employment at the Long Bien night market in Hanoi "Each night, I can earn nearly US$7 by transporting about one ton of goods. Like most migrant workers, I do not have a written contract with any employer." (UN Women 2013). For the most vulnerable, employment can only be found in the most exploitative segments of the informal economy where women resort to jobs in unregistered industrial workshops or "sweatshops" or as sex workers at risk of being targeted for human trafficking (ILO 2011).

Subgroups among the Urban Poor: The Elderly

The EAP is home to over one-third of the world's population aged 65 years and older. The majority of this share of the population resides in China. The rapid aging of the region is a result of declining fertility rates combined with heightened life expectancy over the past few decades. This phenomenon is also reflected in the lowest-income populations in EAP. This demographic transition has led to some important policy challenges for EAP governments. Some of the issues that will need to be addressed include:

(i) the shrinking and aging labor force
(ii) the need for improved health care systems accounting for the specific needs of the elderly
(iii) the activation of a strong pension system, including opportunities for those that work in the informal sector which accounts for many of the urban poor

The government systems and policies needed to manage the demographic change will also have to be flexible in accommodating rapid urbanization. By 2030, the UN projects that based on the old-age dependency ratios for urban areas, the populations of all countries in EAP,[4]

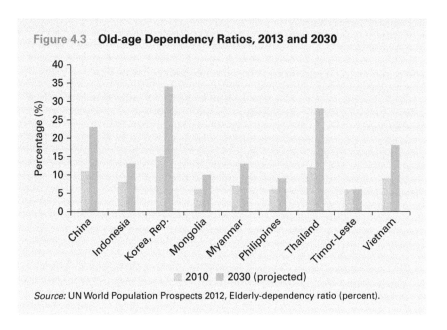

Figure 4.3   **Old-age Dependency Ratios, 2013 and 2030**

■ 2010   ■ 2030 (projected)

Source: UN World Population Prospects 2012, Elderly-dependency ratio (percent).

except Timor-Leste and Papua New Guinea, will be categorized as aging.[5] In many of these countries, the elderly population is projected to more than double (figure 4.3).

The EAP region is commended for its ability to mitigate many of the challenges that arise from a growing elderly population. Overall, poverty rates increase with age, but in many EAP countries they have been decreasing over time. For instance, Indonesia and Vietnam saw poverty rates for populations 60 years and older fall from around 40 percent in 2006–08 to below 30 percent in 2009–12 (World Bank 2016a).[6] These numbers indicate the progress that the region has made in ensuring that country-specific policies and programs are put in place to manage the impending demographic changes. However, there has been little research on the challenges faced by the aging poor who are residing in urban areas. Unlike the rural poor, these people are living in cities where provisions are being made for the elderly. However, the governments' focus on policies such as building robust pension programs and health care systems only benefit formal-sector workers. Those working informally and residing in slums (that is, the urban poor) typically have limited access to social protections, as they often have no income, few savings, growing health needs, and in some cases, disabilities.

In most EAP countries, income from work in urban areas is the primary source of old-age support. The exceptions are urban Mongolia and China, where the total incomes of people aged 60 and over are generated from public transfers—though this is something of an anomaly, resulting from strong social assistance country systems. In other countries, the secondary source of income for most of the elderly living in urban areas is private

---

Box 4.5   **Inside Korea's Impoverished Elderly Population**

Korea has the highest rate of impoverished elderly among the 34 developed countries—nearly half of Korea's elderly population live in poverty. For a country which is more than 80 percent urban, this indicates a large percentage of aging city dwellers who lack access to resources for quality living. This rise in the population of elderly poor population resulted from the 1997–98 economic crisis and was compounded by the more recent global economic downturn. The most vulnerable, living homeless on the streets of Seoul, are part of the generation that fought in the Korean War.

Over time, the social structure has deteriorated and children are less likely to take on the responsibility of caregiving. The elderly are left to provide for themselves and live off of their minimal savings. Furthermore, in an effort to remove this burden from their families, many seniors commit suicide. Korea has the highest rate of elderly suicide in the world.

The Korean government has recognized the challenges faced in providing for the aging population and has made adjustments to the National Pension system that was established in 1988. As the system is relatively new, there is some catching up needed for it to make adequate payments to seniors. The program has been expanded to provide assistance to the poorest of the poor; however, the monthly payments are only one-quarter of the desired minimum needed for the quality life.

Regardless, Korea is making steps towards improved access to the pension program and to curb the increase in the numbers of the elderly poor. Over 90 percent of pension coverage of seniors is projected by 2060, and the government is paying close attention to avenues through which to expedite this process.

Sources: OECD 2013; NPR 2015.

transfers, such as those from family members. This pattern indicates the importance of ensuring that there are programs to support retired urban populations, specifically the elderly urban poor, who typically fall outside the formal system (box 4.5).[7]

Going forward a main difficulty many EAP countries face is that they have to meet the challenges of an aging population with lower levels of wealth. Stronger economies can better provide the necessary services for the elderly. Countries such as Japan and Korea have greater income per capita and a largely formalized labor sector, where more than 75 percent are contributing to pensions (World Bank Pension Database 2013). As a result, they are better equipped to manage some of these aging challenges than countries such as Thailand, which has a low formalization rate (Packard and Nguyen 2014). Emerging economies with less income per capita, such as China, Indonesia, and Vietnam, also have rapidly increasing old-age dependency ratios, and will need to creatively manage challenges that come with this demographic transition.

Although much data have been collected on the EAP demographic transition, there has been very little focus on the urban elderly and even less on the urban elderly living below the poverty line. Despite the data gaps, it is apparent that as these changes are occurring, and within the urban poor, the elderly are particularly vulnerable, especially if they are no longer able to work.

Subgroups among the Urban Poor: Migrants

Negative View of Governments towards Rural-Urban Migration

Urbanization has a positive correlation with national GDP (World Bank and IMF 2013; World Bank 2009), and its economic benefits are widely recognized. At the same time, the benefits of remittances from migration are also hailed as a critical source of rural development. Yet national governments articulate much concern over the pace of urbanization and often hold rural-urban migration responsible for negative outcomes of urbanization such as congestion or crime and violence.

This negative view of migration has led to a desire by national policy makers to create barriers for the free movement of rural populations to cities. For instance, in 2013, 84 percent of governments in less-developed regions had policies to lower migration from rural-to-urban areas, compared with 41 percent in 1996 (United Nations 2014.) Such policies are particularly popular in Asia and Africa, regions where the majority of urban growth is projected to take place over the coming decades. In EAP, the middle-income countries of Indonesia, the Philippines, Thailand, and Vietnam wanted to reduce rural-urban migration. Even countries with low urbanization levels such as Cambodia had policies in place to reduce rural-urban migration.

Interestingly, one exception to this trend is China, where policies since the1990s have aimed to raise the level of rural-urban migration and increase the pace of urbanization. However, policies under the hukou have also been in place which controlled that migration (box 4.6).

Box 4.6   Policies That Have Excluded Migrants in the EAP

Policies that result in the socioeconomic exclusion of migrants in urban areas are not limited to China, but have been experimented with—to different extents—in other EAP countries, such as Indonesia and Vietnam.

As with China, Vietnam's population management policies prior to the Do Moi reforms of 1986 limited urbanward migration flows through a household registration system and housing policies. Under the system, every citizen was expected to register his/her place of birth and place of residence, as well as other basic demographic information, such as age, sex, marital status, education, and occupation. Residential registration status, whether permanent or temporary, determined eligibility for social services such as health care and school. While permanent residents could access these social services for free or at subsidized costs in their registered locality, temporary residents had to pay for these services in full. Changing registration status was difficult, and this process created a class of temporary migrants who were unable to register themselves in urban destinations and struggled to access state support. While this hukou-type of movement control loosened after Vietnam's economic liberalization reforms in the late 1980s, allowing the increased migration of rural populations, it did not translate into ease of change to residence status. Large numbers of migrants are still unable to fulfill conditions required, making such routine activities as registering births and accessing basic health and education services quite complex and bureaucratic.

Source: Asia Foundation and the Korean Development Institute 2011.

Marginalization of Rural Migrants and Links to Social Exclusion

The unequal treatment of unregistered migrant populations in China has manifested itself in the form of inter-generational socioeconomic exclusion that has been documented by a large body of scholarly literature. Migrants without hukou have unequal access to social and public services compared with those who have it. Recent estimates based on Chinese Census data show that 4 in 10 urban residents do not have access to the same package of public services and social participation (including grassroots democratic voting) as the others with nonfarm hukous (World Bank and the Development Research Center of the State Council, the People's Republic of China 2014). They also often experience worse working conditions and lower wage levels—average wages for urban migrants were estimated to be 43 percent less than those for urban residents in 2011. In addition, only 10 percent of migrants own urban housing, compared with 90 percent of the permanent urban population (World Bank and the Development Research Center of the State Council, the People's Republic of China 2014). This inequality in homeownership is due to a mix of hukou-related restrictions and exclusion from the mortgage finance market, which make it difficult for migrants to achieve a better standard of living.

In the case of Vietnam, unregistered migrants have had to resort to more expensive private providers for secure social services such as health care. This leads to the exacerbation of existing inequalities and the deepening of urban poverty. A United Nations 2010 assessment of internal migration in Vietnam found that the exclusion of migrants is particularly detrimental to migrant children, women, and families with children, as they have little or no access to formal support structures, and are separated from social networks they may otherwise have relied on. Given the added pressure on migrants to send remittances home, they are more likely to be unwilling or unable to pay for medical attention. While systematic studies documenting the conditions of unregistered migrants in Vietnam are scarce, especially since these populations are under-represented in national surveys, data shows that health outcomes for unregistered migrants were worse than those for urban local populations (Nyugen and White 2007).

Even in countries where policies do not formally discriminate against rural migrants, negative perceptions and the rhetoric of political parties blaming migrants for urban challenges result in stigmatizing stereotypes. Research on social exclusion in urban areas has documented extensive cases of stigma faced by migrants, who are blamed for increased crime, the growth of slums, housing shortages, overburdened basic infrastructure and services, congestion, and increasing exposure to environmental hazards (Garland, Massoumi, and Ruble 2007). Such stigmatization is particularly aimed at low-skilled, low-income migrants working in the informal sector. At the same time, high-paying professionals who are equally attracted to large cities for jobs do not experience the same kind of stigma but are rather seen as adding value to cities.

The divergence in the experiences of these two categories of migrants is a clear result of the differences in their purchasing power. This situation further translates into a residential disadvantage faced by low-income migrants, given the lack of affordable housing options. In this context, migrants are forced to find shelter in the informal settlements with insecure tenure, which doubly delegitimizes their presence as urban citizens. Such dynamics result in "a template for urban development that does not include the interests of the urban poor, let alone rural populations aspiring to come to cities" (McGranahan et al. 2016).

While migrants do not necessarily start out as poor, they can fall into poverty traps as they struggle to navigate the exclusionary barriers that increase the opportunity cost of their integration into the urban fabric. Longitudinal data from Brazil, for example, shows systematic evidence of municipalities actively restricting the provision of services to neighborhoods with high proportions of rural migrants (Feler and Henderson 2011). Anti-migration policies are largely unsuccessful, such as not planning for migrants or not providing access to services as a way to discourage them. The neglect of not planning for increasing urban populations results in sprawl, slums, and social divisions which ultimately can affect city competitiveness. As such, discrimination against migrants to the cities has implications beyond the well-being of migrant individuals and is detrimental to the overall trajectory of urban development.

Mixed Impacts of International Migration

The EAP region consists of labor-sending countries (source countries), labor-receiving countries (destination countries), and countries such as Thailand that both send and receive workers. In labor-sending countries, remittances help reduce poverty significantly by increasing income for migrants' families, loosening credit constraints for migrants, and insuring migrants' households against shocks. While urban-specific data on international migration in the region are lacking, there are indications of impacts on the welfare of labor-sending households in cities. In Indonesia, for example, where most skilled laborers come from cities rather than rural areas, brain drain consequences may be more serious. Skilled migrants could nonetheless improve knowledge links as part of the return process (Feler and Henderson 2011).

For some receiving countries, such as China, migrant workers form a significant proportion of the workforce, especially in labor-intensive sectors such as construction, fishing, household services, manufacturing, and plantation agriculture. They thus help relieve acute labor shortages, boost growth, and maintain competitiveness. In developing host countries, rapid urban growth can create housing, sanitation, and other burdens that can lead to unrest if not managed appropriately. Indonesia has attempted to mitigate this problem by requiring migrants to show proof of employment and housing to enter the city (Feler and Henderson 2011).

Along with intraregional trade and finance, international migration will become part of the drive towards "deep" economic integration in the region. The region is also facing the onset of one of the most rapid demographic changes in history. Rapidly aging, labor-receiving countries, such as Thailand in the long term, may have to cope with a decline in domestic labor supply, at the same time as rising demand for services increases the demand for labor in cities (Feler and Henderson 2011).

Social Inclusion: Programs Targeting Urban Women, the Elderly, and Migrant Populations

Broad policies aimed at promoting inclusion in cities include better provision of infrastructure and services to promote equitable access, nondiscriminatory labor and residency policies, and good governance, which gives all groups a voice in decision making. There are a number of programs targeted to the subgroups among the poor in the EAP that are highlighted, below, as interesting examples to consider for replication.

Targeting Low-Income Women in Urban Areas

The *World Development Report 2012: Gender Equality and Development* (World Bank 2012b) suggests that gender equality is smart economics; it can enhance economic efficiency and improve other development outcomes.[8] Investing in interventions that promote gender equality and ensure equal rights to low-income women in particular will be important to achieve inclusive development in urban areas in EAP. Some adaptation of existing programs can ensure that they reach low-income women, while the introduction of new programs can also play an important role.

Health and Safety

Security and Urban Transportation in China. The project design of the Liaoning Medium Cities Transport Project was significantly altered after female-only group discussions highlighted safety concerns held by women who predominantly walked or rode bicycles, as opposed to men who drove cars. City officials were able to accommodate their suggestions, making low-cost adjustments to the lack of streetlights, the poorly designed underpasses, and the long waits at bus stops that characterized the initial design (World Bank 2010).

Early Warning Communication in South Africa. A community-based early warning system was designed in South Africa with the assumption that after reporting danger or a threat to one part of the community, the information would spread to all relevant parties. Following a gender analysis, it was discovered that while men preferred climate information to be transmitted by radio, women showed a strong preference for information transmission through schools or by a public official, and as these alternatives allowed them the ability to immediately ask questions and engage in a discussion (World Bank 2014b).

Community-Level Preparedness in Indonesia. The testing of evacuation routes in Indonesia that were designed without a gender analysis revealed that women with children could not reach designated safe areas within the allotted time; as a result, the routes were subsequently revised. In the Aceh Besar and Aceh Jaya districts, a staircase design used in evacuation routes was modified to include handrails and shorten the height of steps to accommodate women holding babies and children or assisting the elderly (World Bank 2014b).

Worker's Rights and Improved Economic Opportunities

Homeworker's Protection Act in Thailand. Homenet Thailand, a national network of home-based workers and nongovernmental organizations (NGOs), led lobbying efforts to legalize social protection policies for its constituents. In 2011 the government of Thailand passed the Homeworker's Protect Act, which mandates fair wages (including equal pay for men and women) for workers completing orders for industrial enterprises in their homes. The law also obliges enterprises to provide a contract and establish a committee providing workers access to courts in the case of a labor dispute. Following the passage of the law, Homenet focused its efforts on educating workers on their rights and publicizing the new legislation (WIEGO 2013).

Agency and Participation

Community-Driven Infrastructure in Indonesia. A gender mainstreaming strategy was developed and incorporated in Indonesia's National Community Empowerment Program (PNPM), which provides block grants for small-scale infrastructure projects to low-income communities. Among the methods employed to enhance women's participation in this community-driven process were focus group discussions, support for women who were part of revolving loan fund groups, and gender awareness training. New projects require 30 percent female participation in community groups and 35 percent for the BKM (Badan Keswadayan Masyarakat [Community Boards of Trustees]) to ensure that women's voices are heard when planning for upgrades in community infrastructure and services (Azarbaijani-Moghaddam 2014). Additional changes were made in subsequent programs to encourage additional female participation—for example, holding all-female meetings and providing childcare at meetings (World Bank 2013).

Land Titling Legislation in Southeast Asia. Countries throughout the EAP have sought to improve gender equity in land titling through legislation. For example, the 2004 Land Law in Vietnam dictated that new land certificates and titles must include the names of both spouses. The results of the law were mixed across ethnicities, with ethnic minorities being more reluctant to name women on titles. A similar program in Lao

PDR achieved success only after a concerted effort to engage women and raise community awareness about land titling and women's rights (World Bank 2012a).

Regulatory Policies and Programs for the Elderly in Urban Areas

With the projected doubling of the age-dependency ratio in the region, many EAP countries have formulated policies and programs to adapt to these demographic shifts.

In Mongolia, for example, due to its socialist history, there are inclusionary policies favoring the elderly, such as universal pension coverage and a robust health care system. In 2012, there were more hospitals in Mongolia than in Europe, and through health financing, there are options for capitation payments to manage health care costs (WHO 2012).

In Korea, the government has been focused on improving benefits for childcare and maternity leave; this process has enabled more women to participate in the labor force, increasing economic participation and encouraging longevity in the work force.

In the past three years, China has also reformed its social protection programs for the elderly to specifically target the elderly urban poor, providing social pensions and budget-financed matching contribution schemes for informal sector workers (box 4.7). There have also been aggressive policies to promote labor participation by increasing the minimum wage and encouraging urbanization to lessen the urban-rural wage gap (ADB 2014). Reluctance to raise payroll taxes has pushed China to increase pension schemes through budgetary support, promoting this as a national priority (The Chinese University of Hong Kong SAR, China 2008).

In Thailand, the Community Organizations Development Institute (CODI) slum upgrading program incorporates welfare support for the elderly (box 4.8). Other interesting programs and policies to increase

---

Box 4.7   Approaches to Inclusion of the Elderly in China

Inclusive Construction with the Elderly in Mind. China is the most rapidly aging country in the EAP region; the number of individuals over 65 years will reach 200 million by 2025 and exceed 300 million by 2050. In Shanghai, the elderly population is growing at about 5.6 percent annually, and in 2012 accounted for 25.7 percent of its total population. Many of these elderly residents live on their own and depend heavily on government subsidies for care. Furthermore, the quality of housing facilities occupied by senior citizens is often old or outdated. Accidents are the leading cause of death among senior citizens in Shanghai.

The government has recognized that the substantial need for suitable senior housing will require efforts from the public and private sectors, as well as nonprofits. In response, in 2010, Habitat for Humanity China, in partnership with Shanghai's Civil Affairs Bureau and Senior Citizens' Foundation, launched the Age-Friendly Housing Project.

(Box continues on next page)

Box 4.7   Approaches to Inclusion of the Elderly in China *(continued)*

The project targets communities with the following:

Higher proportions of elderly families	Higher proportions of aging public housing	Greater numbers of families living under the minimum living standard	Higher proportions of disabled residents	Greater frequencies of in-house accidents

Elderly residents are provided with necessary renovations to improve the safety of their homes, specifically from fire and accidents, and to ensure complete accessibility. This process has included the installment of handrails and grab bars, anti-slip flooring, and other types of repairs. Many of the elderly urban poor who receive support through the project would normally lack support from their families, have limited financial security, and may have illnesses and disabilities.

The project does more than provide secure housing for the elderly urban poor; it also increases awareness within the local communities and involves them in the process to help alleviate the challenges being faced by this age cohort. The community plays an important project role by helping to mobilize resources to support the rehabilitation of these homes. This process has included event planning and the creation of partnerships to engage sponsors. There is also community involvement in the design, contracting, and construction activities.

The project began in 2011 by offering renovations to 25 elderly residents in the Yangpu and Zhabei districts.

Source: Habitat for Humanity China and Colliers International 2015.

Box 4.8   Pro-poor Slum Upgrading in Thailand's Community Organizations Development Institute

With support from the Community Organizations Development Institute (CODI), the urban poor in communities in Thai cities are empowered to address their development needs. CODI manages a community development fund and disburses money allocated from the government to assist the urban poor through upgrading of grants and loans.

Many of CODI's activities are branded as physical improvement, however, social interventions are also integrated in the poverty alleviation investments. The community development fund provides community welfare funding targeting the elderly, school fees for youth, and food for HIV-positive community members, and others who have various sickness.

The welfare support has been particularly helpful for the elderly, who are often vulnerable and fall into poverty without adequate pension support, labor opportunities, or lack of service—challenges faced by several newly aging Asian economies. Thailand is the third most rapidly aging population in the world, in 2010, over 10 percent of the elderly were poor (World Bank 2016a).

To tackle the problems facing the elderly poor in urban areas, CODI set up an elderly welfare fund to finance a variety of projects, including grants for health care, food and funeral expenses, social activities such as exercise groups, music and temple visits, and a revolving fund for income-generation and healthcare needs. An innovative use of the welfare funds was illustrated in Satun, where the elderly decided to use a portion of their CODI funds for a communal rubber plantation to offer the opportunity for elderly to generate income.

Source: Boonyabancha and Mitlin 2005.

Table 4.2   **Targeted Programs for the Elderly in East Asia**

Country and Program/Policy	Description
Korea, Rep. Social Insurance Program	One program target is the non- or low-income-earning elderly, as it provides insurance and pension packages to help stabilize the bottom 70 percent of the elderly population.
Japan Long-Term Care Reform	In this mandatory social insurance system for long-term care, the benefits are in the form of institutional or community-based services. These are offered as services not cash allowances and are aimed at covering all caregiving costs for the elderly.
Indonesia PT TASPEN	Cash assistance for the vulnerable elderly from the formal and informal sector. Although this is a universal program, the cost-sharing formula benefits formal workers because their contributions are greater than informal workers.
Thailand 500 Baht Universal Pension Scheme	The program targets elderly who are not residing in public facilities or receiving permanent income from sources such as government pensions or government-employed persons. Flexible arrangements were introduced to encourage informal workers and the self-employed to contribute at varying levels or attain a waiver without penalties.

Source: World Bank 2016a.

flexibility in light of the aging challenges and particular effects on the urban elderly poor are highlighted in table 4.2.

Programs for Migrant Populations in Urban Areas

A focus on migrant populations is crucial for social inclusion in urban areas. As discussed in previous sections, this process includes the following: removing restrictions on internal mobility; removing obstacles linked to migration status for access to basic services such as health and education; and addressing various forms of economic, political, and cultural discrimination against migrants. And it includes facilitating the full integration of migrants in host societies by tackling stereotypes and promoting intercultural dialogue and understanding.

Rural-urban migrants are also disproportionately young. Age-responsive support in housing, education, health services including sexual and reproductive health, and employment are therefore essential. Safe and generative urban spaces for youth have been linked to greater access to training, health services, and a space for youth to have their voices heard in local governance.

Despite the known economic benefits of migration, a number of countries across the region constrain the movement of people and perpetuate strong negative biases against rural-urban migrants (table 4.3). Rather than restricting migration outright, the *World Development*

Table 4.3   Migrations Policies Recognizing Agglomeration Benefits

	Migration of unskilled labor	Migration of skilled labor
Internal migration	**Neutral,** but discouraging if agglomeration economies are unlikely. Policies should encourage migration for economic reasons and discourage migration in search of public services. Remove explicit and implicit restrictions as well as place-based service entitlements.	**Strongly supportive,** particularly to capture agglomeration gains where these are likely. Invest in services in peripheral areas to build portable human capital. Increase the flow of labor market information, so migrants arrive better informed of employment possibilities.
Cross-border migration in regional neighborhoods	**Supportive,** particularly for welfare and diversification gains from remitted earnings.	**Supportive,** where markets in regional neighborhoods are integrated and gains from agglomeration can spill over to the sending country.
Cross-border migration outside regional neighborhoods	**Supportive,** particularly for welfare gains from remitted earnings.	**Neutral,** as there a possible foregone agglomeration from an accelerated brain drain, but with possible gains from knowledge transfer of return migrants, and strong incentives for human capital investment from the prospect of migrating.

Source: World Bank 2009.

Report 2009: Reshaping Economic Geography (World Bank 2009) recommends policies that improve the quality of migration. These policies focus on providing quality services (healthcare, education, and so on) in outlying, economically lagging areas, which eliminates many of the "push" reasons families might have for migrating to cities.

Regional examples of policy interventions that enhanced the agglomeration benefits of migration are highlighted below:

Building the Human Capital of Rural-Urban Migrants in China. Nearly half of the rural population of Anhui Province in China has sought employment in cities and the nonfarm sector. Recognizing that migrants had been used to fill the most menial and lowest-paying jobs in the urban labor market, local governments partnered with the World Bank to offer vocational and skills training in the provinces of Anhui, Ningxia, and Shandong. The training programs were leveraged to build relationships with urban employers, who saw the benefits of hiring already-trained workers. As a result, a new market of labor brokers developed to match rural-urban migrants with better job opportunities in the cities. In Anhui Province alone, more than 57,000 migrants received training from 2009 to 2014 through 10 project-supported schools. And 98 percent of graduates received occupational qualification certificates, and the percentage of graduates entering employment within six months increased from 51 percent to 98.2 percent. Initial wages received by graduates doubled from 1,430 Yuan to 3,300 Yuan a month.

Facilitating Remittance Services for Internal Migrants in the Philippines. The geography of the Philippines, comprising 2,000 inhabited islands, has lent itself to high rates of internal (and international) migration, driven by an employment search. Indeed, two-thirds of the population lives and works in select urban areas, while sending remittances back to family living in a different province. There is limited use of formal banking, with only a 31 percent bank penetration rate, while mobile phone penetration is high at 120 million mobile connections and 71 percent unique subscribers. The high rates of migration and mobile phone use, and limited formal banking seem naturally conducive to the creation of a mobile money market. SMART money, launched in the Philippines in 2001 by Smart Communications in partnership with Banco de Oro, was in fact the world's first deployment of mobile money. A second remittance and banking service, GCash, was launched in 2004. While driven by these two companies, mobile banking innovation continues to be fostered in an enabling regulatory environment promoted by the Bangko Sentral ng Pilipinas (BSP). BSP regulations have allowed for nonbanks to offer financial services, flexibility in ID cards needed to verify users of the service, legal certainty, and formalized rules for mobile money and the testing of various business models. As a result, banking infrastructure has expanded its reach to underserved populations and allowed for the safe transfer of money between migrants and their families (GSMA 2009).

Addressing Disparities in Living Standards in Japan. Rural-urban migration in postwar Japan, which had been high in the 1950s and 1960s, tapered off in the mid-1970s when the government took policy action to improve disparities between urban centers and lagging areas. In 1970, the government introduced the New Economic and Social Development Plan and the New Integrated Spatial Development Plan (Shin-Zenso). In industrial areas, these plans continued to invest in basic services and social intuitions including public utilities, medical facilities, and schools. However, there was also a focus on achieving a minimum level of living standards across less developed areas. The government earmarked budget transfers to local governments as well as pooled public funds through the Fiscal Investment and Loan Program for large-scale investment in basic services. As per capita income converged between leading urban centers and other areas, labor migration rates leveled off.

Notes

1. Paraphrased from World Bank (2015b).
2. http://www.humanium.org/en/world/right-to-identity/.
3. Youth labor force participation in the EAP for females is 62.3 percent, compared to 57.5 percent for males. For Asia more broadly, the figures

are 46 percent for females and 60.2 percent for males. Statistics are from 2009 (Packard and Nguyen 2014).

4. The countries analyzed include: Australia, Cambodia, China, Indonesia, Japan, Korea, Lao PDR, Malaysia, Mongolia, Myanmar, New Zealand, Papua New Guinea, the Philippines, Thailand, Timor-Leste, and Vietnam.

5. United Nations Population Division (cited in Packard and Nguyen [2014]).

6. Numbers are approximated for income poverty, however, consumptive reflects a similar pattern.

7. Giles and Huang (2015), based on data from CHARLS (2011); IFLS (2007); KLoSA (2010); ThaiSES (2011and World Bank East Asia and Pacific Standardized Household Surveys, various years—as cited in World Bank [2016a]).

8. First, removing barriers that prevent women from having the same access as men to education, economic opportunities, and productive inputs can generate broad productivity gains. Second, improving women's absolute and relative status feeds many other development outcomes, including those for their children. Third, leveling the playing field—where women and men have equal chances to become socially and politically active, make decisions, and shape policies—is likely to lead, over time, to more representative and more inclusive institutions and policy choices and thus to a better development path (World Bank 2012b).

References

ADB (Asian Development Bank). 2014. "Urban Poverty in Asia." ADB, Manila.

———. 2015a. *Inequality in Asia and the Pacific: Trends, Drivers, and Policy Implications*. London: Routledge.

———. 2015b. "Women in the Workforce: An Unmet Potential in Asia and the Pacific." ADB, Mandaluyong City, Philippines. ADB.

Asia Foundation, and the Korean Development Institute. 2011. "Social Mobility: Experiences and Lessons from Asia." Korean Development Institute, Seoul.

Azarbaijani-Moghaddam, S. 2014. "Gender Inclusion Strategies in Program Nasional Pemberdayaan Masyarakat (PNPM)." World Bank, Jakarta, Indonesia.

Bell, K. C. 2014. "A Review of the Land Sector in East Asia: Lessons for Land Governance and the Spatial Enablement of Government and Societies." World Bank Conference on Land and Poverty. World Bank, Washington, DC.

Boonyabancha, S. 2016. "How to Scale-Up Community-Driven Informal Settlement Upgrading: Sharing at the World Bank March 31, 2016." Presentation.

Boonyabancha, S., and D. Mitlin. 2005. "Addressing Poverty and Avoiding Dependency: Loan-funded Welfare Support in Thailand."

Chant, S. 2007. "Gender, Cities and the Millennium Development Goals in the Global South." New Working Paper Series, Gender Institute, London School of Economics, London.

Chen, M. A. 2014. "Informal Economy Monitoring Study Sector Report: Home-Based Workers." WIEGO, Cambridge, Massachusetts.

Chinese University of Hong Kong. 2008. "A Qualitative Study on 'Hidden Elderly' in Hong Kong." Chinese University of Hong Kong, Hong Kong SAR, China.

Feler, L., and J. V. Henderson. 2011. "Exclusionary Policies in Urban Development: Under-servicing Migrant Households in Brazilian Cities." *J Urban Econ.* 69 (3): 253–72, May 1.

Garland, A. M., M. Massoumi, and B. A. Ruble, eds. 2007. "Global Urban Poverty." Woodrow Wilson International Center for Scholars, Washington, DC.

Gentilini, U. 2015. "Entering the City: Emerging Evidence and Practices with Safety Nets in Urban Areas." Social Protection and Labor Discussion Paper, No. 1504. World Bank, Washington, DC.

Giles, and Y. Huang. 2015. "Are the Elderly Left Behind in a Time of Rapid Economic and Demographic Change?" Background paper for the *East Asia and Pacific Regional Report on Aging.* World Bank, Washington, DC.

GSMA. 2009. "Mobile Money in the Philippines—The Market, the Models and Regulations." http://www.gsma.com/mobilefordevelopment/wp -content/uploads/2012/06/Philippines-Case-Study-v-X21-21.pdf.

Habitat for Humanity China and Colliers International. 2015. "Aging China: Opportunities in Real Estate for Senior Housing." Gensler, March.

ILO (International Labour Organization). 2011. "Women and Labour Markets in Asia: Rebalancing towards Gender Equality in Labour Markets in Asia." ILO Regional Office for Asia and the Pacific, and ADB, Bangkok.

Lipton, M. 2002. "Access to Assets and Land in the Context of Poverty Reduction and Economic Development in Asia." Conference paper. Bangkok.

McGranahan, G., et al. 2016. "Inclusive Urbanization: Can the 2030 Agenda be Delivered without It?" *Environment and Urbanization* 28 (1), April. International Institute for Environment and Development, London.

Morton, M., et al. 2014. *Gender at Work: A Companion to the World Development Report on Jobs.* Washington, DC: World Bank.

NPR (National Public Radio). 2015. "A Forgotten Generation: Half of South Korea's Elderly Live in Poverty." April.

Nyugen, L. T., and M. J. White. 2007. "Health Status of Temporary Migrants in Urban Areas in Vietnam." *International Migration* 45 (4): 101–34, October.

OECD (Organization for Economic Co-operation and Development). 2013. "Report on Integrated Service Delivery for Vulnerable Groups." DELSA/ELSA/WP1(2013)8. OECD, Paris.

Packard, T. G., and T. Van Nguyen. 2014. "East Asia Pacific at Work: Employment, Enterprise, and Well-being." *East Asia and Pacific Regional Report*. World Bank, Washington, DC.

Rex, H. C., and Z. Trohanis. 2012. "Making Women's Voices Count: Integrating Gender Issues in Disaster Risk Management Overview and Resources for Guidance Notes." East Asia and the Pacific Region Sustainable Development Guidance Note, no. 0. Gender and Disaster Risk Management. World Bank, Washington, DC.

Tacoli, C. 2012. "Urbanization, Gender and Urban Poverty: Paid Work and Unpaid Carework in the City." Human Settlements Group, International Institute for Environment and Development, London.

Taylor, A. 2011. "Women and the City: Examining the Gender Impact of Violence and Urbanization; A Comparative Study of Brazil, Cambodia, Ethiopia, Liberia and Nepal." ActionAid, Johannesburg.

United Nations. 2014. "World Population Policies." United Nations, New York.

UN Habitat. 2003. "Global Report on Human Settlements 2003: The Challenge of Slums." United Nations Human Settlement Programme, Nairobi.

———. 2009. "Global Report on Human Settlements 2009: Planning Sustainable Cities." United Nations Human Settlement Programme, Nairobi.

UNICEF. 2012. "Maternal and Child Health. Issue Brief." UNICEF, Jakarta, Indonesia.

———. 2015. "Advancing WASH in Schools Monitoring." UNICEF, New York. http://www.unicef.org/wash/schools/files/Advancing_WASH_in_Schools_Monitoring(1).pdf.

UN Women. 2013. "Women Migrant Workers in Viet Nam Take Steps towards Better Rights and Services." http://www.unwomen.org/en/news/stories/2013/12/women-migrant-workers-in-viet-nam-take-steps-towards-better-rights-and-services, December 17.

Yuen, B. 2009. "Revisiting Urban Planning in East Asia, South-east Asia and Pacific." UN Habitat, Nairobi.

WHO (World Health Organization). 2012. "Health Service Delivery: Mongolia 2012." Ministry of Health. WHO, Ulaanbaatar.

WIEGO. 2013. "Winning Legal Rights for Thailand's Homeworkers." http://www.wiego.org/resources/winning-legal-rights-thailands-homeworkers.

World Bank. 2009. *World Development Report 2009: Reshaping Economic Geography.* Washington, DC: World Bank.

———. 2010. *Making Transport Work for Women and Men: Tools for Task Teams.* Washington, DC: World Bank.

———. 2012a. "Toward Gender Equality in East Asia and the Pacific: A Companion to the World Development Report." *East Asia and Pacific Regional Report.* World Bank, Washington, DC.

———. 2012b. *World Development Report 2012: Gender Equality and Development.* Washington, DC: World Bank.

———. 2013a. "A Diverse and Dynamic Region: Taking Stock of Social Assistance Performance in East Asia and the Pacific." World Bank, Washington, DC.

———. 2013b. "Indonesia: Evaluation of the Urban Community-Driven Development Program." World Bank, Washington, DC.

———. 2014a. *East Asia Regional Study 2014.* Washington, DC: World Bank.

———. 2014b. "Presentation: World Bank, Gender Mainstreaming DRM and Urban Operations." Feb 19. World Bank, Washington, DC.

———. 2014c. "The Economic Cost of Stigma and the Exclusions of LGBT People: A Case Study of India." World Bank, Washington, DC.

———. 2015a. "Achieving a System of Competitive Cities in Malaysia." World Bank, Washington, DC.

———. 2015b. "Inclusion Matters: The Foundation for Shared Prosperity." World Bank, Washington, DC.

———. 2016a. "Live Long and Prosper: Aging in East Asia and Pacific." *East Asia and Pacific Regional Report.* Washington, DC: World Bank.

———. 2016b. "Social Inclusion in China." Draft report. World Bank, Washington, DC.

———. 2016c. "Toward Inclusive Urban Service Delivery in Ulaanbaatar, Mongolia." World Bank, Washington, DC.

———. Forthcoming. "Urban Poverty in Ulaanbaatar: Understanding its Dimensions and Addressing the Challenges." World Bank, Washington, DC.

World Bank, and Development Research Center of the State Council, the People's Republic of China. 2014. "Urban China: Toward Efficient, Inclusive, and Sustainable Urbanization." World Bank, Washington, DC.

World Bank, and IMF (International Monetary Fund). 2013. *2013 Global Monitoring Report 2013: Rural-Urban Dynamics and the Millennium Development Goals.* Washington, DC: World Bank.

CHAPTER 5

Guiding Principles for Promoting Poverty Reduction and Inclusion in East Asia and the Pacific's Cities

Introduction

The previous chapters of this report have highlighted the challenges of fostering inclusive cities in the East Asia and the Pacific (EAP) region, but have also documented many effective programs and policies aimed at tackling urban poverty and inequality that are being implemented across different countries and cities in the region. That being said, the major challenges which persist in most countries can, if unaddressed, pose threats to future economic growth, stability, and social cohesion.

Fortunately, inclusive urbanization is being recognized as an increasingly important and central development theme, as demonstrated by the strong support of global leaders for the Sustainable Development Goals (SDGs). SDG number 11 is to "Make cities and human settlements inclusive, safe, resilient and sustainable," and the New Urban Agenda calls for the provision of basic services for all citizens. It fully respects the rights of refugees, migrants, and internally displaced persons regardless of their migration status, among other important priorities.

Yet how these goals will be implemented remains to be seen. Policy makers at the national and local levels will need to work together in orienting policies and programs towards more inclusive cities that foster opportunities for improving the living conditions of the urban poor. The private sector and civil society have an equally important role to play, particularly in EAP countries. EAP countries such as Japan, Korea, and Singapore serve as excellent models for promoting inclusive urbanization through slum improvements and other programs, and can play an important role in continuing to foster the exchange of critical knowledge in the region.

This section draws on global experience to present a set of key guiding principles for policy makers. Implementation of these principles will need to be tailored to the very diverse country and city contexts in the EAP region. To help frame priorities for different country and city circumstances, a typology drawing from the *World Development Report 2009: Reshaping Economic Geography* (World Bank 2009) is used. Categories of urbanization level—incipient, intermediate, and advanced—help to characterize some of the key differences that would affect policy and program priorities for inclusive urbanization (table 5.1). For example, a country or city that is the early stages of urbanization would have very different characteristics and needs than a highly urbanized place. Factors such as size, density, wealth, and capacity are important distinguishing elements across places at different levels of urbanization and thus would affect how priorities are sequenced when identifying strategies for an inclusive cities strategy.

Incipient urbanization refers to places that are in the early stages of urbanization and typically still in lower-middle income status. Though poverty levels may be higher, there is an opportunity to put in place key policy and programs that will affect future urbanization with the aim of creating inclusive livable cities. Such places in EAP at the country level may include Cambodia, Lao PDR, and Myanmar; and at the city level, examples might include smaller cities such as Vientiane (Lao PDR), Siem Reap (Cambodia), or Hai Duong (Vietnam). These places tend to have lower density, and lower levels of wealth and lower capacity, which means they may require specific financial and technical support.

Intermediate urbanization is characterized by countries that are around 50 percent urbanized or medium to large cities that are growing at a rapid pace. Examples at the country level include China, Indonesia, the Philippines, and Thailand; and at the city level, Phnom Penh (Cambodia), Yogyakarta (Indonesia), Yangon (Myanmar), Cebu City (the Philippines), or Hai Phong (Vietnam). For such places, urbanization has largely taken place and they may have middle-income status, but there is substantial need to address substandard housing, deficiencies in service delivery, and inequality for some groups. There may limited financial resources and capacity for such investments requiring innovative financing mechanisms

Table 5.1 Typology for Country and City Urbanization Levels

Urbanization level	Definition at the country and city level	Characteristics
Incipient	Country: Urban share of 25 percent City: Smaller towns and cities	Rapid urbanization, low density, low inequality Lower level wealth and capacity
Intermediate	Country: Urban Share of 50 percent City: Medium to large cities	Rapid urbanization, mixed density Mid-level wealth and capacity
Advanced	Country: Urban share of more than 75 percent City: Highly urbanized large cities and metropolitan areas	Slowing urbanization, high density, complex urban environment Higher wealth and capacity

as well as capacity support to design and implement programs and policies effectively.

Advanced urbanization refers to countries that are more than 75 percent urbanized. In EAP such countries include Malaysia, Japan, and Korea. At the city level, advanced urbanization would include large highly urbanized metropolitan areas such as Beijing (China), Jakarta (Indonesia), Manila (the Philippines), Bangkok (Thailand), or Ho Chi Minh City (Vietnam). Though these places may have higher-middle-income status, and much wealth and substantial institutional capacity, in some places there may still be high levels of urban poverty and the backlog of those living in slums is substantial, requiring urgent attention.

The guiding principles outlined below in table 5.2, highlight important priorities for all urbanization levels, but the specific policy or program to be implemented may depend on a city's or country's size, density, wealth, and capacity. Table 5.3, below, summarizes the full set of examples covered in this report.

Table 5.2 Guiding Principles for Promoting Inclusion of the Urban Poor by Urbanization Level

Guiding Policy Principals	Incipient	Intermediate	Advanced
Promoting Economic Inclusion			
Connect the urban poor with job markets	- Investing in primary education	- Develop strong labor market information systems - Invest in vocational skills training - Invest in public transportation to allow for mobility to jobs	- Improve quality of education and skills training; invest in vocational and higher education; - Provide targeted job training programs particularly for unemployed youth - Expand investments in public transportation to all areas to expand access to jobs
Encourage pro-poor economic development	- Encourage entrepreneurship and migration - Expand access to credit through microenterprise programs - Institute and enforce policies that promote the rights of informal workers such as legalizing space for informal work and creating laws that protect home-based workers		
Build resilience to external shocks	- Support community initiatives for resilience building	- Invest in disaster planning and early warning systems in high-risk areas - Develop targeted safety net programs	- Expand early warning systems for disaster risk - Expand and improve targeted safety nets - Develop and implement targeted programs to reduce environmental degradation - Retrofit infrastructure - Develop insurance pools

(Table continues on next page)

Table 5.2   Guiding Principles for Promoting Inclusion of the Urban Poor by Urbanization Level *(continued)*

Guiding Policy Principals	Incipient	Intermediate	Advanced
Promoting Spatial Inclusion			
Invest in integrated urban planning	- Invest in spatial planning that is well-integrated with transportation planning that facilitates spatial connections between jobs and low-income housing.	- Invest in transportation infrastructure and connective policies to facilitate density and encourage affordability, and enhance mobility for all - Invest in cycle lanes and sidewalks - Proactively plan for urban expansion including in sites and services in designated locations - Invest in open public spaces	- Deepen investments in transportation infrastructure, connectivity, cycle lanes and sidewalks; - Invest and maintain public spaces - Resettlement of urban poor in high-risk areas - Ensure there are open green spaces in low-income areas
Ensure affordable land and housing	- Define and enforce land rights to include secure land tenure and property rights - Improve land administration	- Expand administrative jurisdictions to coordinate infrastructure investments - Refine and enforce land use regulations that maintain affordable land prices such as Transfer of Development Rights (TDR), special assessment districts, mixed use development, cross-subsidy schemes, and land pooling - Develop and implement land titling programs - Proactively plan for urban expansion, including in sites and services - Prevent informal settlements in high-risk areas - Introduce housing finance programs for low-income groups	- Land use regulation and land taxation - Implement land titling programs - Enable expansion of housing finance for low-income groups

(Table continues on next page)

Table 5.2   Guiding Principles for Promoting Inclusion of the Urban Poor by Urbanization Level *(continued)*

Guiding Policy Principals	Incipient	Intermediate	Advanced
Provide equitable access to infrastructure and basic services	- Invest in basic infrastructure services (water and sanitation)	- Universal provision of basic infrastructure services: clean water, sanitation, solid waste collection, electricity, affordable transportation Expand opportunities for private financing of infrastructure	- Implement improvements in quality of universal provision of basic infrastructure services - Institute slum upgrading programs and integration into the city

Promoting Social Inclusion

Open the rights of all citizens to the city	- Reform or eliminate exclusionary policies for urban migrants		
Target marginalized subgroups among the poor		- Invest in targeted social safety net programs for the poorest	- Deepen and improve targeted social safety net programs for the poorest
Strengthen local governance and embrace citizen engagement	- Invest in strong leadership, capacity building, and enforcement of governance priorities for urban management at the national and local levels - Encourage opportunities for participation in local-level decision making		
		- Implement targeted programs to reduce crime and violence - Work with civil society groups on policies and programs in low-income neighborhoods	- Deepen and improve targeted programs to reduce crime and violence - Support civil society groups that implement policies and programs in low-income neighborhoods
		- Build better information systems on current living conditions and future areas of growth through surveys and remote sensing data. - Effectively use information systems for policy making and planning	- Mainstream data collection initiatives - Conduct specialized studies on subgroups requiring further analysis

Promoting Economic Inclusion for the Urban Poor

Connect the Urban Poor with Job Markets

Employment is critical to poverty reduction and economic inclusion, especially given the heavy reliance of the urban poor on cash incomes. Fostering opportunities for employment and income generation helps to build the resilience of the urban poor in the face of informality, job losses, and wage reductions in urban industries, particularly in the absence of agriculture production to fall back on. It can also reduce the threat of social instability, as income gaps widen and inequality grows. This threat is of particular concern in countries with high youth unemployment rates including Fiji, Indonesia, the Philippines, Tuvalu, and Vanuatu.

A starting point is to build skills through improving the urban poor's access to education. For places at incipient urbanization levels, this means investing in universal access to quality primary education. As labor markets across the region are shifting towards higher-skilled workers, education is a key bridge between the urban poor and good jobs. Recognizing this, Shanghai, China, for example, initiated a policy to provide universal compulsory education for migrant children. For cities and countries with intermediate and advanced urbanization levels, the government can go further by bringing together industry and education, and by promoting university offerings and vocational training programs that impart sought-after skills and meet labor market demands.

A second area important to connecting the urban poor to jobs is through providing the infrastructure that enables better mobility in poor communities. The urban poor are constantly navigating the trade-off between easy access to employment, and secure and affordable housing. For those who live at the urban periphery, commutes to work can be costly. There is a need in countries such as Indonesia. Mongolia, and the Philippines to reconsider policies that favor car-oriented development over public transportation systems, and to ensure that public transit is accessible to communities both at the periphery and contained in slums. Hanoi, Vietnam, is a good example of a city that has facilitated densification and the connection between peri-urban areas and the city center by modernizing road networks just outside the city. In addition, the government simultaneously invested in slum upgrading, which overall provided better living conditions. Coupled with improvements in access to jobs, this scenario provides a good example of how cities can address multiple dimensions of exclusion.

Encourage Pro-Poor Economic Development

Across the region, rural-urban migrant populations are incorrectly associated with increasing urban poverty. Governments have responded by enacting policies to prevent the entry of migrants into cities. Rather than preventing poverty, these policies enhance it by increasing the vulnerability of excluded groups. Vietnam provides a salient example of these exclusionary policies, where those without residency status cannot access credit and formal financial institutions. Even among "legal" residents, the urban poor remain underserved by banks. Many of the urban poor are self-employed, and without access to credit, cannot easily access capital to grow their businesses. Microenterprise initiatives work to fill this gap, but their reach is limited. Programs to expand credit in Indonesia and the Philippines have been beneficial, however, these programs often target specific communities or neighborhoods rather than the urban poor more broadly.

Across all urbanization levels, programs to encourage entrepreneurship and migration, and expand access to credit through microenterprise programs are important. Similarly important are programs for promoting the rights of informal workers, given the high prevalence of informality in the region, particularly among the urban poor. Such policies include legalizing space for informal work as in Indonesia, creating laws that protect home-based workers as in Thailand, and organizing informal workers to protect livelihoods in the Philippines (Cebu City). In these examples, governments found success only after engaging with poor communities and ensuring that new laws and policies were supported by the appropriate enforcement mechanisms.

Build Resilience to External Shocks

The impacts of natural hazards and economic shocks have hit EAP countries hard over time, with the greatest impacts for the urban poor. Fluctuations in cash incomes are more consequential in urban areas than in rural areas, as the loss of work and wages have immediate impacts on household expenditures. For incipient cities and countries, investing in basic infrastructure and services for all can mitigate the impacts on the urban poor. Community-led initiatives are also extremely important to help low-income communities cope with shocks. In times of natural disaster or other shocks, the urban poor have proven to be resilient. Examples of communities organizing themselves to cope with hardships include job-sharing arrangements in the informal construction sector in Vietnam; informal savings and credit groups in Cambodia and Laos PDR; and community-organized distribution of food or expenses in Cambodia and Vietnam.

As urbanization reaches the intermediate and advanced stages, investments in social safety net programs, disaster planning, and early warning systems can help the urban poor preserve economic gains. In Jakarta, for example, the Flood Early Warning System has been used to coordinate standard operating procedures and build local capacities to manage disaster risk using participatory planning approaches. This system ensured that urban residents were being included, regardless of income or community status. In China, Fiji, Indonesia, and the Philippines, social safety net programs are designed to offer disaster preparation activities for subgroups among the poor that are most vulnerable to shocks, and to provide assistance for low-income residents affected by disasters.

Policies can build on these efforts and provide formal funding both for preparedness measures, such as insurance pools, and rehabilitation initiatives.

The Catastrophe Deferred Drawdown Option (CAT-DDO) in the Philippines provided an opportunity to draw down on insurance options as a response to Typhoon Yolanda; some of the funds were used for low-income communities to make post-disaster conditional cash transfers and operate cash for work programs. Building-back-better workfare programs were used in Aceh, Indonesia, after the 2004 earthquake; they used community contracting for reconstruction works and training for incremental housing construction to ensure low-cost approaches for building-back-better in low-income communities.

Promoting Spatial Inclusion for the Urban Poor

Invest in Integrated Urban Planning

Spatial planning that is well integrated with transport planning can help reduce inequality in access to urban opportunities and amenities at all urbanization levels. The pattern of a city's physical layout or urban form is one of many factors that affect the urban poor's ability to access economic opportunities in their cities. This access may be fostered by ensuring a spatial match between jobs, markets, public transportation, health and education services, recreational areas, and affordable housing. In high-density, spatially efficient cities, time that the poor would otherwise spend commuting can instead be spent generating income, and household resources that would have been spent on commuting costs can otherwise be spent on food, education, health care, or other basic needs.

As countries and cities reach intermediate urbanization stages, investments in urban planning are required to proactively influence growth patterns and avoid problems of sprawl, slums, and congestion, which all negatively influence urban life. Proactively planning for urban expansion can help cities to avoid the mistakes of many megacities and prevent future slum formation. Ensuring affordable and reliable public transport can expand housing and job opportunities for low-income residents and reduce commute times. For instance, China stands out for its proactive urbanization policies, which have included the massive construction of affordable housing in urban areas. This approach enabled low-income households to purchase lots at a relatively low price and incrementally build housing. That being said, the design of these settlements has been criticized for its sprawling spatial form with large blocks which makes markets, amenities, and transport more difficult to access.

At the advanced urbanization stage, it is important to deepen investments in transport infrastructure, prioritizing public transport corridors and connectivity to facilitate easy connections between jobs and housing for the poor and enhancing access to economic opportunities. Design also needs to allow for cycle lanes and sidewalks, as a significant portion of the urban poor rely on cycling or walking. Involving local governments and civil society in the planning process through consultations, disclosing the plans as they are developed, and establishing channels to receive feedback from the public will help to ensure local needs are met and equity considerations are included. Korea and Singapore provide many important lessons in this regard (boxes 5.1 and 5.2).

In the process of designing and implementing urban plans, there are a number of good practices that governments can pursue to promote better equity and inclusion within cities. Several sites and services projects offer

---

Box 5.1   Urbanization and Spatial Transformation Phases in Korea

The policies that Korea implemented during its decades-long transformation from a predominantly rural to an urban economy provide a framework of good practice for the support of urbanization in its incipient, intermediate, and advanced stages. An overview of policies and interventions follows:

Incipient Urbanization Priorities: Provision of Basic Social Services and Improvement of Land Markets
The most successful and lasting policies implemented during incipient urbanization were the ones targeting basic services.

- Education: In 1960 when nearly 75 percent of the population was rural, 35 percent of adults over the age of 15 had no schooling. As the population urbanized (75 percent urban in 1990, rising to 80 percent urban in 2009), the percentage of adults without education dropped to 15 percent in 1980, and to less than 5 percent by 2000.
- Healthcare: A similar transformation to education occurred in healthcare. In 1980 4 percent of all children were immunized against measles. By 1989, that number had risen to 95 percent.
- Land use: There was strong support from the central government for land use conversion of agricultural land for industrial purposes.

Intermediate Urbanization Priorities: Institutions and Infrastructure for Increasing Density and Reducing Congestion
As urban areas grew in size and became more congested, administrative jurisdictions were expanded to better coordinate infrastructure investments.

Larger jurisdictions facilitated investments in subway and expanded bus systems, paved road networks, and other connective infrastructure; they also increased transportation between urban areas, helping to create a network of cities with specialized local economies.

Advanced Urbanization Priorities: Institutions and Investments for Higher Density and Shorter Distance, and Targeted Investments to Address Divisions
Once Korea had reached an advanced urbanization stage, targeted policies for slum upgrading and poverty reduction were more successful. Priority was given to the following:

- In-situ slum upgrading and subsidies for relocation
- Investments in connective infrastructure in low-income areas

This sequence of policies in line with Korea's spatial transformation allowed it to develop into an advanced urbanized economy.

Sources: Korea Research Institute for Human Settlements 2011; World Bank 2009.

a prospective approach for growing cities in EAP, where anticipation of growth involves proactively investing in the rights of way and basic infrastructure services in designated locations. Public spaces play an important role in strengthening social and cultural interaction, fostering a sense of belonging and pride in an area, and forging social ties by bringing the community together. In poor areas, public spaces are especially important, serving as an extension of small living spaces; pathways for public transport, water supply, electricity, drainage and street lighting; venues for informal trade and commerce such as hawking and street vending; and centers of religious and cultural exchange, recreation, and social interaction.

The urban poor often live in the most vulnerable parts of the city, putting them at high risk to the impacts of climate change and natural disasters. There are many approaches to building resilience through urban planning and management, which need to become standard practice for cities, particularly in high-risk areas. The identification of risk-prone areas, prevention of new construction, and the resettlement of high-risk communities can mitigate the impacts on the poor.

Ensure Affordable Land and Housing

The shortage of affordable housing options has resulted in growing slum populations across EAP cities, particularly where low-income residents have few options for financing home purchases or for affordable rentals. At the policy level, housing is found to be comparatively more affordable in countries where property rights are protected and construction permitting is rapid. Targeted subsidy and lending programs can also help to reach the poorest. Singapore's successful experience in addressing slums, for example, is attributed to institutional reform and significant investments in housing and infrastructure (box 5.2).

At the incipient urbanization levels, policies that define and enforce land rights to open up land access and improve tenure security are priorities for reducing urban poverty. For instance, in Kampong Speu province in Cambodia, which is at an early urbanization stage, residents benefited from a land registration and titling program which formulated policies for land administration and management, developed mechanisms for dispute resolution, and established a national land registry system. Lessons from the experience of this land titling program in Cambodia, as well as programs in Laos PDR, Thailand, and other parts of the world, suggest that these programs are associated with enhanced security and consequently increased housing renovation (Durand-Lasserve et al. 2006). Property titles have increased household investment, but the bulk of the investment is financed without the use of credit. Tenure security has also been found to have a significant impact on the market value of land. The "formalization" norms will vary significantly across countries.

Intermediate urbanization levels require a particular focus on land use regulations that maintain affordable land prices. Restrictive regulations such as minimum plot sizes, maximum floor area ratio, and outdated

Box 5.2   **Singapore's Inclusive Urbanization Experience**

International experience shows that slum upgrading and improvement is sustainable only when accompanied by sufficient citywide transportation infrastructure and institutions that are effective in providing basic services. Singapore provides a unique example of a government successfully address-ing all three challenges concurrently.

When Singapore became independent in 1965, 70 percent of the country's population lived in badly overcrowded conditions, and one-third were squatting on the city fringes. Unemployment aver-aged 14 percent, GDP per capita was less than $2,700, and half of the population were illiterate. Falling mortality rates and migration from the Malay Peninsula implied rapid population growth, further increasing the pressure on both housing and employment; 600,000 additional units of housing were needed, and private supply was less than 60,000.

Today, less than 40 years later, Singapore's slums are gone. In their place is one of the cleanest and most welcoming cities in the world. The secret? First, institutional reforms made the government known for its accountability. Then the government became a major provider of infrastructure and services. Land scarcity made good planning an imperative. Multiyear plans were produced, imple-mented, and updated. Finally, the housing authority (HDB) was mandated to undertake a massive program of slum clearance, housing construction, and urban renewal. Public housing became an integral part of all development plans. At the program's height, HDB was building a new flat every eight minutes. Of Singapore's population, 86 percent now lives in publicly built units. Most own their flats, encouraged by special housing funds financed from the Employees Provident Fund, a manda-tory retirement scheme. Serviced land was made available. Through the Land Amalgamation act, the government acquired almost one-third of city land. Slum dwellers were relocated to public housing. For a city-state in a poor region, it is not an exaggeration to assert that effective urbanization was responsible for delivering growth rates that averaged 8 percent a year throughout the 1970s and 1980s. It required a combination of market institutions and social service provision, strategic invest-ment in infrastructure, and improved housing for slum dwellers.

Source: World Bank 2009.

zoning can result in higher land prices. Tools to address these may include transfer development rights, special assessment districts, density bonuses, mixed use development and cross-subsidy schemes. Land pooling has also been used successfully to open up access to land. For example, in Thailand under the Baan Mankong program, slum dwellers facing imminent eviction collectively organized and bargained successfully for a share of the land they occupied through the Community Development Organizations Institute (CODI) (Boonyabancha 2009). The occupied land was divided into two portions, and a developer was given the right to build on one por-tion of the site and land occupants were re-housed on the other portion, with a promise of secure tenure on their new plots or in their new housing.[1] Such an approach has been replicated, but implementation is dependent on strong institutional arrangements.

Housing programs for the urban poor are also very important at both the intermediate and advanced urbanization levels. These programs can include opening up access to housing finance as was recently launched in

Indonesia through the ambitious housing program, *Satu Juta Rumah* (One Million Homes), which aims to improve access to affordable housing through targeted assistance for mortgage down payments, assistance for incremental home improvements, and the expansion of access to housing finance. Rental programs such as rental housing subsidies in China, which combines rental subsidies with new rental developments to provide housing units for low-income households, or CODI in Thailand, which uses cooperative land ownership and long-term leases to community cooperatives to allow low-income communities to secure land titles, are also important approaches for affordable housing options for the urban poor.

Provide Equitable Access to Infrastructure and Basic Services

Aligned with the importance of spatial planning is equitable access to infrastructure and basic services to promote spatial inclusion. Though overall urban areas fare better than rural in this regard, there are still major gaps. Investments in clean water, sanitation, and solid waste collection have tremendous impacts on health, productivity, and welfare. Ensuring affordable transport provides access to income-earning opportunities as well as services such as schools, clinics, and hospitals.

At early urbanization levels, investments in clean water and sanitation are top priority. Laying down network infrastructure can anticipate future growth and prevent costly retrofitting or upgrading later. As urbanization further develops to the intermediate stages, investment needs will grow substantially to include prioritization of universal provision, including in low-income areas, of basic infrastructure services—clean water, sanitation, solid waste collection, electricity, and affordable transport. Such investments will require new financing sources through the private sector and public-private partnerships (PPPs) and other innovative approaches. For example, in the Philippines, water and sanitation have been privatized under two concession contracts with incentives to work with small-scale private service providers. A result of the partnership has been innovation in the extension of access to low-income residents without the use of subsidies. Alternative arrangements include paying connection fees in installments or through a higher water tariff; the use of shared meters to reduce connection costs; and establishing connections in informal settlements through the use of hoses and other low-cost mechanisms.

When cities and countries reach advanced urbanization, quality improvements will be needed for basic infrastructure, as well as slum upgrading programs which provide neighborhood-based interventions aimed at priority infrastructure needs. In Indonesia, Thailand, and Vietnam, internationally recognized flagship programs are being scaled up. For instance, through the Vietnam Urban Upgrading Project the urban poor have gained access to better water and sewerage connections, roads, lakes, canals, and bridges. The project combined the provision of infrastructure with strong community engagement, emphasizing strong community-level participation, and in-situ upgrading over resettlement, allowing residents to maintain their communities and livelihoods. It helped households in the upgraded areas to obtain a certificate of tenure or land use certificates, and supported the poorest households with home-improvement or income-generation loans to alleviate the pressure on their finances due to a lack of credit.

Other countries such as Cambodia, Mongolia, and the Philippines have a substantial need for slum upgrading that requires urgent attention. Successful approaches focus on incorporating participatory processes, where local participation can help to ensure pro-poor investments and program sustainability. Efforts to maintain households and communities in place rather than relocation have also been shown to be important in sustaining livelihoods and social networks.

Promoting Social Inclusion for the Urban Poor

Recognize the Rights of all Citizens to the City

An essential part of the development of inclusive cities, at any urbanization level, is building on the recognition that all citizens, regardless of identity, income status, or whether they were born in rural or urban areas, can have equal access to urban services and own property. This recognition helps to empower people and give them a sense of belonging in cities. Local governments can play an important role in encouraging this access; however, they can also create barriers with policies that exclude low-income communities, informal workers, women, and migrants.

Policies such as the *hukou* system in China, and other exclusionary policies for urban migrants in Cambodia, Indonesia, and Vietnam have created divisions in society and prevented many migrants from benefiting from urbanization. In the case of China this is now changing with recent relaxation of the hukou, particularly in smaller cities. Though the full effects are yet to be seen, this change would seem to be a positive move for many urban migrants. Similar policy changes in other countries could improve equity and opportunity for urban migrants.

To facilitate inclusion and ensure that the urban poor's perspectives are taken into account, local governments can seek input from a broad representation of civil society.

Target Marginalized Subgroups among the Urban Poor

While social protection programs exist for the urban poor, they are not always universally affordable. As countries get to intermediate and advanced urbanization levels, it is important to target programs to those that are marginalized for various reasons that affect their inclusion in the city and their opportunities for poverty reduction. This report covered three such groups given their large size—migrants, women, and the elderly. By providing a mechanism for vulnerable groups to achieve increased accessibility, social safety net programs, specifically conditional cash transfers, and cash-for-work opportunities, can similarly boost poverty reduction and inclusion in cities.

Such programs become particularly important to foster social inclusion at intermediate and advanced urbanization stages when divisions in urban areas tend to become more acute. Targeted programs for women to improve safety in public transport have been implemented in Liaoning Province, China, through simple approaches such as better streetlights, redesign of underpasses, and shorter wait times at bus stops. In Indonesia's national community empowerment program, design elements have been included to boost female participation such as holding women-only meetings and providing childcare arrangements. In Malaysia during the 1980s and 1990s, the government implemented targeted interventions in social programs for marginalized people including investments in human capital, urban infrastructure, and skills development, and promoted gender equity. As a result, urban poverty decreased from 18.7 percent in 1979 to 2.4 percent in 1997, demonstrating the important benefits of such policies.

For the elderly, Indonesia, Japan, Korea, and Thailand all have policies and programs targeting low-income elderly in urban areas. These programs provide cash assistance through insurance or targeted programs. In Shanghai, China, for example, there is an interesting program designed to improve age-friendly housing through renovations to improve safety, as well as social support for those that may not have help from families.

For migrants, China has notably offered vocational training in Anhui, Ningxia, and Shandong to rural migrants. The programs were leveraged to build relationships with urban employers who saw the benefits of hiring already-trained workers.

More broadly there are programs in Indonesia, the Philippines, and elsewhere that provide income support and training opportunities for those who fall outside the formal economy or newcomers experiencing discrimination. These countries recognized that their social protection programs were mainly aimed at rural areas and have designed specific approaches to target the urban poor. In cities with high urban inequality and the proliferation of pockets of poverty—even those not reflected in national statistics—pro-poor policies to eliminate social exclusion can facilitate important welfare advantages.

Strengthen Local Governance and Embrace Citizen Engagement

Building inclusive cities requires good local-level governance through transparent and fair decision making, and sufficient resources to successfully implement programs and policies on the ground. Engaging the urban poor in decision-making processes is important in strengthening policies, enhancing service delivery, and ensuring social stability in cities. Research shows that the urban poor have less access and representation in the political system than the urban nonpoor; that they have fewer opportunities to shape and influence their governing institutions; and that they endure a far more hostile, fearful relationship with institutions of urban law and order (Desai 2010). In many EAP cities, particularly those at the intermediate and advanced urbanization stages, wealth and poverty coexist in close proximity and intra-city disparities can result in exclusion from growth opportunities and in some cases, can result in crime and violence. Empowering urban dwellers to actively engage and contribute in their cities is a powerful way of promoting social inclusion.

Finding ways to embed social integration in the decision-making process can quell social unrest and ensure a sense of belonging in the city. EAP has benefited from a regional program targeting inclusive slum upgrading for the urban poor—the Asia Coalition for Community Action (ACCA). The ACCA program achieves inclusion first by conducting citywide surveys to assess the needs of communities. It then establishes a city/community development fund with input from community architects and planners to provide grants for small infrastructure investments and large housing projects. Through ACCA, Fiji was able to mobilize support for the urban poor to organize urban upgrading projects that benefited roughly 10,000 informal residents living in Lautoka, the country's second largest city. Similarly, in Indonesia, through the Urban Community-Driven Development Program in (PNPM), urban residents have taken a proactive role in identifying community priorities, improving relations with local governments, and designing and implementing community improvements.

Encouraging citizen engagement is an inclusionary way to take the voices of the marginalized into account and to ensure all priorities are being addressed. The urban poor can thus be integrated into the city's fabric, and the challenges of providing basic needs and services for the marginalized can be addressed from a physical and social perspective.

Investing Further in Knowledge on the Urban Poor and Slums

Further evidence-based urban analysis is needed for cities to correctly assess and understand trends related to living conditions, to identify future challenges, and to develop plans accordingly. In preparing this study, a number of knowledge gaps and several priority areas for further work were identified. Among these are more extensive city-level studies on low-income populations and the characteristics of slums over time, analysis on subgroups among the urban poor such as LGBTI people and migrants, and analysis on urban mobility and access to livelihoods by the urban poor.

Such analysis and planning are dependent on reliable and easily accessible data, and sufficient capacity to conduct in-depth analysis. Basic information on the location of low-income settlements, high-risk areas, access to basic services, and high-growth areas can be challenging or expensive to collect for resource-constrained cities. Yet the benefits of investing in basic information are critical to ensure good planning; urban data systems allow cities to move from making reactive decisions to developing proactive solutions to the many urban challenges.

Among the data resources that are particularly useful for evidence-based planning in cities and for understanding issues related to urban poverty and informal settlements, are the following:

(i) remote sensing, which uses satellite imagery to locate infrastructure, identify natural hazards, and delineate urban extent
(ii) community mapping, which can be used to survey and develop maps of all the informal settlements and assess their service accessibility, empowering stakeholders to map services and think about local solutions to accessibility issues
(iii) census data, which provide valuable information about housing characteristics, access to basic services, education levels, and employment
(iv) household surveys, which offer a more in-depth understanding of living conditions by expanding the amount of information gathered from households
(v) data derived from other sources, such as cellular networks or citizen feedback on social media

Data sets from surveys and other methods developed by municipal governments also need to be stored and shared to be best used. Often, developed data are not shared with other municipal agencies or are considered proprietary to each agency. Breaking down the barriers between agencies and creating unified data standards will give municipalities and their agencies access to all data to develop more informed, evidence-based decisions. Many of the case studies highlighted in this study demonstrate the value and importance of such data in designing programs and policies to promote inclusive cities (box 5.3).

Box 5.3   Analyzing Urban Poverty and Informal Settlements in Metro Manila and Ulaanbaatar

The lack of comprehensive, accurate, up-to-date data on locations of slums and their characteristics is a constraint to proper planning and addressing the urban poor's needs. A number of data resources and analytical approaches have been used for the two in-depth case studies conducted in the context of this study. While the work of carrying out specially designed household survey can be time consuming and expensive, the wealth of information has enabled in-depth analysis.

Metro Manila, Philippines
Metro Manila has a large number of diverse slums in many locations. Identifying and delineating their boundaries at the city scale without any base information is challenge for any city but a much bigger one a complex urban context such as that of Metro Manila. Accordingly, the study used the following approaches to analyzing urban poverty and slums in Metro Manila,
    Geospatial Analysis. A unique geospatial approach was applied, which used advanced semi-automated Object-Based Image Analysis (OBIA) to process very high resolution satellite images at

(Box continues on next page)

Box 5.3   Analyzing Urban Poverty and Informal Settlements in Metro Manila and Ulaanbaatar *(continued)*

spatial resolution of 50 cm and identify and delineate the slums at scale and in a short time frame (World Bank 2016a). A statistical analysis of various slum settlement attributes related to objects found inside slums was combined with a linear index and other spatial relations into a model. Then a basic analysis of the characteristics, such as spatial distribution of slums and accessibility to public infrastructure, was further carried out as slums were overlaid with other GIS map layers. This geo-referenced database of slums formed the basis for a spatially representative random sample survey of slum households.

Household Survey in Informal Settlements. A household survey was carried out in three local government units in 2015/2016 as resources did not allow for a full sample of the entire Metro Manila region. The city of Manila in the east and center, Quezon City in northwest, and Muntilupa on the southern shores of the Metro were included in the sample, each with different characteristics that, together offer a representative sampling of the metropolitan area. A total of 2,606 households were interviewed, corresponding to a population of 11,840 persons.

For the purposes of the analysis of the diversity of slum types, the sample was also stratified based on the following typology classification of slums:

Metro Manila Slum Typologies

- Highly dense
- Linear dry (combining linear along railway and other linear type of settlements)
- Wet
- Pocket
- Mixed (merged with low density and under-the-trees categories, with the latter being verified and categorized as needed during the household listing process)

Ulaanbaatar, Mongolia

Mongolia's rapid urbanization has resulted in a concentration of urban poor in Ulaanbaatar in recent years, particularly in ger areas, with a number of service delivery and social problems which had not been well understood. The World Bank study uses a mixed methods approach, combining quantitative, qualitative, and spatial analyses. Availability of rich spatial data and the use of spatial techniques further are further used to create a better understanding of the locational distribution of urban poor and the nature of poor places. The analysis uses the following data resources and analytics, several of which were generated specifically for this study as well as a World Bank report (World Bank 2016b).

Household Survey on Service Delivery in Ulaanbaatar. This survey was a geo-referenced, citywide random sample of 3,000 households using a two-stage random sampling design, stratified by ger and nonger areas. The sample collected information on socioeconomic indicators; migration status; access to water, sanitation, and solid waste collection; functionality of streetlights; access to health clinics and schools; social capital; and neighborhood conditions. Data collection was carried out in 2014.

Analysis of the 2010, 2012, and 2014 Household Socioeconomic Survey Data. The data were collected by Mongolia's National Statistical Agency, with a focus on results for Ulaanbaatar.

Focus Group Discussions. There were18 focus group discussions held with residents from different Ulaanbaatar districts on the perceived quality, accessibility, and outcomes of health and education as key locally-provided social services. The analysis of focus group discussions allowed for a more nuanced understanding of how poverty is experienced and the mechanisms that serve to perpetuate poverty, particularly when interpreting quantitative data.

(Box continues on next page)

Ethnographic Study. An ethnographic study was also commissioned under the project, which delves deeper into the understanding of vulnerability in Ulaanbaatar's urban setting. It captures the experiences of two vulnerable groups, namely, recent migrants living near a landfill site and a ger-area community that was established partially on a cemetery. Both groups face stigma from local residents in Ulaanbaatar, and the in-depth study allows insights into their lived urban experiences and coping strategies.

Spatial Data and Analytics. Extensive spatial data were secured from the Ulaanbaatar City Master Planning Department, which form the basis for the majority of the spatial analyses examining access to services. The analyses include GIS layers of the distribution of public transit nodes and networks, schools, clinics, streetlights, building footprints, residential classifications, and so on. In addition, the National Statistical Office of Mongolia provided access to a poverty map that estimated poverty at the subdistrict level (for example, *khoroo* level or an urban ward). The poverty mapping was conducted using the decennial census and household survey data through the application of a robust small-area-estimation methodology. The findings allow for urban poverty comparison across districts and khoroos.

Sources: World Bank forthcoming a; World Bank forthcoming b.

Table 5.3   **Summary of Policy and Program Examples Aimed at Promoting Inclusion in EAP**

	Country	Policy	Description
		Connecting people to jobs	
Economic Inclusion	Vietnam	*Integration of peri-urban villages through road networks*	As Hanoi experienced rapid urbanization, it facilitated the densification of surrounding peri-urban villages by modernizing road networks just outside of the city. This process not only allowed formal developers access to new land, but also improved connections to the urban center from peri-urban areas.
	China, India, Philippines	*Using online outsourcing and microwork to target unemployed youth*	Impact-outsourcing involves breaking up tasks into lower-skilled microwork. For example, managed service platforms such as Samasource specifically target and train disadvantaged youth to complete web-based tasks such as image recognition, transcription, and data enrichment that can be completed on inexpensive devices.

(Table continues on next page)

Table 5.3   Summary of Policy and Program Examples Aimed at Promoting Inclusion in EAP *(continued)*

Country	Policy	Description
Building skills and access to education		
Vietnam	*Supporting street-vendors through private sector-led trainings*	Recognition of the existing sales networks of street vendors led Bel Access to create a comprehensive program complete with technical training, optional uniforms, distribution at wholesale sites, assistance integrating into the formal sector, and partnerships with microcredit institutions to convert street vendors into Bel Access salespeople. The 70 vendors who completed the skills training course saw an average 15 percent rise in income after three months.
China	*Inclusive urban education*	Shanghai achieved the provision of universal compulsory education for migrant children through a program of building new schools as well as paying for the enrollment of migrant children into private schools. Private schools are generally of lesser quality than public schools; however, the government of Shanghai actively audited private schools to determine which could accommodate migrant children.
Pro-poor economic development		
Indonesia	*Formalizing spaces for street vendors*	Without legally designated work spaces or permits, street vendors had long been subjected to threats of eviction and extortion in the form of bribes. Over a series of 54 meetings between the mayor and vendor representatives, the two parties agreed that the vendors would move to a location that was easy for customers to reach and where the city would provide facilities including permanent shelters and connections to municipal water and electricity grids. Nearly 1,000 vendors moved on the relocation day, which was marked by a citywide celebration and parade.
Philippines	*Organizing informal workers to protect livelihoods*	By organizing under the Cebu City United Vendors Association, informal vendors were able to create a platform to lobby city authorities for security of livelihoods and reduced harassment. In 2000, the mayor created a working committee to study the conditions of street vendors and the implications of legalized trading in some parts of the city. In addition, the city administration agreed to a policy that any demolitions of vendor stalls could not occur without a consultation with the vendor, allowing them time to arrange for a relocation site.
Access to credit and finance		
Philippines	*Integrated finance and social services*	The Quezon City government created an alternative livelihood project for waste-pickers whereby workers were organized in cooperatives, through which they could collectively receive assistance in the form of education, skills training, and access to finance. Joint financing and skills training was also available to workers seeking to develop minor business ventures and find alternative livelihoods.

(Table continues on next page)

Table 5.3   Summary of Policy and Program Examples Aimed at Promoting Inclusion in EAP *(continued)*

	Country	Policy	Description
Building resilience			
Economic Inclusion	Indonesia	*Building-back-better workfare programs*	After the 2006 earthquake in Aceh, community contracting was used as a tool for rehabilitation and reconstruction in post-disaster conditions. Community and local workers were trained and employed for reconstruction works; community mobilization, technical assistance, and training for incremental housing construction were used to ensure that the community members had a low-cost solution for building back better.
	Philippines	*Insurance and catastrophic risk pools*	The government took out two World Bank Disaster Risk Management Development Policy Loans with a Catastrophe Deferred Drawdown Option (CAT-DDO). Comprehensive financial planning established under the first CAT-DDO, offered the Philippines an opportunity to draw down on insurance options. In times of disaster, communities had liquidity to make post-disaster conditional cash transfers and to run cash-for-work programs.
	China, Indonesia	*Strengthening disaster planning and early warning systems*	The China Meteorological Administration Weather Alert System uses SMS to provide comprehensive forecasting and warning information. Similarly, the Jakarta Flood Early Warning System has been used to coordinate standard operating procedures and build local capacity to manage disaster risk.
Social safety net programs for disaster relief			
Economic Inclusion	Philippines	*Conditional cash transfer (CCT)*	Two of the identified target groups for the modified urban CCT program are evacuees and households displaced as a result of disaster or conflict. The program offers cash transfers to vulnerable persons and provides social welfare programs that offer disaster preparation activities to protect against future impacts.
	China	*Urban Di Bao: minimum livelihood guarantee system*	The Urban Di Bao social protection program ensures that the poor have access to basic needs, including disaster relief. In times of disaster, the program funds emergency supply items such as water, food, heat, medication, and clothing, and makes provision for temporary shelter or resettlement.
	Indonesia	*Indonesia social protection policy*	The Ministry of Social Welfare has implemented social assistance in the form of disaster relief in Surakarta and Makassar cities to combat the adverse impacts of hazards faced particularly by the urban poor. Furthermore, Indonesia builds the financing of basic safety nets into the post-disaster recovery process.

(Table continues on next page)

Table 5.3 Summary of Policy and Program Examples Aimed at Promoting Inclusion in EAP *(continued)*

	Country	Policy	Description
		Housing the urban poor	
Spatial Inclusion	Philippines	*Land banking and "in-city" relocation*	Iloilo city initiated plans for a flood-control project, which required the relocation of 3,500 squatters from canals and low-lying, flood-prone areas. Working with the Homeless People's Federation and the Iloilo City Urban Poor Network, the city developed a progressive housing policy that ensured no eviction without relocation and that all relocation would occur within city limits. To achieve this, the city purchased land parcels from private owners and "banked" them to accommodate future relocation and social housing needs.
	Thailand	*Land titling and rental cooperatives*	The Community Development Organizations Institute (CODI) uses various ownership structures including cooperative land ownership and long-term leases to community cooperatives to allow low-income communities to secure land titles. The collective approach also discourages speculators from purchasing individual housing units from the poor to sell to higher-income groups. CODI finances its programs using a mix of its own funding, government subsidies, and pooled savings from residents.
	China	*Rental housing subsidies*	The Cheap Rental Housing Guarantee Plan (CRH) combines rental subsidies with new rental developments to provide housing units for low-income households. Municipal and local governments administer the program and bear the primary costs. The central government has stipulated that 5 percent of net gains from land conveyance fees be allocated towards the program—though with limited enforcement mechanisms, the program remains perpetually underfunded. Nevertheless, the program has done a good job targeting low-income tenants and enforcing strict development standards.
	Philippines	*Community mortgages*	Through the formation of community associations, low-income households can access subsidized mortgages from the state-run Social Housing Finance Corporation. These associations are also charged with collecting loan payments and enforcing sanctions and penalties. Since 2001, the program has provided loans to over 77,000 households, with a repayment rate of 75 percent— high for comparable schemes in the region.

(Table continues on next page)

Table 5.3   Summary of Policy and Program Examples Aimed at Promoting Inclusion in EAP *(continued)*

	Country	Policy	Description
		Broadening the reach of infrastructure and service provision	
Spatial Inclusion	Vietnam	*Urban infrastructure upgrading*	More than 200 low-income areas were identified, and communities were asked to evaluate what improvements would be most beneficial. In-situ upgrading of water supply, drainage, road paving, household electricity connections, and sanitation and solid waste management proved to be less costly than clearing and moving these households to hard-to-access relocation sites. The initiative also included a microfinance component to be used for home upgrades or income-generation purposes, helping to address some of the credit access barriers often experienced by the urban poor.
	Indonesia	*Community-driven infrastructure development*	Program Nasional Pemberdayaan Masyarakat (PNPM), provides block grants for community-level infrastructure and extends to all 11,000 urban wards in Indonesia. The program provides both financial and technical support to poor communities, allowing them to address immediate infrastructure needs.
	Philippines	*Partnering with small-scale private service providers (SPSPs)*	Water supply and sanitation have been privatized under two concession contracts with incentives to work with SPSPs. A result of the partnership has been the innovative development of the extension of access to low-income residents without the use of subsidies. Alternative arrangements include paying connection fees in installments or through a higher water tariff; the use of shared meters to reduce connection costs; and establishing connections in informal settlements through the use of hoses and other low-cost mechanisms.
	India	*Using mobile phones to track water usage and availability*	The social enterprise NextDrop uses a system of SMS notifications to alert utilities about water outages and customers about the timing and availability of water delivery services. From a customer perspective, accurate information helps to reduce wait times and allows households to plan their water usage, while utilities receive real-time information about their distribution system. Importantly, this system uses mobile phone technology that is already widely used among the urban poor.
	Indonesia	*Decentralized wastewater treatment systems*	The community-managed DEWATS allow for rapid improvements in sanitation facilities in high-priority informal settlements. These systems are most effective when communities and local government share costs and responsibilities for their operations and maintenance.

(Table continues on next page)

Table 5.3 Summary of Policy and Program Examples Aimed at Promoting Inclusion in EAP *(continued)*

	Country	Policy	Description
	**Transport policies to connect the urban poor**		
Spatial Inclusion	Philippines	*Mapping public transit routes*	Using open source tools, a database was created that meets the General Transit Feed Specification (GTFS), an internationally recognized standard for mapping transit routes. The database includes both bus and informal *jeepney* routes, and can be downloaded on smartphones or accessed through web- or SMS-based trip-planning tools.
	China	*Linking non-motorized transport and bus rapid transport*	A greenway was developed alongside the BRT corridor, complete with pedestrian walkways and a bike-sharing system consisting of 5,000 bikes across 109 stations. The BRT lines and bike-sharing stations are integrated, and passengers can use the same smart card to access both. The corridor also extends from some of Guangzhou's most-developed areas to peripheral neighborhoods where future development is anticipated.
	China	*Improving pedestrian facilities*	Disabled residents were asked to field test the design of bus stops, intersections, and sidewalks to ensure accessibility. Multiple consultations during the project design and implementation phases allowed city planners not only to incorporate many of the suggested improvements, but also show low-income residents that their ideas regarding traffic management, road safety, and pedestrian mobility were taken into consideration.
	**Social protection programs**		
	China, Vietnam	*Reforming residency status registration*	In China and Vietnam, there have been reforms to exclusionary systems allowing for better access to social protection. The *hukou* in China and *ho-khau* in Vietnam were designed to base access to services such as education and health on legally registered urban residency. These systems are undergoing changes to accommodate the most excluded and vulnerable, but still encounter challenges.
	Indonesia	*Conditional cash transfer*	The Keluarga Harapan Program (PKH) is a conditional cash transfer which includes the urban poor. The program has been most impactful in improving the use of and behavior towards healthcare in urban settings. Also, the blanket program is providing many lessons in how to assist local government in re-centering service delivery and social integration for the urban poor.

(Table continues on next page)

Table 5.3 Summary of Policy and Program Examples Aimed at Promoting Inclusion in EAP *(continued)*

	Country	Policy	Description
Targeting low-income women in urban areas			
Social Inclusion	China	*Security and urban transportation*	The Liaoning Medium Cities Transport Project design was significantly altered after female-only group discussions highlighted their safety concerns; the women predominantly walked or rode bicycles, as opposed to men who drove cars. City officials were able to accommodate their suggestions, making low-cost adjustments to the lack of streetlights, the poorly designed underpasses, and the long waits at bus stops that characterized the initial design.
	South Africa	*Early warning communications*	A community-based early warning system was designed with the assumption that after reporting danger or a threat to one part of the community, the information would spread to all relevant parties. Following a gender analysis, it was discovered that while men preferred climate information to be transmitted by radio, women showed a strong preference for information transmission through schools or by a public official, as these alternatives allowed them the ability to immediately ask questions and engage in a discussion.
	Indonesia	*Community-level preparedness*	The testing of evacuation routes designed without a gender analysis revealed that women with children could not reach designated safe areas within the allotted time, and the routes were subsequently revised. In the Aceh Besar and Aceh Jaya districts, design of a staircase used in evacuation routes was modified to include handrails and shorten the height of steps to accommodate women holding babies and children or assisting the elderly.
	Thailand	*Worker's rights and improved economic opportunities*	A national network of home-based workers and nongovernmental organizations led lobbying efforts to legalize social protection policies for its constituents. In 2011 the government of Thailand passed the Homeworker's Protect Act, which mandates fair wages (including equal pay for men and women) for workers completing orders for industrial enterprises in their homes. The law also obliges enterprises to provide a contract and establish a committee providing workers access to courts in the case of a labor dispute.
	Indonesia	*Gender mainstreaming for community-driven infrastructure*	Focus group discussions, revolving loan fund groups, and training on gender awareness were used to enhance women's participation Indonesia's National Community Empowerment Program (PNPM), which provides block grants for small-scale infrastructure projects to low-income communities.

(Table continues on next page)

Table 5.3 Summary of Policy and Program Examples Aimed at Promoting Inclusion in EAP *(continued)*

	Country	Policy	Description
	Targeting elderly in urban areas		
	Korea	*Social insurance program*	One of the program's target groups is the low-income or non-earning elderly, as it provides insurance and pension packages to help stabilize the bottom 70 percent of the elderly population.
	Japan	*Long-term care reform*	This mandatory social insurance system for long-term care provides benefits in the form of institutional or community-based services, not cash allowances. The benefits are aimed at covering all caregiving costs for the elderly.
	Indonesia	*Cash assistance*	Cash assistance is provided for the vulnerable elderly from the formal and informal sector. Although this is a universal program, the cost-sharing formula benefits formal workers through their contributions as they are greater than those of informal workers.
	Thailand	*Universal pension scheme*	The program targets elderly who are not residing in public facilities or receiving permanent income from sources such as government pensions or government-employed persons. Flexible arrangements have been introduced to encourage informal workers and the self-employed to contribute at varying levels, or to attain a waiver without penalties.
	Targeting migrants in urban areas		
Social Inclusion	China	*Building the human capital of rural-urban migrants*	Recognizing that migrants had been used to fill the most menial and lowest-paying jobs in the urban labor market, local governments partnered with the World Bank to offer vocational and skills training in three provinces. The training programs were leveraged to build relationships with urban employers, who saw the benefits of hiring already-trained workers. As a result, a new market of labor brokers has developed to match rural-urban migrants with better job opportunities in the cities.
	Philippines	*Facilitating remittance services for internal migrants*	The high rates of migration and mobile phone use, and limited formal banking in the Philippines were conducive to the creation of a mobile money market. SMART money, launched in 2001 by Smart Communications in partnership with Banco de Oro, was the world's first deployment of mobile money. Over time, the banking infrastructure has expanded its reach to underserved populations and allowed for the safe transfer of money between migrants and their families.
	Japan	*Addressing disparities in living standards*	The government earmarked budget transfers to local governments as well as pooled public funds through the Fiscal Investment and Loan Program for large-scale investment in basic services. As per capita income converged between leading urban centers and other areas, labor migration rates have leveled off.

Note

1. http://web.mit.edu/urbanupgrading/upgrading/issues-tools/tools/Reg-of -land.html.

References

Boonyabancha, S. 2009. "Land for Housing the Poor — By the Poor: Experiences from the Baan Mankong Nationwide Slum Upgrading Programme in Thailand." *Environment and Urbanization* 21 (2), 2009. International Institute for Environment and Development, London.

Desai, R. 2010. "The Political Economy of Urban Poverty in Developing Countries: Theories, Issues, and an Agenda for Research (June 30, 2010)." Wolfensohn Center for Development Working Paper No. 20. https://ssrn.com/abstract=1658580.

Durand-Lasserve, A., et al. 2006. "The Formalization of Urban Land Tenure in Developing Countries." In *Urban Land Markets: Improving Land Management for Successful Urbanization*, 101–32. Edited by S. V. Lall, M. Freire, B. Yuen, R. Rajack, and J.-J. Helluin. New York: Springer.

Korea Research Institute for Human Settlements (KRIHS). 2011. "Urbanization and Urban Policies in Korea." KRIHS, Seoul.

World Bank. 2009. *World Development Report 2009: Reshaping Economic Geography*. Washington, DC: World Bank.

———. 2016. "From Satellites to Settlements: Identifying Slums from Outer Space within Metro Manila's Complex Urban Landscape." Draft. World Bank, Washington, DC.

———. 2016b. "Toward Inclusive Urban Service Delivery in Ulaanbaatar, Mongolia." World Bank, Washington, DC.

———. Forthcoming a. "Navigating Informality: Perils and Prospects in Metro Manila's Slums." World Bank, Washington, DC.

———. Forthcoming b. "Urban Poverty in Ulaanbaatar: Understanding its Dimensions and Addressing the Challenges." World Bank, Washington, DC.

Appendix: Country Profiles

Cambodia

Key Development Statistics
Population: 15.38 million

GDP per capita: US$1,094.60

Urbanization Rate
Urban population density: 8,600
(persons/ square kilometer)

Urban population growth:
2.6 percent

Rural-Urban Statistics
Urban population: 20.5 percent (3.14 million)

Rural population: 79.5
percent (12.18 million)

Largest Urban Areas
Phnom Penh: 1.6 million   Baat Dambang: 228,681   Siem Reap: 264,034

Sources: WDI 2014; World Bank 2015a; General Population Census of Cambodia 2008.

Cambodia is in the early urbanization stages and remains primarily agrarian. It has among the smallest urban populations in the region, growing from 920,000 people to 1.4 million between 2000 and 2010. Phnom Penh is the country's only major urban area, and total urban land, approximately 160 square kilometers in 2010, comprises only 0.1 percent of Cambodia's land mass. Cambodia shares a number of urbanization characteristics, such as low urban area and population, with its neighbor Lao PDR, with the exception of urban population density. In this respect,

Cambodia has a much higher density, with 8,600 people per square kilometer, than the 3,200 people per square kilometer seen in urban areas in Lao PDR (World Bank 2015a).

Where urbanization has occurred, it has been largely unplanned for and unregulated. As a result, Phnom Penh has seen an increase in traffic congestion, flood risk, and squatter and slum settlements. Without urban planning interventions, Cambodia will continue to experience widening spatial and economic disparities within its cities.

Who Are the Urban Poor?

According to the 2008 Census, 25.6 percent of Cambodian households were headed by women. In urban poor communities, however, 38.3 percent of households are headed by women, of whom 27 percent were single mothers or widows. Two recent studies, the 2012 Phnom Penh Urban Poor Assessment and 2014 Phnom Penh Multiple Indicator Assessment of the Urban Poor, have indicated that poverty levels in Phnom Penh are considerably higher than officially reported (29 percent compared to 12.8 percent using the adjusted absolute poverty rate for Phnom Penh). These studies provided the following additional insights into growing urban poor communities:

- Nearly one in four households care for vulnerable children (orphans, abandoned, or with disability) and one in five households has members with chronic diseases. This demographic composition puts much social pressure on families.
- Most people in urban poor communities are employed in low-skill occupations with 60 percent of households earning less than $75 per month.
- More than two-thirds of the urban poor are indebted, with loan payments constituting a significant portion of monthly expenditures, though much of which payments go towards the loan interest.

Slums and Urban Housing

Since 1980, the Phnom Penh city administration has identified 516 different urban poor communities. Common settlement sites are along major infrastructure and transportation lines in and out of the city, including main roads, railways, and sewage systems. These sites are often public lands where households have constructed simple one-room houses. Houses are built on stilts in flood-prone areas.

The government has focused efforts on access to roads, electricity, and water supply, which 96 percent, 92 percent and 85 percent of households enjoy, respectively. Less commonly supplied are sewage systems and garbage collection services at 72 percent and 60 percent respectively. Furthermore, awareness of sanitation and environmental issues is low among urban poor communities, and contaminated water along with environmental hygiene remain concerns within poor neighborhoods (UNICEF 2012).

Suburbanization and the Rise of Satellite Cities

Phnom Penh has also witnessed the growth of self-contained "satellite cities" in peri-urban areas. These cities offer luxury accommodations and full infrastructure and service provision. For example, the Grand Phnom Penh International City development will include 4,500 houses, half-a-dozen residential apartment towers, a golf club, water park, public gardens, access to an international-grade school and a state-of-the-art hospital. The price for a villa in this development ranges from $120,000 to $850,000 (Strangio 2014).

Without pushing for comprehensive city infrastructure, Phnom Penh risks seeing development only for the wealthy. Currently, these satellite cities are not included in any broader development plan and do not coordinate infrastructure with surrounding neighborhoods.

Jobs and Migration

According to the 2008 census, the Phnom Penh population was about 1.2 million, with 400,000 migrants arriving within the five years leading up to the census. Migrants to Phnom Penh are overwhelmingly young and female, which is changing the city's age and gender structure.

These migrants, along with the wider urban poor population, tend to find low-paid and low-skilled or service-oriented work. Occupations are heavily segregated by gender, with women working in manufacturing—particularly in the garment industry—and as vendors, while men work primarily in construction and transportation. "White collar professionals" are rare due to the generally low education levels among the urban poor.

National Programs and Policies Targeting the Urban Poor

Prior to about 2008–09, there were few policies or programs with an explicit focus on urban development, much less the urban poor. However, following a new decentralized government structure and subnational governance reform with the goals of promoting local development and reducing poverty, a number of urban planning initiatives have been under development—though yet to be realized (table A.1).

Table A.1   Urban Planning Initiatives under Development in Cambodia

	Objectives	Results
Rectangular Strategy Phase III 2014-2018[a]	The government's socioeconomic policy agenda with a national target of 1 percent poverty reduction per year	Priority areas: Developing human resources to ensure competitiveness in an increasingly open regional labor market; investing in transportation infrastructure; improving trade facilitation; expanding low-cost energy; developing and increasing value-added agriculture; and strengthening governance and capacity in public institutions
National Strategic Development Plan 2014–2018[a]	Implementation plan for RS III; includes urban-specific components	Preparation of a draft law on Land Management and Urban Planning as well as Master Plan for Urban Infrastructure Development
Urban Poverty Development Fund[b]	Product of collaboration between community leaders, nongovernmental organizations (NGOs) and the Asian Coalition for Housing Rights. Established a revolving fund and savings groups to provide loans to poor communities for housing, land, and income-generation activities.	In 2009 UPDF was supporting 2,000 savings groups in 26 cities with more than US$2 million disbursed in loans to the urban poor.

a. ADB 2012a.
b. ACCA 2014.

China

The scale of urbanization in China is unprecedented, with 100 million new residents in cities in the past decade alone (World Bank and the Development Research Center of the State Council, the People's Republic of China 2014). Urban spatial expansion to accommodate growing populations resulted in an increase of urban land from 66,000 square kilometers in 2000, to 89,000 square kilometers in 2010. For perspective, the amount of new urban land development in China over a decade is more than double the total urban land in Indonesia (the country with the next most-urban development in the region) (World Bank 2015a).

Government oversight and direction have allowed China to avoid many of the pitfalls commonly associated with rapid urbanization, namely widespread unemployment and poverty. In fact, during the past 30 years, an estimated 500 million people have risen out of poverty thanks to economic opportunities found in cities. Nevertheless, inequality has grown due in large part to the incomplete integration of rural-urban migrants. With urbanization projected to reach 70 percent by 2030 (with an estimated 1 billion people living in cities), policies to promote more balanced and inclusive urbanization will become essential to both sustaining and expanding the gains already made in poverty reduction (World Bank and the Development Research Center of the State Council 2014).

Who Are the Urban Poor?

Rural-urban migrants. China's cities are home to an estimated 234 million rural-urban migrants, who typically work in construction, manufacturing, or service-sector jobs, and live in dorms or rent low-cost, substandard housing.

Migrants often hold rural *hukou* (China's system of household registration), leaving them without access to local public-sector services including education, healthcare, and childcare. In 2014, 53.7 percent of China's population lived in cities, but only 36 percent had urban hukou.

Unemployed and laid-off workers. While the official numbers for registered unemployed in cities has remained at 4 percent, this figure excludes workers who are still "attached" to state-owned employers but do not work or receive a salary. According to the *China Workforce Statistic Yearbook*, there are more than 30 million cumulative laid-off workers. A lack of transferable skills results in large numbers of these workers remaining unemployed and economically vulnerable.

Displaced farmers. During the past 20 years, the use of farmland for urban development has left some 53 million farmers without land and their farm-based livelihoods. The combination of low compensation, limited alternative employment opportunities, and the increasing cost of living in cities has contributed to widespread social unrest (World Bank and the Development Research Center of the State Council 2014).

Nonfarmer urban residents have also seen the transformation of their rural communities into urban land and often suffer from relocation or displacement. For example, the development of 4.3 million m^2 in just three years in the city of Chengdu affected more than 30,000 households, with 20 percent of the resettled residents reporting damage and suffering caused by their relocation (GHK Ltd. 2004).

Low-income university graduates are an urban demographic, estimated at more than 3 million people, that is widely referred to using the term "ant tribe" in reference to their cramped living quarters and underemployment in poverty-level work, despite their intelligence and university training. Originally found in Beijing and Shanghai, the "ant tribe" has now spread to other major cities including Chongqing, Guangzhou, Taiyuan, Wuhan, Xi'an, and Zhengzhou, with their numbers increasing annually by 200,000–300,000 (Zhang 2013).

Urban Villages and Urban Housing

The term "slum" itself is not used in official documents or by the Chinese media to describe domestic housing developments. Instead, substandard housing in China is referred to as "urban villages," "dilapidated housing," or "shantytowns." With one-quarter of its urban residents living in urban villages or substandard housing, China is home to the largest urban village population in the world. According to modeled UN data, the population was 191 million in 2014, up from 131 million in 1990.[1] Given the sheer scale of urbanization in China, though the proportion of the population living in urban villages is declining, absolute numbers have continued to rise.

Urban villages or *chengzhongcun* (literally "village in the city") are directly linked to the dual urban-rural land market. As cities expanded, local governments developed modern infrastructure and buildings on agricultural land acquired from rural collectives. However, acquiring the associated rural residential properties and relocating households proved difficult and expensive, so these collective villages were often left out of urban master plans. As a result, high-rises and skyscrapers in city centers, or high-end gated villa communities in the suburbs were built around these villages. The villages themselves are governed by village committee and are not accountable to the development or management control of municipal authorities.

Dilapidated housing is a general term to describe old and dilapidated settlements. Cities across China use various criteria to categorize dilapidated hosing within their municipal boundaries including the year when the structure was built, the quality of structure evaluated by designated agencies, the location of structure in flood-prone urban areas, and so on.

Shantytowns are generally settlements constructed by state-owned industries during the planned economy era. At present, they are located in either resource-exhausted cities or stand-alone industrial communities and comprised of the following: i) medium- to large-scale clusters of low-rise, highly dense, and dilapidated housing in mature urban districts; and ii) dilapidated settlements located in old, state-owned factories, mines, farms, logging areas, and so on (Jia 2016).

The infrastructure and service delivery available to residents of substandard housing are often lacking, and households are subject to poor sanitation, water supply, ventilation, drainage, and waste management conditions. Overcrowded living conditions also have negative impacts on the health and safety of low-income urban residents. Despite their many shortcomings, urban villages and shantytowns play critical roles in both the formal and informal urban economy by housing the many thousands of rural-urban migrants who comprise the labor force for the construction, manufacturing, and service sectors driving economic growth and development. In addition to affordable housing, residents of these settlements provide informal services such as boxed lunch cooking, transportation, domestic help, waste collecting, sorting, and recycling that help to keep cost-of-living manageable throughout the city.

Urban Villages and Rental Markets in Cities

Renting housing in urban villages has proven a valuable source of income for residents who are no longer able to farm after the acquisition of their agricultural lands for urban development. A common phenomenon in major cities across China, residents of urban villages have subdivided residential buildings to rent to migrants looking for affordable housing in close proximity to job opportunities.

To maximize rental income, residents have rebuilt and expanded houses, in some cases up to eight stories high. As these settlements are outside the jurisdiction of municipal authorities, the design and construction of buildings are not constrained by the application, inspection, and approval procedures for building height, floor-area-ratio, width of corridors, stairways and exit, public space and public safety (Song and Zenou 2012). This scenario has resulted in the development of high-density neighborhoods that are inadequately served by public utilities and often lacking in basic facilities.

Government authorities have identified the need to increase affordable rental housing, however housing policy is largely focused on building and selling new housing units. This option is not viable for migrants who lack urban hukou as well as the income necessary to support such a purchase. About half of China's 200 million migrants are estimated to live in 50,000 urban and suburban villages across the country (World Bank and the Development Research Center of the State Council 2014). For example:

- A survey conducted in 2008, with support from the Beijing Municipal Land Authority, identified 867 urban villages in the Beijing municipal area, mostly located in suburban districts, occupying 18.7 percent of the municipal territory and 49.5 percent of total residential land (Zheng et al. 2009).
- In Guangzhou, an estimated 138 urban villages covering about 20 percent of the municipality, house around 70 percent of migrants and 40 percent of the total urban population (Lin and De Meulder 2012).
- In Shenzhen, urban villages occupy roughly 4 percent of the city's actual land, but are home to an estimated 50 percent of its population (World Bank and the Development Research Center of the State Council 2014).

National Programs and Policies Targeting the Urban Poor

The urban hukou system was historically a barrier to delivering social services and program to the urban poor. In 2014, a National New-Type Urbanization Plan was put forth with concrete targets for rural-urban residency reform, which will include a full system of social security for migrants.

China also has a long history of upgrading substandard housing development; shantytown upgrading projects have been implemented in major cities for nearly 20 years. Since 2008, shantytown upgrading programs have become part of the national agenda and have been adopted by every province in China. However, decentralization has led to uneven funding and application of upgrading policies. While recent redevelopment projects have prioritized the in-situ resettlement of original residents and emphasized fair compensation, the knock-down-and-rebuild redevelopment approach is also commonly used (Jia 2016). Table A.2, below, details urban planning initiatives.

Table A.2   **Urban Planning Initiatives in China**

	Objectives	Results
Urban Dibao Program[a]	Piloted in 1993 and expanded to all cities by 1999, the Urban Dibao Program provides regular cash and in-kind transfers to poor households based on local poverty lines. Initially intended to support laid-off workers following the reform of state-owned enterprises, the program now focuses its support for the elderly living in poverty and the working poor. Benefits extend only to registered residents, thereby excluding migrants.	In 2012, Urban Dibao covered 23.12 million beneficiaries, accounting for 3 percent of the total urban population.
National New-Type Urbanization Plan (2014–20)[b]	With the overarching goal of increasing the urban population ratio to 60 percent, this plan includes measures to formally recognize migrants by reforming hukou. Restrictions will be lifted gradually in cities with populations < 1 million, loosened for 1 to 3 million, allow for limited registration for 3 to 5 million, and strictly controlled in megacities.	Target of school enrolment rate for children of migrant workers at 99 percent by 2020; free vocational training for migrant workers, unemployed, and urban poor; and 23 percent coverage of affordable housing for urban residents.
Urban Resident Basic Medical Insurance (URBMI)[c]	Launched nationwide in 2009, this voluntary health insurance program covers beneficiaries who do not qualify or receive insurance through employers in the formal sector. The program specifically targets students, children, the elderly, unemployed, and informal workers.	Insurance coverage for urban populations not covered by employers has grown from 12.4 percent in 2000 to 51.3 percent in 2010.
Social Housing Subsidies[a]	A comprehensive rural and urban program that includes low-cost rental housing, assisted home ownership, public rental housing, and shelter improvements. Fiscal support for the program has increased from RMB 10 billion in 2007 to RMB 380 billion in 2012. The 12th Five-Year Plan targets 35 million units of social housing, bringing total coverage to 20 percent of households.	By 2012, the program met the housing needs of 31 million urban households (12.5 percent of total urban households), with an additional 5 million urban households receiving rental subsidies.
Shantytowns Upgrading (State Council, 2013)[b]	Shantytown upgrading in 2013–17, (about 10 million households in total), including about 8 million households in urban districts, 900,000 in standalone state-owned factories and mines, 300,000 in state-owned logging, and 800,000 in state-owned farms.	The 2016 State Council memo on "Further Strengthening Urban Planning and Management" included the goal of completing nationwide shantytown upgrading in three years.

a. World Bank and the Development Research Center of the State Council, the People's Republic of China 2014.
b. Jia 2016.
c. Giles et al. 2013.

Indonesia

Key Development Statistics

Population: 254.5 million   GDP per capita: US$3,491.90

Urbanization Rate

Urban population density: 9,400   Urban population growth: 3.5 percent
(people/ square kilometer)

Rural-Urban Statistics

Urban population: 53 percent   Rural population: 47 percent
(134.87 million)   (119.57 million)
8.3 percent of the urban population 14.2 percent of rural population live
live in poverty   in poverty

Largest Urban Areas

Jakarta: 8.5 million   Bandung: 6.9 million   Surbaya: 6.1 million
Sources: WDI 2014; World Bank 2015a.

Indonesia ranked among the top 10 fastest urbanizing countries in the world during 1990–2014, and has the second-largest urban population in East Asia after China. Over the past decade, Indonesia has seen an average growth rate of 5.4 percent, which has bolstered its status as a middle-income country and nearly halved poverty from 24 percent in 1999, to 11.3 percent in 2014. Nearly 21 million of the 23.8 million new jobs created between 2001 and 2014 were in the service sector, predominantly in urban areas (World Bank 2015c). However, despite sustained growth, the pace of poverty reduction has slowed in recent years, with the number of poor people decreasing by only 2 percent per year since 2002. Inequality, on the other hand, is noticeably on the rise, with Indonesia's Gini coefficient increasing from 0.30 in 2000, to 0.41 in 2014. Some 28 million Indonesians live below the poverty line (IDR330,776 or US$22.6 per month), while 40 percent of the total population is clustered around the line and vulnerable to falling into poverty in the event of economic shocks (World Bank 2015b). Sustained levels of high inequality are not only socially and politically destabilizing, but threaten future economic growth as poorer populations struggle to move into the middle/consumer class, find productive work, and invest in future generations.

Who Are the Urban Poor?

The World Bank estimates indicate that 36 percent of Indonesians living in poverty (over 10 million people) live in urban areas, with the number of urban poor projected to surpass that of rural poor by 2030. The urban poor are concentrated in the Java and Sumatra provinces, and as in other countries, are characterized by low education levels, low-skill and

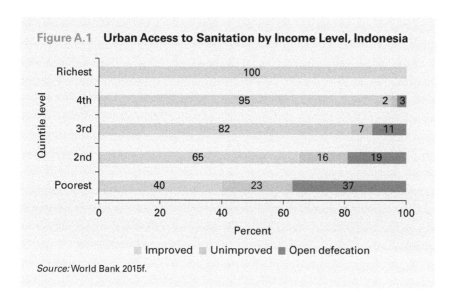

Figure A.1   **Urban Access to Sanitation by Income Level, Indonesia**

Source: World Bank 2015f.

low-wage labor or informal sector jobs, insecure housing, and limited access to infrastructure and services.

Only 42 percent of urban households have access to a public water supply network and barely one-third have a household connection to the public utility company. The urban poor in Indonesia pay at least 10 to 30 times more to buy clean water from private providers, compared with the prices paid by wealthier households for water from water utilities (World Bank 2016c). In addition, 28 percent of urban Indonesians do not have access to improved sanitation facilities and 13 percent still practice open defecation (World Bank 2016b). The inequality of access to basic services is especially apparent when compared across income levels. Access to piped water supply for the poorest quintile is 9 percent and improved sanitation facilities is 36 percent, as compared to 50 percent and 100 percent, respectively, for the richest quintile (World Bank 2015bf) (figure A.1).

Slums and Urban Resilience

The most visible manifestations of urban poverty are slums, which house an estimated 22 percent of Indonesia's urban population, or approximately 29 million people. Indonesia's cities, built around waterways and coastlines, are prone to a number of natural disasters including floods, landslides, fires, and droughts. In addition, in coastal areas, seawater rise has the potential to exacerbate flooding and coastal erosion, leading to damage to structures as well as causing salt intrusion in groundwater or river water supplies. Within cities, densely populated slums tend not only to be located in areas vulnerable to natural disaster, but also lack the infrastructure and capacity to respond to and recover from increasingly frequent disasters. Indeed, about 30 percent of roads and 50 percent of drainage networks within slums are considered to be in poor condition (World Bank 2016c) (box A.1).

Box A.1   **Urban Risk Profile, Balikpapan, Indonesia**

The resource-rich seaport city of Balikpapan, located in East Kalimantan Province, is a hub for fishing and tourism. With a population of 557,579 and growth rate of 1.32 percent, this medium-sized city is seeing industrial and urban development on reclaimed wetlands. Balikpapan has a poverty rate of 4.7 percent and an estimated 6,022 households live in slums.

Slums concentrated along the west coast (Balikpapan Bay) and south coast (Makassar Strait) account for 61.12 percent of all slum areas in the city. These communities, which include floating slums, are at risk of water inundation from rising sea levels. Slums have also developed in the hilly and river basin areas of the city, which are vulnerable to landslides and flooding respectively, particularly during the rainy season. Overcrowding has contributed to a growing number of fires, with emergency response times averaging 30–45 minutes.

Infrastructure investments are necessary for slum communities to develop resiliency to natural disasters, especially in the context of climate change. Priority areas for investment include the following: (i) seawalls to protect vulnerable coastal areas, and (ii) fire response paths to ensure easy emergency access and evacuation.

Source: World Bank 2016b.

Jobs and Informal Labor

Since 2002, the majority of employment growth has occurred in urban areas, primarily in the service sector which saw the creation of 19.5 million new jobs. Jobs in the service sector, however, tend to require low-skill labor and remain vulnerable to economic shocks. Wholesale, trade, hotel and restaurant—the lowest-productivity industries within the service sector—employ 21 percent of total workers. Among these workers, fewer than 10 percent have a tertiary level of education and more than 60 percent have no formal contracts (World Bank 2015c). So while economic growth and job creation have helped to reduce poverty, informality and the poor quality of jobs are preventing a large segment of the population from achieving economic security (box A.2).

National Programs and Policies Targeting the Urban Poor

There are a number of longstanding government programs aimed at providing social assistance to the poor. The two largest programs are *Raskin* (rice subsidy) and *Jamkesmas* (healthcare), which are implemented nationally. The effectiveness of these programs is diluted both from distribution losses and "leakage" or mistargeted subsidy delivery. For example, Raskin is meant to provide food support to 15 million poor households. In urban areas, Raskin coverage extends to 70 percent of households in the first income quintile (poor and near poor). However, about 60 percent of the total subsided rice goes to families that are neither poor or near poor

(World Bank 2012a). In addition, losses sustained during the distribution process from central procurement to communities, leave households with an average subsidy of 5–6 kg, when monthly consumption averages 50 kg. (World Bank 2015c). Consequently, this program does not sufficiently support vulnerable populations or provide adequate protection from food price shocks.

Infrastructure programs targeting the urban poor are delivered primarily through PNPM Urban, a national program aiming to improve local governance and service delivery. PNPM Urban follows a community-driven development approach and provides block grants directly to poor communities for small-scale infrastructure projects. The program is successful in engaging local communities and delivering infrastructure improvements. However, given the limited scale of the projects, there is still room for local governments to provide more coordinated service delivery and upgrading of slums and informal settlements (table A.3).

Box A.2   Perspectives on Poverty and Finding Jobs in Indonesia

"[Poverty] is increasing now because the job availability is different than before. Now it is difficult finding a livelihood and job." (man, Astana).

"It is the economic sector, since there are many jobless people in this RW and they live in a dirty area…In RW 3 there are many jobless people and unskilled laborers." (man, Jakarta Barat)

"There are a lot of young people here who do not know where to channel their ideas. Hence things like [getting] drunk and fighting which are negative… it is rare here for youth to have high school education. Most of them only get the first elementary school and get unemployed." (woman, Cirebon)

"Even with a bachelor's degree, you still have difficulty getting a job. (woman, Cengkareng, Timur)

Source: World Bank 2012a.

Table A.3   Urban Planning Initiatives in Indonesia

	Objectives	Results
BSM (Beasiswa Untuk Seswa Miskin)	Cash transfers to low-income students in public secular schools	2010 target: 2.77 million elementary, 1 million junior secondary, and 750,000 in senior secondary and vocational school
Hibah Water And Sanitation	Provides incentives for local governments and water utilities to install new household water connections, focusing on low-income households. Also includes sewerage/sanitation component.	Scaled up to reach 1.2 million households

(Table continues on next page)

Table A.3   Urban Planning Initiatives in Indonesia *(continued)*

	Objectives	Results
Jamkesmas	Health cards are distributed based on need. Cards entitle holders to free health services in health centers and hospitals.	Health service fee waivers for 18.2 million households
Neighborhood Upgrading and Shelter Sector Project (NUSSP)	ADB-funded project to support slum upgrading using a community-driven development model	Improved shelter for about 800,000 households or 3.1 million people from 2005–10
PKH (Program Keluarga Harapan)	Conditional cash transfer program for very poor households with children, contingent on mother attending pre- and post-natal health checkups, uses professional medical service during childbirth and for check-ups for young children, and enrolls older children in school	816,000 households in 2010
PNPM Urban	Small-scale, community-driven development focusing on infrastructure as well as credit for small or microenterprises and social protections	Financed more than 31,100 km of small roads, 8,800 km of drainage, rehabilitation of 126,800 houses, 164,800 units of solid waste and sanitation facilities, and 9,450 health facilities.
Raskin (Beras Untuk Orang Miskin)	Targeted rice subsidy for poorest rural and urban households	2010 target: 17.5 million households
Sanimas	Assist local governments and urban communities with planning, implementing, and maintaining community sanitation systems.	
Slum Alleviation Policy And Action Plan (SAPOLA)	Supports development of a national slum upgrading action plan focusing on enabling local governments to improving living conditions in slums	

Source: World Bank 2013.

Mongolia

Key Development Statistics

Population: 2.9 million

GDP per capita: US$4,129.40

Urbanization Rate

Urban population density: 3,400
(persons/ square kilometer)

Urban population growth:
2.8 percent

Rural-Urban Statistics

Urban population: 71.2 percent
(2.07 million)
Urban poverty headcount: 18.8 percent
Urban population in slums: 42.7 percent

Rural population: 28.8 percent
(837,403)
Rural poverty headcount:
26.4 percent

Largest Urban Areas

Ulaanbaatar: 1.38 million

Darkhan: 180,000

Sources: WDI 2014; World Bank 2015a.

Relative to other East Asian countries, Mongolia has among the least total area of urban lands, with 270 square kilometers in 2010. Urban development has been concentrated almost entirely in the capitol city of Ulaanbaatar, which is home to nearly half of Mongolia's population. Mongolia's urbanization has been shaped by two factors: rural-urban migration, and current land administration policies. Migration patterns are two-fold: economic opportunities and better access to education and health services in Ulaanbaatar create a pull-factor for rural households; while extended *dzud* conditions (summer drought followed by severe winter weather) lead to loss of crops and livestock, further simultaneously pushing migrants towards the city. The land administration policies are such that all registered citizens receive a plot of land, contributing to the growth of *ger* areas, or areas with detached housing rather than apartment units. This process has huge implications for the urban development patterns seen in Ulaanbaatar, which has thus far been low-density and sprawling.

Who Are the Urban Poor?

Ulaanbaatar is home to approximately 33 percent of Mongolia's poor population, with approximately 16 percent of the city's households living below the poverty line. The city has a higher proportion of poor than any other subnational administrative location type. Inequality levels in Ulaanbaatar have remained high, with a Gini coefficient steadfast at 0.33 between 2010–14. Key determinants of income poverty include residential location, employment status, and educational attainment, with poverty highest among households living in gers, with unemployed and less-educated heads of household.

It is notable that migration status is not a determinant of poverty when controlling for age, gender, education status, employment —status, and residential location. However, given that a majority of migrants live in ger districts, they experience poor service delivery and infrastructure, which contributes to a higher incidence of multidimensional poverty. In addition, they face difficulties in registering their urban residency to acquire land. Among migrant households, 60 percent are multidimensional poor, compared with 48 percent of nonmigrant households.

Gers and Urban Housing

The city classifies Ger areas by three zones—central, mid-tier (middle), and fringe—for future developments in terms of their locations, connectivity to engineering networks, and housing types. Within the official classification, the definitions are as follows:

- Central ger areas are those where a connection for centralized engineering networks is feasible and will be redeveloped with high-rise and mid-rise buildings.
- Mid-tier ger areas are planned for redeveloping with low-rise and mid-rise buildings and connected to partial engineering networks.
- Redevelopment for fringe ger areas is planned in phases via land readjustment schemes with onsite networks.
- "Non-ger areas" typically contain apartment buildings with scatterings of plots with single houses and ger structures.

There is a clear spatial dimension to the distribution of urban poor in Ulaanbaatar across its districts and *khoroos*. Approximately 38 percent of people living in ger residences are poor, compared with less than 1 percent of those living in apartments. Poor households seem to be evenly spread out across the three classifications of ger areas rather than being concentrated in the fringe areas, contrary to the accepted narrative in Ulaanbaatar. This narrative equates urban poverty with migrant status.

A contributing factor to poverty is the spatial inequality in service delivery, particularly within ger areas. Nearly 100 percent of apartment dwellers (the majority of whom are close to the city center) have flush toilets, while most ger dwellers use unimproved sanitation facilities (including open pit latrines and open defecation). In addition, World Bank surveys have found that only 19 percent of households in the lowest income quintile have piped water, compared with more than half of those in the highest quintile. Households in the lowest quintile are more dependent on water delivery to kiosks via trucks. Kiosks served by trucks are known to face severe water shortages during winter and rainy months when the heavy vehicles cannot access the areas in the steeper topography, particularly in fringe ger areas that lack proper roads.

National Programs and Policies Targeting the Urban Poor

In 2013, Mongolia spent 2.78 percent of GDP on welfare transfers, making it one of the few countries in the region that spent a relatively generous amount of social transfers. The government has maintained a poverty-targeting method that has registered about 90 percent of all households in the country. The programs are fragmented, with 71 programs administered through a variety of ministries. Nearly half of all citizens are the direct beneficiaries of at least one program. Social welfare programs do not specifically target urban areas, but rather vulnerable populations or groups that the government deems vulnerable or deserving (elderly, disabled, orphans, pregnant mothers, veterans with state honor, and so on) throughout the country (table A.4).

Table A.4 **Urban Planning Initiatives in Mongolia**

	Objectives	Results
National Development Strategy 2007–2021	Overarching goal of increasing welfare and reducing poverty through accelerated development and sustained economic growth	Urban policies include: Prioritize urbanization to (provinces) to reduce pressure on Ulaanbaatar; Equitable distribution of urban services between formal and nonformal areas
40,000 Houses Program	Government funding for subsidized mortgages and for the construction of apartments	10,115 mortgages and construction of 8,900 apartments representing 25 and 30 percent of total loan origination and unit construction respectively from 2007–11
Food Stamp Program	A group of government programs that targets the bottom 5 percent of households (the only current social assistance program that currently targets poverty)	Provides MNT 10,000 (US$5) per adults and MNT 5,000 (US$3) per month per child

Source: World Bank forthcoming.

Myanmar

Key Development Statistics

Population: 53.44 million   GDP per capita: US$1,203.80

Urbanization Statistics

Urban population density: 7,500   Urban population growth:
(people/square kilometer)   2.5 percent

Rural-Urban Statistics

Urban population: 33.6 percent   Rural population: 66.4 percent
(17.93 million)   (35.51 million)
34.6 percent of the urban population   An estimated 70 percent of the
live in poverty   nation's poor live in rural areas.

Largest Urban Areas

Yangon: 5.21 million, 34 percent   Mandalay: 1.225 million,
poverty rate   33 percent poverty rate

Sources: WDI 2014; UNSD Demographic Statistics; World Bank 2014b.

Myanmar is one of the least developed countries in the region, due to a legacy of isolation under military rule and economic sanctions. With the launch of major political and economic reform in 2011, however, Myanmar has the potential to capitalize on its rich natural resources and favorable geography adjacent two large markets, China and India. Urbanization is still at a nascent stage, however, with limited urban build-up from 2000 to 2010. Urban lands cover just 0.1 percent of the area of Myanmar (World Bank 2015a). Though it has no large urban centers by East Asian standards, Myanmar's biggest city, Yangon, has seen its population grow rapidly from 3.4 million in 2010, to 5.21 million in 2014.

Who Are the Urban Poor?

While poverty remains largely concentrated in rural areas (roughly 70 percent), the cities of Yangon and Mandalay display surprisingly high poverty rates at 34 percent and 33 percent, respectively (World Bank 2014a). An inequality analysis shows a higher Gini coefficient in urban areas than in rural areas or the country at large (figure A.2). UN Habitat estimates that 46.5 percent of all urban populations live in informal settlements or slums.[2] While these settlements are not comparable in size or scope to the over-crowded slums found in megacities throughout the region, they nonetheless share characteristics of poor infrastructure and service delivery, limited mobility, and insecure land tenure.

Public infrastructure for the delivery of basic services such as water and electricity has suffered from years of underinvestment. As an

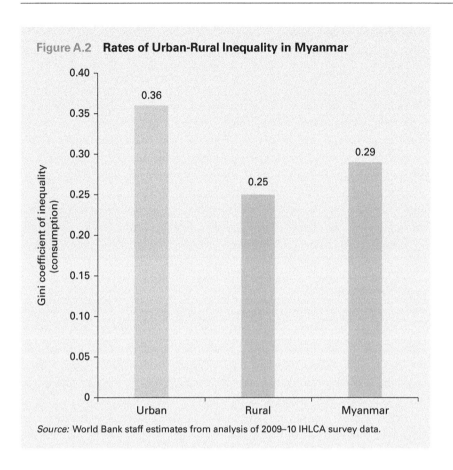

Figure A.2   **Rates of Urban-Rural Inequality in Myanmar**

Source: World Bank staff estimates from analysis of 2009–10 IHLCA survey data.

example, Mandalay's main water system was built in the 1990s, and though the pumping station is functional, the water it provides is untreated and supplied only intermittently. Furthermore, water is supplied to only one part of the city core, making it unlikely that coverage extends to the urban poor in informal settlements (ADB 2015). Survey data show that within urban areas, 93 percent of the population has access to improved water supply and 84 percent to improved sanitation facilities (WHO/ UNICEF Joint Monitoring Programme 2015). Comparisons with comparable countries in the region, however, show that while water and sanitation figures are similar to those of Thailand, the infant mortality rate is more in line with that of Cambodia. Furthermore, township data indicate that diarrhea is still a major killer of children under the age of five (World Bank 2014b). Both statistics are inconsistent with reported coverage for improved sanitation and call into question the reliability of official data and information available regarding the urban poor.

Jobs and Informal Labor

Urban poverty is further compounded by the rising cost of living, and limited access to stable and well-paid jobs. The "depth and severity" of urban poverty is relatively low, with many households clustered near or just below the poverty line, indicating that poverty might quickly decline with expanded economic growth and employment opportunities. However, economic growth has been driven by capital-intensive resource extraction, primarily of natural gas, rather than more labor-intensive sectors. These types of industries attract the majority of foreign direct investment (FDI) and are encouraged by a cash-strapped government. With a limited number of labor-intensive sectors outside of agriculture, the urban poor are left to find informal work and the majority are employed as casual laborers in construction or other service industries, including restaurants and tea shops (World Bank 2014b).

Rural-Urban Migration

Labor and mobility patterns among the landless and rural poor are changing due to urbanization, and an increasing number are seeking work in urban areas, namely Yangon and Mandalay. Though there are limited data on national migration trends, a regional survey shows internal migration from about one in four households from the Ayeyarwady region and one in five households from the Magway region (World Bank 2016a). On the whole, economic opportunity is the driving force behind migration, with regional variations on the type of work sought (seasonal or permanent). Migrants tend to be male, better educated than their peers, and strikingly young, as seen in table A.5. Many of the households sending members to the city exist at subsistence levels, and migrants cannot afford to move without guaranteed employment. In particular, female migrants rely on networks of villagers who have already migrated to secure employment and lodging prior to moving. Despite such measures, distance from family and community support networks still leave young migrants vulnerable to abuse and exploitation (box A.3).

Table A.5 Composition of Migrants by Gender and Age in Myanmar

	Age: 11–20		Age: 21–30		Age: 31–50	
	Male (%)	Female (%)	Male (%)	Female (%)	Male (%)	Female (%)
Ayeyarwady	49.30	60.80	34.30	28.40	16.40	10.80
Magway	43.40	38.80	35.50	45.50	21.20	15.70

Source: World Bank 2016a.

Box A.3   **Increased Vulnerability among Youth in Myanmar**

While seeking to understand higher rates of new sexually-transmitted disease (STD) cases among youths under the age of 19, a team from the government of Mongolia and UNFPA visited a brothel in the slum area of a township in Ayeyarwady Division. The following notes are from the visit:

> We interviewed three sex workers who were 17 to 19 years of age. All were migrants from other towns. The three girls started working at the brothel two months ago. When asked how and why they chose to do this work, one 17-year-old said that she lived in a village hit by Cyclone Nargis. She lost both parents and her remaining family struggled for survival. When a lady came to her village and promised her a job in the city she followed her and was brought to the brothel. The second girl said that because both her parents were divorced and both remarried, she was brought up by her elderly and impoverished grandmother. Life was tough and survival was difficult, so she was forced to resort to sex work to live. The third girl was from a suburban area of Yangon. She reported that she started sex work because her family had economic problems and could not survive. One of the sex workers never attended school, and the other two attended only up to primary school.

> At this particular brothel, they received only 500 kyats (about US$0.50 per client), and provide services for 5–10 clients per day. All three respondents said that they use condoms consistently and are able to obtain condoms from their pimp, but the girls had no knowledge about HIV/AIDS and STIs whatsoever. All three expressed a desire to quit sex work if they had alternative livelihood options.

Source: UNFPA 2010.

Policies and Programs Targeting the Poor

Public spending on social assistance and other programs targeting the poor is low (0.57 percent of GDP), and coverage of the main government programs extends to only 3.25 percent of the population (Infante Villarroel 2015a). Furthermore, its largest programs provide social security assistance to formal workers and government employees, almost certainly excluding the vast majority of the urban poor. Reform and development frameworks, such as the Framework for Economic and Social Reform (FESR) or the Social Protection Strategic Plan (SPSP), are being developed by the national government and across different ministries. However, roles and responsibilities for the administration of new programs are still being defined (table A.6).

Enrollment in several social programs is predicated on possessing a national identification card. While all citizens over the age of 10 are entitled to the card, only 69.3 percent of eligible citizens have one, and coverage is particularly low among poor and vulnerable groups including urban migrants (Infante Villarroel 2015b). Furthermore, when assistance is available for the urban poor, administrators have trouble identifying target populations. For example, when a pilot child health and maternal voucher scheme was applied in urban areas, there was a stigma associated with poverty, and the vouchers were underutilized. Administrators had trouble identifying poor women in the middle of the income distribution (Dutta and Okamura 2015).

Table A.6   Urban Planning Initiatives in Myanmar

	Objectives	Results
National Electrification Plan[a]	Goal of achieving universal electricity access by 2030	
Essential Health Services Access Project[b]	Increase coverage of essential health services of adequate quality, with a focus on maternal, newborn and child health	
National Community-Driven Development Projects (2010)[c]	Improve access to basic services and essential infrastructure for an estimated 7 million people across 62 Myanmar townships. Received additional $400 million in 2015 to scale up program. Targets rural villages.	Goal: Expand services to 7 million people
Pilot School Grants Program (2014)[b]	Expands national funding for schools and provides stipends and financial support for 100,000 poor students.	
Maternal and child health voucher scheme[b]	Provision of food and supplements for pregnant women and fortified foods for children.	Piloted in one township with 1,346 beneficiaries
Livelihoods and Food Security Trust Fund (LIFT) (2009)[d]	30 partners implementing 58 project encompassing social protection CFW, microfinance, and so on; target is rural poverty.	Administered $206 million to 130 programs across 170 townships Estimated reach: 3 million people

a. ABD 2015.
b. Infante Villarroel 2015a.
c. Infante Villarroel 2015b.
d. www.lift-fund.org.

Papua New Guinea

Key Development Statistics

Population: 7.5 million

Urban poverty headcount ratio: 39.9 percent

GDP per capita: US$2,088.35

Per capita annual growth: 6.3 percent

Urbanization Rate

Urbanization rate: 4.5 percent

Urban population growth: 2.1 percent

Rural-Urban Statistics

Urban population: 13 percent (0.97 million)

11.2 percent of the urban population lives in poverty

Rural population: 87 percent (6.49 million)

Largest Urban Areas

Port Moresby: 0.32 million, 5.9 percent poverty rate

Lae: 0.12 million

Slum Population

Urban areas: 19 percent (1.65 million)

Port Moresby: 45 percent (0.7 million)

Sources: WDI 2009 and 2014; PNG HEIS 2009/10; UN-Habitat 2001, 2010.

Papua New Guinea (PNG) is the world's most diverse country, with more than 800 languages and many indigenous communities. The country is 462,860 square kilometers in area and about 78 percent is classified as forest. Much of the spatial growth is occurring in mountain highlands, coastal lowlands, and islands. It is considered a lower-middle-income country with a GDP at market rate of US$16.93 billion.

Over the past few decades the PNG urban population has been growing steadily. By 2030, the annual growth rate will be at 2.1 percent, triple the average for the region in 2014 (figure A.3),[3] and about 20 percent of PNG's population will reside in urban areas.[4] A percentage share of the urban population has been underestimated as the census does not factor growth in peri-urban areas and some urban centers are not yet classified. The high urbanization rate has been a result of the increased mobility in and around cities after colonialism ended in 1975. In comparison with rural areas, in 2000, 70 percent of urban migrants had moved between provinces and 17 percent between districts within their provinces of birth. This latter number is significantly lower than the 41 percent of rural migrants that moved.[5] Many migrate to the capital, Port Moresby, which is more than twice the population of the second largest city, Lae. A little more than 400,000 people,

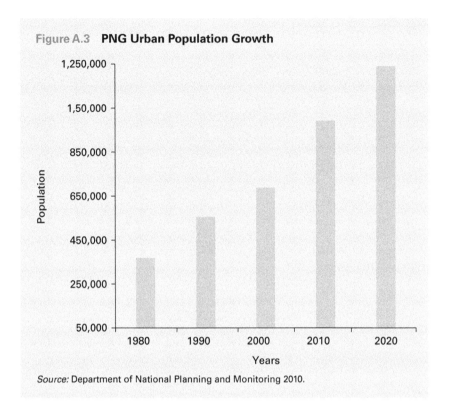

Figure A.3   **PNG Urban Population Growth**

Source: Department of National Planning and Monitoring 2010.

or 7 percent (UN Habitat 2010) of the national population, reside in Port Moresby; it is the key center for government, economic activity, and education.

Port Moresby has received significant investments in development and infrastructure to target economic growth. PNGeans are attracted to the city center in search of better service provision and opportunities. There are ongoing transportation-specific improvements being made, however, there is no direct road connection from the capitol to the provinces, and many villages in the highlands are only accessible by air or foot. Hence, once rural residents move to Port Moresby, there are few who have the capabilities to return home. Another factor leading to its growth as national capital was the influx of migration away from Rabaul in East New Britain in the 1980s and early 1990s as a result of volcanic activity. Rabaul was once one of the most important urban settlements and home to over 17,000 PNGeans in 1990, but after the destruction from the 1994 eruption, the population was reduced to 3,000 and the city's functions moved to Port Moresby. This change contributed to the capital's swift growth. However, this urbanization is occurring rapidly at rates that exceed the supply for housing, land, and economic opportunities for migrants into the city. The urban poor account for one-third of PNG's population. Prosperity and livability in urban areas are low and the capital city, Port Moresby was rated the third worst livable city in the world (EIU 2015).

In comparison to the rest of the East Asia and Pacific (EAP) region, PNG has one of the highest poverty rates, with almost 40 percent of the population living below the poverty line. The ADB characterizes it as "poverty of opportunity," in a reference to the lack of access to education, health services, and income-earning opportunities (ADB 2016). Hence, poverty trends are characterized by the high inequality levels. The country has the 7th most-unequal income distribution in the world, with the richest 20 percent holding over 50 percent of the national income (IMF 2015). A large portion of the poor reside in predominantly rural areas; however, urban poverty has been on the rise, leading to severe challenges. It takes urban residents an average of 12 years to exit from poverty. With the high inequality of the capital, it will take urban residents, on average, 20 years to move above the poverty line (Gobson and Olivia 2002). However, the factors resulting in the rise of the urban poor in the capital have changed over time. Between 1986 and 1996, urban poverty stemmed from rising inequality and deteriorating growth. The incidence of poverty increased in the decades that followed but for an additional reason, namely the proliferation of stagnating incomes and higher prices, with a larger portion of the population continuing to become poorer (Gobson and Olivia 2002). Urban poverty is thus now more widespread and more severe.

Urban Unemployment Is Highest in Port Moresby

With only 2 percent of PNG adults in formal employment in urban areas (Cammack 2008), there is a growing informal sector. The informal sector is an integral contributor to PNG's economy and is a source of income for many urban families. Over 90 percent of PNGeans living in Port Moresby work in the informal economy, mostly selling betel nut, lime, cigarettes, cooked food, gravel and sand for construction, and handicrafts, and providing services like shoeshines and repairs, and more recently, selling recyclables. The informal economy is their only way to make an income. In an effort to acknowledge the informal sector's importance in boosting PNG's economy, to tap into and facilitate a vibrant economy, and to promote financial inclusion, the government developed the National Informal Economy Policy, 2011–2015. This policy has had some moderate traction, although there is still great stigma attached to the informal marketplace. The government is now formulating other ways to better leverage the economic opportunities provided through informality. In general, the informal and formal economies are difficult to differentiate as families use both to sustain their livelihoods (box A.4).

A high percentage of youth move to urban centers for better opportunities. Young men, in particular, have been affected by the shift in the PNG economy away from traditional occupations of hunting and gathering to new sectors, and are thus forced to leave rural areas. The influx of youth moving into the urban centers has outstripped the job opportunities, and most have no choice but to find work in the informal markets.

Box A.4   **Creating Inclusion for Women in Informal Marketplaces in PNG**

Women compose 80 percent of the market vendors in the capital and many are often targets of violence, especially by police. A UN Women study found that 55 percent of the women and girls who responded had experienced some form of violence in the marketplace, such as physical assault, robbery, sexual harassment, sexual violence, verbal abuse, threats, or intimidation. Until 2004, street vending was illegal, but even now with its legalization and the government's encouragement for a more vibrant informal sector, there are still stigmas attached to vending and, as a result, many women remain vulnerable to violence.

Despite the grave situation that many of these women face, there have been a variety of initiatives being mobilized to advocate for better safety measures in the markets, as follows:

- Port Moresby employed **city rangers**, young men who are stationed in and around marketplaces to implement the Informal Sector Development and Control Act. They work to enforce the protection of the vendors, particularly women and girls, as they conduct their sales.
- The **Yellow Cap Mothers** in Gordon's market are an organized group of women, who speak a range of languages, and advocate for and represent women's rights in the informal settlements. The women have demanded improvements to their environment to reduce their vulnerability and have been working collectively to curb police harassment and extortion.
- As part of the **UN Women: Safe Cities Initiative**, vendors were mobilized to upgrade the Geheru market with features including rehabilitated bathrooms and showers, market stalls and shaded areas, potable running water, and a playground. Mobile pay options were also introduced to reduce the harassment the vendor face during transactions. All these activities have helped create a more inclusionary and safe space for women making a living in this sector.

Source: UN Women 2016.

Attributing to the prevalence of informal work, more than 50,000 youth enter the labor market each year, although only a few thousand new jobs are created (Cammack 2008). Being disconnected from economic opportunities and many lacking education, many of the youth become engaged in criminal activities. In 2004, 36 percent of 1,500 surveyed youth in Port Moresby admitted to having committed an offense for which they could have been arrested (Blank 2008). Young men were most likely to commit a wider diversity of crime activity, and many of these crimes occur as a result of gang involvement. Burglary, petty crimes, carjacking, and assault were the most common among young men; while for young women, the main forms of crime committed were assault and petty crimes (Blank 2008) (figures A.4 and A.5, box A.5).

Land and Housing Markets

In PNG, 97 percent of the land is held under customary ownership and of the rest, 2.5 percent is owned by the state and 0.5 percent under private freehold. The small allowance of alienated land has the best topography and accessibility and is therefore are typically in the urban centers. About 60 percent of the National Capital District (NCD) land is

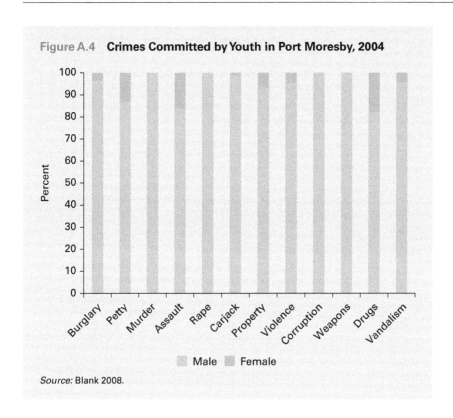

Figure A.4   Crimes Committed by Youth in Port Moresby, 2004

Source: Blank 2008.

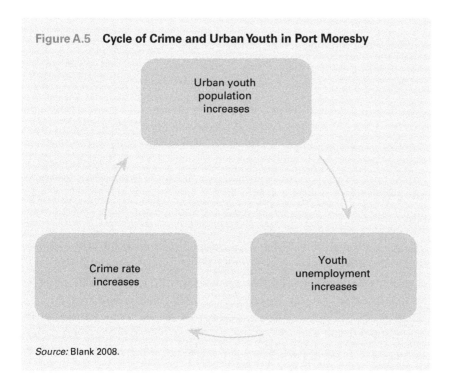

Figure A.5   Cycle of Crime and Urban Youth in Port Moresby

Source: Blank 2008.

Box A.5   How Safe Is It Really? Gangs in the Slums of Papua New Guinea

During the period of independence in the 1970s, there were tremendous waves of migration to urban centers. The pressure of the population change in cities such as Port Moresby and Lae resulted in limited education and employment opportunities, and many migrants were forced into informal settlements. The lack of housing and access to services are particularly prevalent in Port Moresby, where 45 percent of the population lives under these conditions.

Many unemployed youth in cities, young men in particular, lack a sense of inclusion, and limited access to opportunities harbors dissatisfaction and social disorganization. These dynamics drive vulnerable youth towards violence and criminal behavior. The disenfranchised urban poor join what are commonly referred to as "Raskol gangs," and the larger the informal settlement, the greater the gang presence. There is a heightened prevalence of alcohol and drug abuse in the settlements among those without opportunities, and this prevalence fuels violent behavior.

The Raskol gangs operate out of the settlements and command sections of roads in and out of Port Moresby. This scenario is further facilitated by the poor urban planning of the city; there are no roads connecting Port Moresby to other settlements and hence, the gang members find ways to control areas. The motives of the majority of crimes committed include land ownership disputes, money, and inclusion. Weapons are expensive to import and therefore gangs make do with handmade and makeshift weapons including guns, knives, and other sharp materials. There are high incidences of rape and sexual assault as gang initiation. As noted, "One of the leaders of 'Dirty Dons 585' Raskol gang states that raping women is a 'must' for the young members of the gang. In some New Guinean tribes when a boy wants to become a man, he should go to enemy's village and kill a pig. After that his community will accept him as an adult. In industrial Port Moresby women have replaced pigs.'"

The proliferation of crime and gang activity in urban centers, especially Port Moresby, is inextricably linked to urban poverty faced in PNG. Policies and social protection programs targeting the strengthening of formal and informal systems will need to be a high priority to combat the issues of crime and violence in PNG.

Sources: Sokhin 2014; http://www.vladsokhin.com/work/crying-meri/.

classified as alienated, with only 10,000 hectares under customary land tenure.[6] Given the strictly defined predefined arrangements for land use planning in PNG, as well as the high demand for land, terms for land ownership and usage are challenging, leading to the development of unplanned settlements. In the city core (NCD), 79 out of 99 settlements are unplanned,[7] many of which have substandard housing conditions and limited or no access to services.

The government lacks sufficient resources and capacities to plan and allocate for the growing urban population, and this situation has resulted in the development of unplanned underservice settlements. About 45 percent of the settlements in Port Moresby are informal (UN Habitat 2010),[8] a rapid increase from the 19 percent recorded for all urban areas in 2001 (Moreno 2003). Informality has been on the rise due to heightened construction costs and increasing interest rates. More than half of the urban unemployed live in unplanned settlements and substandard conditions (UN Habitat 2010). Land tenure disputes are common, especially on customary land, and residents either have informal arrangements for inhabiting the land, or the government encourages owners to develop the land in a planned way. Regardless, there are pervasive challenges related to land ownership, where disenfranchised landowners are excluded from the process, such as the traditional landowning ethnic minorities—the Ahi in Lae and the Motu Koita in Port Moresby. In addition, the government's land records are poorly maintained or even nonexistent, further muddying land ownership debates. With the lags in the market, there is not necessarily always a shortage of land, although access to adequate infrastructure and services (particularly water, electricity, and sanitation provisions) can be lacking.

A shortage of housing exacerbates the complexity of land arrangements in PNG. In 2000, about 90 percent of PNGeans owned their homes,[9] albeit many of substandard conditions. However, the estimated growth of the urban population between 2010 and 2020 (248,539 more urban dwellers), indicates the need for approximately 46,026 extra homes,[10] and the government will need to establish how best to provide these.

Some strides have been made to address the land and housing challenges. The government initiated the Five Year Strategy and Implementation Plan 2011–2015, and the Customary Land Development Support Unit. These processes have been slow, as the Department of Land and Physical Planning and National Housing Corporation need to better coordinate solutions. Despite this scenario, as urban areas continue to grow, the government will have to better plan the utilization of customary land, as this is in greater abundance (table A.7).

Table A.7   National Policies and Programs Targeting the Poor in Papua New Guinea

National Policies and Programs Targeting the Poor	Objectives	Results
Mid Term Development Plan (MTDP)[a] (2005–10, 2011–15)	The MTDP is a government strategy developed through the Ministry of National Planning and District Development to target sector-level goals identified by Vision 2050 and achievable within the five-year time span. Related to urban improvements, the 2011–15 MTDP highlights the areas of land development, including land administration, housing and land use planning, and law and order, which includes infrastructure rehabilitation and public safety initiatives, access to affordable and reliable public services, and urban development, including housing finance opportunities and master planning. The newest MTDP2 (2016–18) aims to achieve similar goals. Targets: Urban poor and general population	Development of key national development policies, such as the 2013 National Transport Strategy and the Decent Work Country Program (supported by the ILO)

(Table continues on next page)

Table A.7   National Policies and Programs Targeting the Poor in Papua New Guinea *(continued)*

National Policies and Programs Targeting the Poor	Objectives	Results
UN-Habitat Participatory Slum Upgrading Programme[a] (2013–2015)	Developed in alignment with the government's urban development goals outlined in Vision 2050, the US$86,000 program focuses on activities for community mobilization and profiling, the preparation and implementation of community-level planning, city investment prioritization, and general capacity building and strengthening for the government entities. Targets: Slum dwellers and government agencies	
National Informal Sector Policy[b] (2011–2015)	The document passed by the government highlights the importance of the informal economy and provides guidance for safe and sustainable financial inclusion. Targets: Informal sector workers	
Urban Youth Employment Project[c] (2011–2016, 2018)	Jointly funded by the World Bank, government of PNG, and government of Korea, the objectives of the Urban Youth Employment Project for Papua New Guinea are to provide urban youth with income from temporary employment opportunities and to increase their employability. Targets: Urban youth	The program has placed more graduates than scoped and is being scaled up through additional financing from the government of Australia.

a. UN Habitat 2012.
b. UN Habitat 2010.
c. World Bank 2013b.

The Philippines

Key Development Statistics

Population: 99.14 million

GDP per capita: US$2,765.08

Urban poverty headcount ratio:
13 percent

Per capita annual growth:
1.9 percent

Urbanization Rate

Urban spatial expansion:
2.4 percent
6th fastest in East Asia

Urban population growth:
1.3 percent

Rural-Urban Statistics

Urban population: 44 percent
(44.1 million)
27 percent of the urban population
live in poverty

Rural population: 56 percent
(55.0 million)

Largest Urban Areas

Manila: 12.8 million, 25.8 percent
poverty rate

Cebu: 1.54 million, 22.4 percent
poverty rate

Slum Population

Urban Areas: 7.1 percent
(2.9 million)

Metro-Manila: 36.3 percent
(4.0 million)

Sources: WDI 2012 and 2014; National Statistical Coordination Board 2012 and 2014.

The Philippines is one of the fastest urbanizing countries in East Asia, with more than 48 percent of its population residing in urban areas, and urban spatial expansion growing at 2.4 percent per year.[11] Urban areas in the Philippines are highly densified, and the urban population is expected to surpass rural areas. Following this trajectory, by 2050, approximately 102 million people (more than 65 percent of the country's projected total population) will reside in cities (United Nations 2012).

Increasing urban expansion in the Philippines has led to high inequality and concentrations of poverty in cities. Philippine cities currently contribute to more than 70 percent of the national GDP, and the percentage of poor in urban areas is about one-third of that in rural areas. Although cities serve as an important economic hub, for every 1 percent of population growth, the Philippines has only demonstrated less than a 2 percent increase in GDP per capita. This ratio is significantly low in comparison to Vietnam (averaging 8 percent over the past few years) and Thailand (at 10 percent) (World Bank 2014a).

The capital, Manila, together with its surrounding metropolitan areas, characterizes the primary urban agglomeration in the Philippines. There is an absence of medium-sized competitors to the National Capital Region. The second largest urban area in the Philippines, Cebu, is also rapidly emerging, although it has less than one-tenth of the population of Manila.

Around 12.8 million people reside in Metropolitan Manila, and it contributed approximately 36 percent of GDP in 2012.[12] There is high spillover of residents from Metro Manila to peripheral areas, resulting in overcrowding, congestion, and lack of access to the city's resources. In addition, the migrants have difficulties finding jobs and affording the expenses of living in Manila, Cebu, and other urban areas. Many find homes in substandard housing in communities that lack access to basic services and enclaves of informal settlements develop.

Slums and Informality

In 2009, more than 40 percent of the total population resided in informal settlements, and one in four residents in Manila live in informal households. One-fifth of these families reside in locations vulnerable to disaster (UN Habitat 2009), living in public spaces along riverbeds, railroads, public parks, cemeteries (box A.6), and even in tourist areas such as Intramuros, Ermita, and Malacanang Palace (figure A.6).

These squatter families only make up a small portion of the 3.6 million urban households that have limited or no access to basic services, tenure security, or affordable housing. Access to piped water or individual household connections is a prime challenge for the urban poor living in Cebu, Manila, and other large urban areas. Residents of un-serviced communities pay 9–13 times more for the delivery of clean water than those households in serviced areas (Ballesteros 2011). Only 14 percent of informal settlers have access to services.

Box A.6   Living among the Graves

With the lack of available and affordable housing, thousands of informal settler families in Manila are reduced to living in the *Cementerio del Norta*, the largest public graveyard in the country. Some of these residents are unemployed or have low-earning jobs, and are unable to afford homes; they squat on the cemetery's 130 acres of land, living in tombs and mausoleums. The informal cemetery community has no access to running water, electricity, or sanitation.

The plight of Philippines urban residents who have to live in these conditions has been captured by international newspapers. A *Guardian* article featuring one such slum dweller in Cementerio del Norta writes:

The "home" Evangelista lives in is actually a mausoleum housing eight graves. He considers himself lucky—the breezy second story where the deceased's family pays their annual respects doubles as his bedroom. "Look at my view," he says, pointing his cigarette out towards the field of tombstones. He tells me this is the strongest, safest home he's ever had.

The informal families living in the graveyard contribute to the 13 million that reside in substandard conditions, along highways, under bridges, and in alleys throughout the city.

Sources: Hodal 2013a; Hodal 2013b.

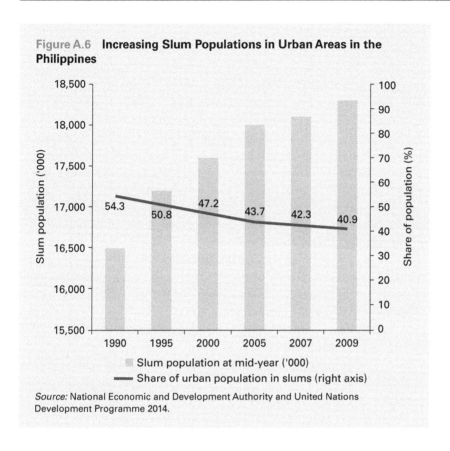

Figure A.6 Increasing Slum Populations in Urban Areas in the Philippines

Source: National Economic and Development Authority and United Nations Development Programme 2014.

The formation and survival of informal settlements have persisted due to the inability of municipalities to plan and provide affordable housing, functional transportation systems, and sufficient jobs for the low-income segments of the urban population. Public investments in infrastructure and regulations on land use for housing, commerce, and industry are spatially uncoordinated, reducing the connections between workers and jobs, and residents and amenities, and this situation adds to sprawl. As a consequence, to be physically close to where jobs are located, much of the urban poor are exposed to excessive risks.

Who Are the Urban Poor?

In Philippine cities, most urban poor take on jobs in domestic labor, tricycle driving, construction labor, factor labor, self-employment, vending, or working in sari-sari stores. Youth are a growing segment of the urban poor population. As a result of demographic transition, the youth cohort in Philippine cities has been increasing; the 2000 census illustrated that twice as many youth have moved from rural areas to cities. However, many of the youth migrating for improved opportunities fall into poverty. In Metro Manila, youth unemployment is more than four times the rate for adults.[13] Women also are a large part of the urban poor.

Land and Housing Market

There is a critical housing shortage in Philippine cities, and in Manila in particular. The Housing and Urban Development Coordinating Council anticipates that in 2017, total housing needs will reach 6.3 million households. The private sector also estimates that 12.5 million housing units will be needed by 2030, given the pace of urbanization in the country and the current demand-supply trends and analysis (HUDCC 2015). This housing need is associated with unmet demand, as well as the lack of housing assistance availability for lower-income households. As a result, there has been a proliferation of slum areas and informal settlements.

A challenge associated with the housing shortage is the lack of coordination between housing policy and city planning in the Philippines. In the Metro Manila greater area, for example, there are 85 municipalities and cities involved in governance, with no clear delineation of roles and responsibilities of national, local, and municipal levels of government. Each municipality is independently managed, and all work on various issues related to decreasing the incidence of urban poverty. Strategies to facilitate land acquisition, opportunities for tenure, and zoning are disconnected, and many go unfunded (table A.8).

Table A.8   National Policies and Programs Targeting the Poor in the Philippines

National Policies and Programs Targeting the Poor	Objectives	Results
Community Mortgage Fund[a] (2004–present)	Provides mortgage financing to assist in securing land tenure through community ownership methods. Social Housing Finance Corporation (SHFC) has recently introduced its high-density housing and a loan program to provide in-city, near city, or near site housing for relocated informal settlers in Metro Manila. The World Bank has provided the SHFC with technical assistance until 2016, to help achieve their goal of serving half a million informal settler families by 2022. Targets: Informal settlers and urban poor	Between 2001 and 2013, 153,000 families were assisted under the program.
Abot Kaya Pabahay Fund[a] (1990–present)	Aimed at implementing a program for social housing and financial support for low-income families. Assists the National Shelter Program and the Community Mortgage Fund in their missions. Targets: Middle-to low-income families.	The National Home Mortgage Finance Corporate (and Home Guaranty Corporation) built 556,000 housing units from 2001 to 2013; however, the homes were above affordability (P545,000 per unit) and the procedures and documentation make this financing option less favorable for informal settler families.

(Table continues on next page)

Table A.8 **National Policies and Programs Targeting the Poor in the Philippines**
(continued)

National Policies and Programs Targeting the Poor	Objectives	Results
Home Development Mutual Fund (Pag-IBIG Fund)[b] (2010–present)	National savings program and affordable shelter financing options for Filipino workers	
One Safe Future (1SF) Program[c] (2014–16)	Grant seed funding of P334.5 million for social housing; envisions an Informal Settler Family-free community in Metro Manila by 2016. The relocation occurs on a site-specific basis using a bottom-up approach. Targets: Six city governments in Manila	
Development of Poor Urban Communities Sector Project (2003–10)[b]	Financed by a US$30.5 million Asian Development Bank loan and set out to provide shelter financing and microcredit facilities for urban poor families. The program works with the private sector to leverage capacities in the implementation of the socialized housing program.	However, it was not able to target the urban poor working and living in the informal sector, instead benefiting salaried employees who are already members of the Home Development Mutual Fund.
National Informal Settlement Upgrading Strategy[d]	World Bank and Cities Alliance financed US$0.455 million grant to assist the government in developing a national slum upgrading strategy and implementation of the policies.	The strategy was prepared and knowledge exchange conferences were being held with experts from Indonesia, Thailand, and Vietnam.

a. Government of the Philippines n.d.
b. ADB 2012a.
c. DILG 2014.
d. Watanabe 2016.

Vietnam

Key Development Statistics

Population: 90.73 million   GDP per capita: US$1,910.51

Urban poverty headcount ratio: Per capita annual growth: 6 percent
3.3 percent

Urbanization Rate

Urban spatial expansion: Urban population growth:
2.8 percent   3.1 percent

4th fastest in East Asia   2nd fastest in East Asia

Rural-Urban Statistics

Urban population: 33 percent   Rural population: 67 percent
(29.9 million)   (66.4 million)

6.6 percent of the urban population
live in poverty

Largest Urban Areas

Ho Chi Minh City: 7.8 million,   Hanoi: 5.6 million, 4.6 percent
2.1 percent poverty rate   poverty rate

Sources: WDI 2013 and 2014; UNDP Urban Poverty Assessment 2010.

Vietnam has the sixth largest urban population in East Asia, however, only 32 percent are concentrated in the two largest cities. The urban population is increasing at a rate of 3.3 percent per annum, almost twice the national population growth rate. Vietnam has been able to harness economic development within its city centers, and the incomes of Hanoi and Ho Chi Minh City (HCMC) are nearly double those earned in rural areas, even after adjusting for living costs. A smaller portion of the urban population resides in the secondary cities and towns; however, these are where the largest percentage (70 percent) of the urban poor are concentrated. Hanoi and HCMC account for only 11 percent of the residents living in urban poverty (figure A.7).

There has been a steady increase in rural-to-urban migration in Vietnam. Youth, in particular, move into cities for better job opportunities and access to services; this process has only become more intensified, whereby 23 percent of youth between the ages of 21–25 living in urban areas had only moved there five years prior.[14] Furthermore, youth unemployment in urban areas has been on the rise (11.5 percent) and surpasses the rate in rural areas (4.1 percent) (Government of Vietnam. 2015). This scenario is in keeping with the high youth unemployment in the country (6.3 percent in 2014), which mirrors the global proportion, but is still above average for the EAP region.[15]

Despite the increase in rural-to-urban migration and the haphazard expansion of cities, especially in Hanoi and HCMC, there are very few

Figure A.7   **Poverty Levels in Vietnam by Class of City**

	Special City	Class 1	Class 2	Class 3	Classes 4 & 5
# of cities in category	2	7	14	45	634
Average population ('000)	4,075	467	225	86	11
Percent of urban population	32.1	12.9	12.4	15.3	27.3
Poverty rate (percent)	1.9	3.8	4.2	5.8	11.2
Share of the urban poor (percent)	11.0	8.8	9.2	5.9	55.0

Source: World Bank 2012b.

slum developments. The traditional sense of slums as visible pockets of poverty and dilapidated buildings is not the reality of settlements in Vietnam's cities. However, there are major issues of illegal construction and poor infrastructure. Up until the late '80s, homes were provided to all citizens through a state-run program. But with the inability to provide enough homes to meet the demand, the government allowed some private construction regulated by minimum standards. Despite these restrictions, homes were constructed illegally; many of them were substandard and did not adhere to building regulations. Regardless, according to official statistics, these buildings received basic services, correlating with the high percentage of city dwellers with access to water and sanitation (approximately 94 percent for sanitation and 99 percent for water [WDI 2014]). However, there is a disconnect between these high percentages of access and the characteristics of low-income settlements that include poorly maintained infrastructure, low-quality housing, unplanned encroachments, and limited wastewater management.

To tackle these emergent challenges, the government is focusing on the process of land titling and tenure security, as well as improving infrastructure.

Slums and Informality

The government has taken a proactive approach to creating housing solutions through a flexible and pluralistic system of housing supply across market segments. Vietnam has been able to achieve this better than other East Asian countries with higher GDPs. This success can be attributed to some of the following:

- Social housing policies in favor of affordable housing provision
- Flexibility with construction techniques (such as floor space and plot size)

- Opportunities for incremental upgrading for individual homes and urban centers
- Densification of peri-urban areas, connecting them to the urban centers and services
- Robust private housing construction and rental housing sectors
- Rich housing finance and subsidy market, targeting the poor
- Mainstreaming of low-income housing strategies into citywide planning initiatives

However, although there are few slums, some urban poor households live in substandard conditions where the housing quality is low and where other conditions of informality have developed.

Who Are the Urban Poor?

Conditions for the urban poor differ in every city, for example, slums along the canals in HCMC, shacks in suburban alleys in Hanoi, or floating fishing boat communities in Hue. Regardless, there are some common characteristics most possess. Unlike the informal settler families in Tondo Manila, the urban poor have land and houses. The issue is nuanced, however, where they do not have legal ownership.

The urban poor are the primary agents of sprawl into smaller cities and towns on the outskirts of Hanoi and HCMC. The inability to legally own land and houses has forced ad hoc construction, although some residents nevertheless have access to basic services. In fact, with the positive economic growth Vietnam has been experiencing in the past few decades, the urban poor typically have jobs, albeit working in the informal sector or for family-owned business and services. These populations have limited access to credit, social protection, and having highly volatile incomes (box A.7).

Box A.7   Women Improving Their Situation in Urban Slums in Vietnam

Pham Thi Minh is one of 6,674 borrowers in Haiphong who is all praise for the US$ 3 million microcredit program (with US$ 2.6M in World Bank support). A retired garment factory worker in her mid-50s, she says: "Our house was in a very bad condition. There was no proper flooring or drainage, no kitchen or toilet. When it rained the roof leaked so badly, we would be completely flooded." It's hard to believe it's the same house which now gleams with tiled flooring, a proper roof, a paved courtyard leading to a separate kitchen with a gas stove, and bathroom with a flushing, seated toilet.

To rebuild her house, Minh borrowed VND10 million (a little over US$540) from the revolving housing fund, with additional contributions from her extended family. It's as though the new surroundings have galvanized her spirit, goading her not only to repay her loan but to work as a cleaner in a school to add new comforts to her home. In her home, there are a refrigerator, a TV, and other furniture and decorations.

Source: World Bank 2010.

Land and Housing Market

Growth projections illustrate that by 2025, HCMC will be home to 9.6 million people and Hanoi 4.8 million. This impeding rapid urban growth will create a heavy strain on the housing market in Vietnamese cities, which are already burdened by the challenge of high living costs. An additional challenge has been the quality of housing stock, whereby 20 percent of Vietnam's households live in poor conditions. Furthermore, with the current increase in the urban population, there is an estimated need for 374,000 additional housing units in cities each year (World Bank 2015e).

The government has created an imbalance in the housing and land market in Vietnam from the state-led collectivization of land through which housing is granted to families. The program created artificially low prices in the housing market, thus deflating the value of the assets and distorting the market. Despite this supply-demand driven approach to providing housing, there is still a deficit in affordable solutions for the poor and near-poor. In general, property prices began to escalate in 2007, which then led to stagnation of the housing market up until 2012. As a result of FDI, the improvement of the global economic climate, and renewed government policies, a stimulate package of US$1.4 billion (VND$30 trillion) was introduced to offer loans for the purchase of social housing. This package has helped target the housing needs of the middle-income homeownership sector, albeit at a high cost to the government (box A.8).

The Housing Law, effective July 2015, is a new approach taken by the government of Vietnam to bolster this growing housing market with reforms to provide increased opportunities to access land and property. The law encourages the development of incremental housing, attracting

---

Box A.8   Doi Moi Economic Policy in Vietnam

The Doi Moi Economic Policy refers to the socialist-oriented market reforms enacted in 1986, which encouraged increased exportation and manufacturing in an effort to open the economy. Trade liberalization in Vietnam boosted the economies of cities significantly and concentrated much of the FDI in Hanoi, HCMC, three neighboring provinces, and Haiphong. Before the program, Vietnam was one of the poorest economies in the world, with a per capital income of US$100. With the policies and reforms attributed to Doi Moi, the per capita income is around US$2,000. Vietnam's economy has grown to low-middle-income status; at its peak, the country experienced economic growth averaging 7.4 percent per annum from 1990 to 2008.

Doi Moi has helped reduce poverty in Vietnam's cities, and the government continues to foster the reduction of income disparities and urban development through a number their policies and strategies.

Sources: World Bank 2011; World Bank 2015d.

Table A.9   National Policies and Programs Targeting the Poor in Vietnam

National Policies and Programs Targeting the Poor	Objectives	Results
Vietnam Urban Upgrading Project	To alleviate poverty in urban areas by improving the living and environmental conditions of the urban poor using participatory planning methods and influencing planning processes to become more inclusive and pro-poor. The housing microfinance component in particular offers credit to the urban poor. Targets: 137 wards in four cities: Hai Phong and Nam Dinh in the north and Can Tho and Ho Chi Minh City in the south	Microfinance lending was provided to 90,000 households.
Government Decision No. 10 Orientation Master Plan for Urban Development (1998–2020)	Increased coverage for piped water and sewerage, transportation, power, housing, and the provision of open space, and recognized the importance of providing security of tenure through the issuance of land use rights certificates to increase the supply of housing and improves the existing stock. The plan also supports improving access to credit and minimizing inequality for the poor. There is a strong effort to enforce better planning and building regulations in improving the housing market. Targets: Medium- and small-sized cities, while containing the growth of the largest cities	
Decree 188	Required a 20 percent land contribution to social housing production to address the high demand in urban low-income populations	
Socio Economic Development Strategy (2011–20)	Promotes the importance of urbanization to economic prosperity. The focus is on bolstering industrialization and urbanization in parallel, while consolidating social inclusiveness.	
The Government Decree No. 72 (2001) and Decree No. 42 (2009)	Develops classifications of different urban areas to rank their roles	Created a hierarchical system to understand cities positionality in classes (used in the table, above, where levels of analysis can be conducted by urban center, such as urban poverty)

Source: World Bank 2011.

investments to increase financing in the housing sector to address shortages, and private sector participation, particularly in providing affordable rental solutions and housing for vulnerable low-income groups. Table A.9 lists national policies and programs targeting the poor in Vietnam.

Notes

1. UN data (2014) on slum population in urban areas.
2. http://urbandata.unhabitat.org/.
3. The EAP region had an annual growth rate of around 1.6 percent in 1990, and this rate has declined to 1.0 percent in 2000, and sustained 0.7 percent from 2010 to 2014.
4. Independent State of Papua New Guinea, National Urbanization Policy 2010-2030.
5. *Ibid.*
6. *Ibid.*
7. *Ibid.*
8. NCD Settlements Strategic Plan, 2007-2011, Port Moresby.
9. Independent State of Papua New Guinea, National Urbanization Policy 2010–2030.
10. *Ibid.*
11. From 1,800 square kilometers in 2000 to 2,300 square kilometers in 2010.
12. Oxford Economics Global Cities Historic Database.
13. ILO estimates based on the Philippines National Statistics Office: Labour Force Survey (April 2012).
14. Vietnam National Census (2009).
15. Trading Economics Vietnam (2011–2016).

References

ACCA (Asian Coalition for Community Action). 2014. "Cities in Asia: Fifth Yearly Report of the Asian Coalition for Community Action Program." Asian Coalition for Housing Rights, Bangkok.

ADB (Asian Development Bank). 2012a. "Cambodia: Urban Sector Assessment, Strategy, and Road." ADB, Mandaluyong City.

———. 2012b. "Philippines: Development of Poor Urban Communities Sector Project" https://www.adb.org/documents/philippines-development -poor-urban-communities-sector-project

———. 2015. "Myanmar: Mandalay Urban Services Improvement Project." https://www.adb.org/projects/47127-002/main.

———. 2016. "Country Partnership Strategy: Papua New Guinea, 2016-2020." ADB, Manila.

Ballesteros, M. M. 2011. "Why Slum Poverty Matters." Philippine Institute for Development Studies, Manila.

Blank, L. 2008. "Rapid Youth Assessment in Port Moresby, Papua New Guinea." World Bank, Washington, DC.

Cammack, D. 2008. "Chronic Poverty in Papua New Guinea." Chronic Poverty Research Centre.

Department of National Planning and Monitoring. 2010. "Papua New Guinea Development Strategic Plan 2010-2030. Department of National Planning and Monitoring." Port Moresby, Papua New Guinea.

DILG (Department of the Interior and Local Government). 2014. "DILG Grants P334M to 'Build Communities' for the Urban Poor." http://www .dilg.gov.ph/news/DILG-grants-P334M-to-build-communities-for-the -urban-poor/NC-2014-1165.

Dutta, P. V., and Y. Okamura. 2015. "Reaching the Poor and Vulnerable in Myanmar: Lessons from a Social Protection and Poverty Reduction Perspective." Myanmar Social Protection Notes Series; Note 11. World Bank, Washington, DC.

EIU (Economist Intelligence Unit). 2015. "A Summary of the Liveability Ranking and Overview." EIU, London.

GHK (Hong Kong SAR, China) Ltd. 2004. "China Urban Poverty Study, Final Report." DFID (Department for International Development). http://www.dfid.gov.uk/countries/asia/China/urban-poverty-studyeng lish.pdf.

Giles, J., D. Wang, and A. Park. 2013. "Expanding Social Insurance Coverage in Urban China." Policy Research Working Paper, No. WPS 6497. World Bank, Washington, DC.

Gobson, J., and S. Olivia. 2002. "Attacking Poverty in Papua New Guinea, But for How Long?" *Pacific Economic Bulletin* 17 (2).

Government of the Philippines. N.d. "Housing Industry Road Map of the Philippines, 2012–2030." Government of the Philippines, Manila.

Government of Vietnam. 2015. General Statistics Office of Vietnam.

Hodal, K. 2013a. "Manila Is a Hotbed of Progressive Housing Solutions." May 27. https://nextcity.org/features/view/slum-lab-manilas-quest-to-build -a-better-informal-settlement.

———. 2013b. "Philippines Cemetery Provides Manila's Poor a Place to Live among the Dead." *The Guardian* (May 23). https://www.theguard ian.com/world/2013/may/23/philippines-cemetery-urban-poor-home.

HUDCC (Housing and Urban Development Coordinating Council). 2015. "Projected Housing Need 2011–2016." Housing Summit, Quezon City, Philippines.

IMF (International Monetary Fund). 2015. "Papua New Guinea: Selected Issues." IMF, Washington, DC.

Infante Villarroel, A. M. 2015a. "Inventory of Social Protection Programs in Myanmar." Myanmar Social Protection Notes Series; Note 3. World Bank, Washington, DC.

———. 2015b. "Inventory of Social Protection Programs in Myanmar." Myanmar Social Protection Notes Series; Note 8. World Bank, Washington, DC.

Jia, Z. 2016. "Urban Upgrading Note, Review of Facts and Policies." Internal policy note. World Bank, Washington, DC.

Lin, Y. and B. De Meulder. 2012. "A Conceptual Framework for the Strategic Urban Project Approach for Sustainable Redevelopment of 'Villages in the City' in Guangzhou." *Habitat International* 36 (3): 380–87.

Moreno, E. L. 2003. 'Slums of the World." Working Paper. UN Habitat, Nairobi.

National Economic and Development Authority and United Nations Development Programme. 2014. "The Philippines Fifth Progress Report - Millennium Development Goals." National Economic and Development Authority, Pasig City.

PNG (Papua New Guinea) Government. N.d. "Medium Term Development Strategy." PNG.

Sokhin, V. 2014. *Crying Meri: Violence Against Women in Papua New Guinea*. Brooklyn, New York: FotoEvidence.

Song, Y., and Y. Zenou. 2012. "Urban Villages and Housing Values in China." *Regional Science and Urban Economics* 42 (3): 495–505.

Strangio, S. 2014. "Phnom Penh's Wildly Opulent Gated Communities Are Fracturing the City." https://nextcity.org/daily/entry/phnom-penhs-wildly -opulent-gated-communities-are-fracturing-the-city.

UNFPA (United Nations Population Fund). 2010. "Report on Situation Analysis of Population and Development, Reproductive Health and Gender in Myanmar." UNFPA and the Government of Mongolia, Ulaanbaatar.

UN Habitat. 2009. "UN-Habitat Country Programme Document 2008-2009 – Philippines." UN Habitat, Nairobi.

———. 2010. "Port Moresby Urban Profile." UN Habitat, Nairobi.

———. 2012. "Papua New Guinea: National Urban Profile." UN Habitat, Nairobi.

UNICEF. 2012. "Phnom Penh Urban Poor Assessment, Phnom Penh Capital Hall." UNICEF.

United Nations. 2012. "World Urbanization Prospects: The 2011 Revision." Department of Economic and Social Affairs/Population Division. United Nations, New York.

UN Women. 2016. "Making Public Transport Safe for Women and Girls in Papua New Guinea." http://www.unwomen.org/en/news/stories/2016/11 /making-public-transport-safe-for-women-and-girls-in-papua-new -guinea#sthash.SSVGF2Ys.dpuf

Watanabe, M. 2016. "Closing the Gap in Affordable Housing in the Philippines: Policy Paper for the National Summit on Housing and Urban Development." World Bank, Washington, DC.

WHO/ UNICEF Joint Monitoring Programme. 2015. "Progress on Sanitation and Drinking Water – 2015 Update and MDG Assessment." WHO/UNICEF Joint Monitoring Programme, USA.

World Bank. 2010. "Women Lead Transformation of Urban Slums in Vietnam." World Bank, Washington, DC.

———. 2011. "Vietnam Urbanization Review." World Bank, Washington, DC.

———. 2012a. "Indonesia Urban Poverty and Program Review." World Bank, Washington, DC.

———. 2012b. "Vietnam Poverty Assessment." World Bank, Washington, DC.

———. 2013a. "Indonesia: Urban Poverty and Program Review" World Bank, Washington, DC.

———. 2013b. Papua New Guinea: Urban Youth Employment Project. http://www.worldbank.org/en/results/2013/08/12/papua-new-guinea-urban-youth-employment-project.

———. 2014a. "Country Partnership Strategy for the Republic of the Philippines for the Period FY2015-2018." World Bank, Washington, DC.

———. 2014b. "Myanmar Systematic Country Diagnostic." World Bank, Washington, DC.

———. 2015a. *East Asia's Changing Urban Landscape: Measuring a Decade of Spatial Growth. Urban Development.* Washington, DC: World Bank.

———. 2015b. "Indonesia's Rising Divide, 2014." World Bank, Washington, DC.

———. 2015c. "Indonesia Systematic Country Diagnostic: Connecting the Bottom 40 Percent to the Prosperity Generation." World Bank, Washington, DC.

———. 2015d. "Taking Stock: An Update on Vietnam's Recent Economic Developments." World Bank, Washington, DC.

———. 2015e. "Vietnam Affordable Housing—A Way Forward." World Bank, Washington, DC.

———. 2015f. "Water Supply and Sanitation in Indonesia: Turning Finance into Service for the Future." World Bank, Washington, DC.

———. 2016a. "A Country on the Move: Domestic Migration in Two Regions of Myanmar." World Bank, Washington, DC.

———. 2016b. "City Risk Diagnostic for Urban Resilience in Indonesia." World Bank, Washington, DC.

———. 2016c. "Indonesia - National Urban Slum Upgrading Program Project 2016." World Bank, Washington, DC.

_____. Forthcoming. "Urban Poverty in Ulaanbaatar: Understanding its Dimensions and Addressing the Challenges" World Bank, Washington, DC.

World Bank, and the Development Research Center of the State Council, the People's Republic of China. 2014. "Urban China: Toward Efficient, Inclusive, and Sustainable Urbanization." World Bank, Washington, DC.

Zhang, X. 2013. "China's 'Ant Tribe' Present Social Survival Situation and Personal Financial Advice." *Asian Social Science* 9 (2): 24–35.

Zheng, S., et al. 2009. "Urban Villages in China: A 2008 Survey of Migrant Settlements in Beijing." *Eurasian Geography and Economics* 50 (4): 425–46.